Put the
Pen Down!

Put the Pen Down!

What Homebuyers and Sellers
Need to Know Before Signing on
the Dotted Line

MARK WEISLEDER

ECW Press

Copyright © Mark Weisleder, 2009

Published by ECW Press
2120 Queen Street East, Suite 200, Toronto, Ontario, Canada M4E 1E2
416-694-3348 / info@ecwpress.com

LIBRARY AND ARCHIVES CANADA CATALOGUING IN PUBLICATION

Weisleder, Mark
Put the pen down!: what homebuyers and sellers need to know before signing on the dotted line / Mark Weisleder.

ISBN 978-1-55022-913-4

1. House buying—Canada. 2. House selling—Canada. I. Title.

HD1379.W356 2009   643'.120971   C2009-904355-6

Front cover design and photo: Brian Greenspan, Wam Interactive Information Inc.
Back cover photo: © Lee Weston Photography
OREA® forms, clauses, and logo used by kind permission of the Ontario Real Estate Association
Text design: Tania Craan
Typesetting: Gail Nina
Printing: Webcom   1   2   3   4   5

Mixed Sources
Product group from well-managed forests, and other controlled sources
www.fsc.org Cert no. SW-COC-002358
© 1996 Forest Stewardship Council

The publication of *Put the Pen Down!* has been generously supported by the Government of Ontario through Ontario Book Publishing Tax Credit, by the OMDC Book Fund, an initiative of the Ontario Media Development Corporation, and by the Government of Canada through the Book Publishing Industry Development Program (BPIDP).

Canadä   ONTARIO ARTS COUNCIL
                CONSEIL DES ARTS DE L'ONTARIO

PRINTED AND BOUND IN CANADA

ECW PRESS
ecwpress.com

To my late parents, Harry and Ida Weisleder,
for being my heroes and role models

To Jodi,
for making my life an adventure

To Hillary and Jillian,
there is no limit on what you can accomplish if you do your best

To Anne, Louis, and Marsha,
having family that loves unconditionally is as good as it gets

Table of Contents

Acknowledgements xiii

Introduction xv
    It's Not Just Location, Location, Location xv
    Why I Wrote This Book xvi
    What You'll Find in This Book xvii

Chapter 1
How to Find the Right REALTOR® 1
    Finding a Salesperson: Referrals and Research 2
    The Professional Team 4
    Agent Services 6
    Viewing Your Home and the Open House 7
    Home Staging 7
    Landscaping 9
    Pre-Staging Home Inspections 10
    Check Your Mortgage in Advance 10
    For Sale by Owner (FSBO) Programs – Are They Worth It? 10
    Can Lawyers Replace the Services of
        Real Estate Salespeople? 14
    The Three Agreement Forms 15
    "Working With a REALTOR®" 15
    The Listing Agreement 19
    The Buyer Representation Agreement 41

Chapter 2
Preparing to Sell or Buy a Home 63
    How Property Is Registered 63
    Property Line, Fences, Trees, and Overhanging Branches 66
    Establishing a Sale Price 70
    12 Questions to Ask Before Selling or Buying a Home 70

Seller Disclosure Obligations 72

Legal or Title Defects 73

Physical Defects 74

Patent Versus Latent Defects 76

Psychological Defects and Stigmas 82

Walking the Property 85

Disclaimer Clauses – Are They Worth It? 87

What to Do Before Buying a Home 89

The Process 92

Professional Advisers 105

Chapter 3

The Agreement of Purchase and Sale 109

Changes to the Standard Form 175

Conditions 176

Questioning Conditions 180

Waving Conditions 183

Representations 185

Warranties 188

Need for an Up-To-Date Survey 190

Chapter 4

Multiple Offers 193

Chapter 5

The Internet and Scams to Watch Out For 199

The Internet Broker 200

Identity Theft 205

No-Money-Down Real Estate Seminars 208

Real Estate Fraud 211

Buyer Tricks to Watch Out For in the Agreement of Purchase
and Sale 214

Property Flips and the Assignment Clause 217

Who Is Your Buyer? 218

Chapter 6

Landlord and Tenant Rights 221

First-Time Buyers Currently Renting an Apartment or House 221

Be Careful Before Signing Any Residential Lease Renewal 222

Selling a Home Occupied by Tenants 222

Make a Deal 225

Chapter 7

Family Law Rights 227

Married Spouses 227

Common-Law Spouses 227

Support Obligations 228

Property Rights for Married Spouses 228

Chapter 8

Resale Condominiums and Other Co-Ownerships 233

Creating a Condominium 233

Declaration 234

Description 236

Making Changes to the Declaration and Description 236

Pre-Sale of Units 237

The Condominium Corporation 238

Payment of the Common Expense Fee 241

Can You Decorate Your Unit? 241

The Status Certificate 242

Buying a Resale Condominium Unit 243

The Condominium Resale Agreement 245

Special Provisions: Approval of Certificate Status 295

Timeshare Agreements 295

Co-Operative Agreements 296

Co-Ownership Agreements 299

Chapter 9

Special Purchases: New Homes, New Condominiums, Buying from a Bank Under Power of Sale 301

New Homes and Condominiums 301

The Tarion Warranty Program 302

Advantages of Using a Real Estate Salesperson 303

The Fine Print 305

The Pre-Delivery Inspection 306

New Condominiums 307

Buying From a Bank Under Power of Sale 309

Chapter 10

The Federal Privacy Act and Do Not Call Legislation 315

The Privacy Act 315

E-Mail Spam 319

Ten Principles of Privacy 320

Methods of Obtaining Your Consent 324

Related Privacy Questions 329

Canada's Do Not Call List 330

Maintaining an Internal List 331

How Do You Register Your Number on the Do Not Call List? 332

How Do Telemarketers Access the Do Not Call Registry? 332

How Does a Consumer Complain? 332

New Telephone Contact Rules 333

Chapter 11

Legal Proceedings: Are They Worth the Trouble? 335

The Legal Process 336

Steps Involved in a Legal Process 340

Insurance Issues 341

Settle! 342

Use Small Claims Court 342

Conclusion

Forewarned is Forearmed: The Fourteen Steps of Success 343

Appendix: Special Clauses to Consider 345

Index 357

Acknowledgements

I would like to thank the following people for all their invaluable assistance in helping me complete this book:

Jack, David, and Rachel and the rest of the crew at ECW Press, for all their support and for putting up with me and my endless re-writes;

Edna Barker, for helping me sound like a real person, not a lawyer;

Brian and the staff at Wam, for all of their creative ideas;

Rick Kojfman, for his wisdom;

Allan Silber, for being a mentor to me;

All my real estate students over the years, for all the questions that forced me to find the answers.

Introduction

IT'S NOT JUST LOCATION, LOCATION LOCATION

Buying a home should be one of the great milestones in any family's life. It is an exciting time, but also a stressful time. There is a sense of great anticipation in starting a new life as a family in a new neighbourhood. Yet change typically accompanies this process — change in schools, in jobs, and change that affects relatives and friends. There are multitudes of choices available to home buyers: new home vs. resale; city, suburbs, or rural properties; detached house, condominium, or townhouse. In addition, for most first-time buyers, the purchase agreement will be the largest financial commitment they have made in their entire lives.

I have unfortunately, on too many occasions, seen a family's excitement diminished because of unwelcome surprises that are discovered after the closing. These surprises include defects in the home itself, problems with boundary lines and other property issues, as well as facts about the neighbourhood that were not properly disclosed. Some of these problems can be readily fixed, while others will take time, effort, and money.

I practiced privately as a real estate lawyer for twelve years and have been a real estate instructor for the past twenty-four years. Based on my experience, most buyers and sellers are not properly prepared when they embark on their first home purchase.

WHY I WROTE THIS BOOK

My first book, *Real Estate Agents Beware*, and its updated second edition, *Real Estate Salespeople, Beware*, were directed to real estate salespeople and brokers. My goal was to help real estate salespeople and brokers provide maximum protection to their clients, both buyers and sellers. As well, I hoped to help agents and brokers avoid legal or disciplinary proceedings.

I realized that most of this information would help sellers and buyers understand the purchase and sale agreement used by sales agents. I also noted that many of the books and seminar material available for home buyers seemed to paint a very rosy picture of the process. These books and seminars imply that, even with very little knowledge or credit, anyone can become a millionaire by purchasing properties that are in distressed situations. Other books and websites imply that sellers can easily sell their properties themselves, so they won't have to pay real estate commissions.

Buying and selling property is not easy. There are many pitfalls; mistakes can be very expensive, and can lead to legal proceedings that drag on for years.

This book simplifies the buying and selling process, so you'll understand the process before you start looking for a home or decide to sell one. My hope is that you'll have to visit a lawyer only once: to pick up your cheque after the deal closes, if you're a seller, or to pick up your keys, if you're a buyer.

This book is not intended to be a self-help manual on how to complete a purchase or sale transaction on your own.

As I indicate many times in this book, buyers and sellers are much better off using the services of professional real estate agents and, when necessary, a lawyer. These professionals know how to protect a client's interests fully and completely in every transaction. The more informed and educated you are, the more you'll understand the real estate transaction.

Some principles discussed in this book are:

    a. being prepared;

    b. being careful; and

    c. practising full disclosure.

Almost all legal decisions discussed in this book involve lack of care, preparation, and disclosure.

WHAT YOU'LL FIND IN THIS BOOK

Chapter 1 describes what you need to look for in a REALTOR®, then examines the two agreements people sign when hiring real estate salespeople: the listing agreement and the buyer representation agreement.

Chapter 2 is about different land-registration systems and their effect on boundary issues. For a seller, this includes disclosure obligations and effective staging of a property. For a buyer, this includes researching the neighbourhood you want to move to and understanding the home inspection, the finance approval processes, and the need for a proper survey, home insurance, and title insurance.

In Chapter 3, we look in detail — clause by clause — at the standard agreement used by most real estate offices in

Canada. I will explain how these clauses have been interpreted by the courts. I'll also explain conditions, representations, and warranties, which often become the focal point in negotiations between buyers and sellers.

Chapter 4 looks at the multiple-offer experience, and how a buyer and seller can properly prepare for this very stressful process, as well as their legal obligations.

Chapter 5 explains what they do not tell you in those get-rich-quick schemes in seminars or on the Internet. It provides tips to avoid being caught up in identity theft or mortgage fraud. It also describes some tricks unscrupulous buyers include in their offers to purchase. These tricksters trap an unwary seller into obligations and conditions they would never knowingly agree to.

Chapter 6 looks at some of the laws relating to landlord and tenant rights as they apply to buyers and sellers of real estate.

Chapter 7 examines family law, especially as it relates to the sale of the matrimonial home.

Chapter 8 is devoted to condominiums and other forms of group ownership, such as timeshares, co-operatives, and co-ownerships.

Chapter 9 is for people buying new homes and condominiums. What do you need to know when you're buying from a builder? Then we turn to people who are buying a home from a bank that is exercising its rights when a mortgage goes into default.

Chapter 10 looks at the Federal Privacy Act and the Do Not Call List, and how they affect a real estate transaction for buyers and sellers. How are these two pieces of legislation related to real estate? Here's an example of a privacy issue: can an agent advertise the sale price of your home after you've bought it? And the Do Not Call list: can agents call you at home to solicit business? Can they call if they find out you're selling your home by yourself?

Chapter 11 describes the legal process and what you will face if you get caught up in a real-estate-related lawsuit. What's really involved in such a legal proceeding? How can you avoid this process? You will also begin to understand why the only winners in any lawsuit are the lawyers.

How to Find the Right REALTOR®

The real estate profession is just that: a profession. Professional REALTORS® complete rigorous educational requirements to enter the profession and to maintain their licenses to practice. They are regulated by local boards, provincial real estate associations, and provincial registrars. In Ontario, for example, the real estate association is known as the Ontario Real Estate Association (OREA) and the registrar's office is known as the Real Estate Council of Ontario (RECO). To learn more about the services provided by salespeople in Ontario, go to the OREA website (www.orea.com) or the RECO website (www.reco.ca). Each province has its own real estate association and provincial registrar, and they generally operate on the same principles.

Although most buyers and sellers refer to real estate professionals as "agents," the legislation in many provinces now refers to them as "salespeople." I will thus use the term salespeople throughout this book.

The required provincial continuing education courses keep salespeople up to date about new issues that affect buyers and sellers, for example, the dangers of radon gas, asbestos, or vermiculite; oil contamination; septic systems; and zoning, parking, and permits. Most buyers and sellers don't know much about these issues; professional salespeople do.

FINDING A SALESPERSON: REFERRALS AND RESEARCH

As in most businesses, there is no better way to find a competent professional than to ask your friends, colleagues, co-workers, neighbours, and relatives for a reference. The most powerful form of advertising is word of mouth. You can also write down the names of salespeople who have signs up in the area you want to move to. Pay attention to the signs that say "sold" on them.

Start your neighbourhood research on the Internet, as well. For example, if you are interested in the High Park area of Toronto, google this area. You will likely see a link to an article or blog written by a local salesperson who is familiar with the area. Smart salespeople know that these kinds of articles will attract more potential buyers to their area. This is the kind of professional who should be working for you.

If a salesperson sounds like a good match, check out his or her website. If you're selling your home, observe how prospective salespeople market their listings: your home will likely be marketed the same way. If you're buying a home, see if the information on the website is current. Does it help you understand how to buy a property? Is it uncomplicated, uncluttered, and easy to follow? The more professional the website, the more you can expect from the salesperson.

When you interview salespeople, pay particular attention to the material they bring to show you. If they show you testimonials from satisfied clients, look for statements such as "very careful," "always returns calls and e-mails promptly," "explained all documents very clearly and completely," and "always follows up on requests." These are salespeople who will protect your interests. Ask if you can contact the clients directly.

If you're selling, ask prospective salespeople how many listings they have in your area, and what percentage of those listings have sold. How does this compare to the average of other salespeople in your area? This information is available publicly. You're looking for proof that the salesperson knows how to price a property correctly, so the property attracts the best buyers sooner. Studies show that "the best buyers" are those who see a property within a short time of its listing, so it is very important that they are priced just right, to generate immediate interest from the right people.

If you're selling, ask the salesperson, on average, how many days it takes for homes in your prospective neighbourhood to be on the market before they sell. Is it thirty days? Forty-five? Ninety or more? Then ask how many days, on average, have the salesperson's listings been on the market before they actually sold?

A good salesperson will show you a comparative market analysis, which includes comparably priced properties in the area you're looking at. The analysis should describe the amenities for each property; often these amenities explain the different sale prices. Amenities include size of building, location, distance to schools, a built-in swimming pool, or a park or ravine behind the backyard. You can use the comparative market analysis to predict the value of your own home. Take a look and tour some of the homes for sale in your area. Your salesperson should be recommending a sale price for your property that makes sense in relation to what properties are selling for in your neighbourhood. Beware of "overvaluing" — it can lead only to disappointment. Of course, you think your home is special and unique. But special and unique are not what determines real value. A competent salesperson will price your home to attract the right buyers quickly.

What constitutes first-class representation? Here are some attributes:

1. Having a team of professionals to assist you, so your buying or selling decision is easier. These include, for example, home inspectors, planners, lawyers, mortgage brokers, movers, and home stagers.

2. Being careful and consistent in gathering and reviewing documents.

3. Listening to your concerns, then making sure those concerns are addressed in the agreement, especially when writing conditions, representations, and warranties. More about this in Chapter 3.

4. Taking notes during conversations; keeping track of important dates; following up regularly to ensure all your concerns are addressed before the transaction is completed.

5. Telling you about all potential conflicts, and informing you about all material facts relating to the transaction.

6. Treating everyone in the transaction fairly, honestly, and with integrity.

THE PROFESSIONAL TEAM

A good salesperson's team will include:

Home or environmental inspectors for determining the physical condition of a property. These days, the home inspection includes wiring, plumbing, electrical and heating systems, roof, furnace, air conditioning unit, and basement water seepage, plus quite a few new issues: mould, hidden oil tanks or other environmental issues, and hazardous chemicals in the landscaping. For rural properties, inspectors assess wells and the septic systems.

Lawyers, to check the wording in an agreement of purchase and sale and to provide or recommend additional conditions, representations, and warranties, in specific circumstances.

Planners, to check zoning, parking, set-back compliance, and permits for renovations or additions. For example, many homeowners rip out an existing backyard deck and build a newer, larger deck without obtaining a building permit. Many of these decks violate zoning bylaws. At any time, a city official can investigate, then demand that you make the deck comply with zoning requirements.

Mortgage brokers, to help you qualify for financing before you buy a new house. Mortgage brokers also show you how much you can borrow so your monthly payment will be manageable. They will then shop around to make sure that you obtain the best available interest rate from a bank or other lending institution.

Insurance brokers, to protect your new investment. Home insurance is becoming increasingly complicated. For example, there are increased premiums (this means you pay extra) for some defects, such as a roof that is more than twenty-five years old, knob-and-tube wiring, asbestos insulation, and a wood-burning stove. Insurance companies will arrange their own inspection of your home before you buy it, to determine whether the coverage they are providing is adequate. This takes time. You need the insurance coverage arranged before your deal is completed.

Real estate salespeople should be able to provide referral and contact information for other professionals who may assist and protect buyers and sellers. These include:

Appliance repair shops
Roofers
Movers

Interior decorators
Carpenters, plumbers, electricians, painters
Landscapers
Pavers

Of course you can ask family and friends about these professionals, as well.

AGENT SERVICES

Before you sign any agreement with a salesperson, they will
explain all the services they provide for sellers and for buyers.
They'll also review the applicable provincial listing or buyer
representation agreement, and explain all their agency obligations.

Take a look at their sample marketing materials. What will
they do besides put a sign on your front lawn? What kind of
flyers will they use? What does their open-house brochure
look like? What is the firm's buyer network like? How professional are their marketing and selling techniques? Think
about these questions as you compare different salespeople:

Will they advertise your property in a newspaper?
Do they distribute flyers?
How many open houses will they conduct?
Do you want your property marketed over the Internet? Will the
salesperon include a video tour?

VIEWING YOUR HOME AND THE OPEN HOUSE

Good salespeople explain the open house process, and how you can make your home more marketable to anyone viewing — or taking a tour of — your home. Sellers, you should not be in the home when it is shown to potential buyers. Leave that to your salesperson. Your salesperson will explain the use of the lock box, which is attached to your door so other registered real estate representatives can show your home to potential buyers when you are not there. To make sure your home gives the best first impression, your salesperson will introduce you to the art of staging a home for sale.

HOME STAGING

Home staging is the practice of making the right cosmetic and other changes to a property at a relatively low cost so your home will show well and generate high offers. In the United States, it has been found that professional home staging can increase a selling price by six percent.

Do your prospective salespeople have expertise, or do they have a company they can refer you to? In general, buyers prefer a furnished room to an empty space; the furniture helps them imagine their own furniture in the house. Buyers place a premium on the kitchen, so if you are considering improvements to your home, start in the kitchen: you may see a positive return on your investment. Aim for conservative: it will appeal to a wider circle of potential buyers.

Some useful staging tips:

1. Start spring cleaning now.
2. Get rid of all your junk and clutter.

3. Wash all your windows.

4. Paint walls fresh, using lighter colours, such as off-white or beige.

5. Open curtains so lots of light gets in.

6. Get your carpets professionally cleaned. If you're thinking of replacing carpets, go for light beige.

7. Remove leaves or extensions from tables to make the rooms look bigger.

8. Remove unnecessary furniture; again, this will make the rooms look larger.

9. Reduce the number of pillows, afghans, throws, and blankets on your couches.

10. Reduce the number of paintings and other wall decorations.

11. Try to limit the number of chairs around your tables. Four to six is ideal.

12. Reduce the number of dishes in the china cabinets.

13. Organize your children's toys in one area, if possible.

14. Make sure all appliances are in good working order.

15. Replace any burned-out bulbs.

16. Replace outdated drapes and blinds.

17. Make minor repairs: dripping faucets, cracks in walls or ceilings, loose doorknobs, and torn window screens.

18. Make sure that all windows and doors open and shut properly.

19. Be aware of smells: stop smoking inside the house and temporarily relocate your pets, if possible.

20. Put decorative towels in bathrooms.

21. Thin out and organize your closets to make them look more spacious.

22. Change the filters in your furnace.

23. Get rid of all old bicycles, paint cans, and any other useless items from your garage.

24. Play light music during showings and light a fire if it's cold outside.

LANDSCAPING

Outside landscaping is becoming an even greater part of the home staging process, as the buyer's first impression of your home will be when they view the front lawn. Some suggestions in this area are as follows:

1. Keep the lawn neat and tidy.
2. Trim all bushes.
3. Remove dead tree branches.
4. Put flower planters near the front door, if in season.
5. Paint or stain the front door and the mailbox.
6. Reseed any bald spots in your grass.
7. Repair any cracked or uneven driveways and walkways.
8. Remove old plastic furniture from the front porch.
9. Make sure your house number is easy to read.
10. Clean your windows.
11. Make sure that all your exterior lights work and that your home is well lit up at night.
12. Make sure your backyard deck is also neat and tidy and that any gate is well oiled.
13. Make sure your doorbell works.

I have heard of sellers even cleaning up their neighbours' front lawns, to make things look appealing to potential buyers.

PRE-STAGING HOME INSPECTIONS

In Chapter 2, I review the issue of whether sellers should complete property condition statements and give them to buyers. In cases where you're are not able to complete these statements, I suggest that you consider obtaining a pre-listing home inspection and give this out to potential buyers. All sellers should consider obtaining a home inspection report before they start staging their property. A pre-listing inspection will identify problems with your home that most buyers will also detect when they do their own home inspection. If you find these problems early and fix them, your home will show that much better to any potential buyer.

CHECK YOUR MORTGAGE IN ADVANCE

If you're selling, find out if your existing mortgage can be discharged on closing or transferred to the property you're thinking of buying. You do not want to sell your home and then find out you have to pay a high penalty to discharge your mortgage. As interest rates continue to fall, the penalty to discharge a mortgage early will rise.

Make sure you get this information in writing from your lending institution, to avoid any surprises later.

FOR SALE BY OWNER (FSBO) PROGRAMS — ARE THEY WORTH IT?

Many sellers are tempted to sell their properties themselves to avoid or reduce real estate commissions. These sellers are getting help from Internet marketers and businesses that offer "For Sale" signs to place on the lawn. This has been going on for years, and the main lesson learned over time is that people selling their own homes rarely get as much for a home as real estate salespeople do.

Remember the old investment principle: "If it seems too good to be true, then it usually is." More about this in Chapter 5.

Researchers in the United States have collected statistics based on actual sales figures.

> From 2001 to 2008, the average net price for a home sale through a traditional REALTOR®, after payment of all commissions, was about twenty-five percent more than the average sale price when the sellers tried to sell their properties on their own. In a buyer's market, when there are many more listings than available buyers and properties take longer to sell, the figures are even worse if you are trying to sell by yourself.

> Most FSBO sales systems, either Internet or the sign-on-the-lawn method, will effectively reach only twenty percent of the potential buyers out there. Who can afford to miss eighty percent of potential customers? In addition, more than sixty percent of all For Sale By Owner properties are sold to friends and family.

> If an FSBO property doesn't sell in the first five weeks, the net sale price for the home is even less.

Why does this happen? When buyers see that you're not using a salesperson, they want to "share" in the potential commission savings. If the average real estate commission across the country is four to six percent, then the buyer will be asking for at least a two to three percent reduction. FSBO sellers don't have the benefit of an up-to-date marketing report, so they don't know what their home is really worth. Most sellers want to believe their property is special, so they "test" the market with prices that are usually ten to twenty percent higher than the price of comparable properties. None of the FSBO kits give sellers the ability to reach as many buyers and sellers as the traditional multiple listing service (MLS®).

Then there are the aggravating telephone calls from buyers who don't have the money to even consider buying a home. They call at all hours, day or night, demanding to see your property. Salespeople know how to make sure all buyers are qualified, so only legitimate buyers see your home, and they see it at a formal showing, and at your convenience.

In addition, unscrupulous buyers and even thieves prey upon people who are trying to sell homes themselves. Professional salespeople make sure every buyer who tours your home has had their background information checked in accordance with the requirements of FINTRAC. (More about this in Chapter 5.)

If you try to sell your home without a salesperson, you won't be prepared for the negative comments buyers typically will make when they tour your home, or for the stress of presentation of offers and the sign-back process. When an offer is presented, and every time that offer goes back and forth between buyer and seller, many legal rights and obligations come into play. Most sellers and buyers are in an emotional state, which I refer to as "F state"— they are usually frustrated, frantic, and flustered. The advice of an objective, calm, knowledgeable professional at this critical moment is essential. This is where top salespersons demonstrate their worth every time.

People who sell their own homes are often unaware of their legal obligation to disclose hidden physical defects in their property. At present these defects include a leaky roof or basement, a furnace that's not working properly, and a basement apartment that does not comply with local fire code or zoning bylaws, and disclosure obligations continue to evolve. (More about this in Chapter 2.) Legal proceedings can take four to six years. (See Chapter 11 for more information.) All these nightmares are possible when you try to sell your house without professional advice. Real estate professionals are constantly upgrading their education to make sure you're properly protected from legal claims.

The cold reality is that unless you have friends or family willing to buy your home, your chances of selling and saving the average real estate commission is slim at best. Sellers lose more in their net sale price than they save on real estate commission, and they're vulnerable to legal claims after closing.

Two simple principles I've learned about purchasing anything: "You get what you pay for" and "Those who act for themselves typically have a fool for a client."

Weisleder's Wisdom on For Sale By Owner (FSBO) systems

1. FSBO systems, in general, produce a net loss to sellers.
2. At most, FSBO systems reach twenty percent of the potential buyers in your area.
3. Sixty percent of FSBO sellers end up selling to family or friends.
4. FSBO sellers are vulnerable to claims by buyers after closing, especially regarding non-disclosure of defects in the home.
5. FSBO sellers will have to cope with aggravating phone calls from unqualified buyers, and with negative comments made by buyers during home tours.
6. FSBO sellers will have to cope with emotional late-night negotiations.
7. Remember, when you act for yourself, you usually have a fool for a client.

CAN LAWYERS REPLACE THE SERVICES OF REAL ESTATE SALESPEOPLE?

Some sellers believe that a lawyer should be the only person negotiating the agreement of purchase and sale. But lawyers are not real estate salespersons; nor are they marketers. They don't have experience in preparing a property for sale, and often they have no real idea of what a property is worth.

When it comes to real estate, there is a saying: "Lawyers kill deals." There is some element of truth to this. Lawyers know that if any error or omission is made in a proposed agreement of purchase and sale that they negotiate, the lawyer will be held responsible. So they protect themselves by sometimes adding unnecessary representations and warranties to protect the buyer. (More on this in Chapter 3.) Often the representations and warranties lead to a breakdown of the negotiations.

There are of course times when legal advice should be sought, especially if you're buying a new home from a builder (see Chapter 9), or when special clauses are required, for example if you need a severance of a property before closing. And it's a good idea to consult a lawyer if you find any change in the printed form of the standard agreement of purchase and sale, or if unusual additional clauses have been added for no apparent reason. (More about this in Chapter 5.) In some provinces, after the agreement is signed by the buyer and seller, the agreement is made conditional on being reviewed and approved by the lawyers for both sides. (There are examples of these conditions in Appendix 1.5.a and 1.5.b.)

THE THREE AGREEMENT FORMS

When you work with a professional real estate salesperson as a buyer or a seller, you'll be asked to sign forms stating that you understand the services provided by the salesperson. If you're a seller, you sign a Listing Agreement, Listing Contract, or Selling Brokerage Agreement, depending on what province you live in; if you're a buyer, you sign a Representation, a Brokerage, or an Agency Agreement, depending on your province. But first, you sign a form called "Working with a REALTOR®." This form lists the duties of your sales representative and explains the main principles of agency.

"WORKING WITH A REALTOR®"

This document ensures that a buyer or seller understands the important concepts that arise in a real estate sales relationship. In some provinces, the document is called "Working with an Agent."

There are five key concepts to learn: "client," "customer," "seller listing services," "buyer representation services," and "multiple representation (dual agency)."

When you are a client of a real estate brokerage company, the real estate brokerage and all salespeople working for that company owe you the highest fiduciary or loyalty duties. These duties are required by common law and agency law, which has evolved over the years. As well, each province has real estate brokerage laws. A brokerage and its salespeople must keep your information confidential and do everything they can to help you buy or sell your property for the best price. Let's say you sign a listing agreement to sell your property. If the listing salesperson learns of a buyer who will probably pay more for the property, the salesperson must inform you. Other examples: a salesperson must obey all lawful instructions, exercise reasonable care and skill in performing duties, disclose all relevant facts relating to the transaction to you, and know when to refer you to another expert for advice. In some provinces, these duties are expressly included in the listing agreement, but the principle remains the same: as a client, you will receive the highest level of loyal service and advice from your real estate salesperson.

The same principles apply when you sign an agreement with a buyer brokerage. The brokerage company and all its salespeople must act exclusively for you to find you the home that best fits your needs, and keep all your information confidential. They will obey all lawful instructions, exercise reasonable care and skill, disclose all relevant facts in a transaction, and know when to refer you to an expert for advice.

The salesperson will also offer his or her professional advice on any matter relating to the transaction, in order to properly protect buyer and seller clients.

Some buyers or sellers don't want to enter into client relationships with real estate brokerage companies. When this happens, the buyer or seller agrees that the brokerage may provide "customer service." The real estate salesperson will have the obligation only to answer inquiries by the buyer or seller in a fair and honest manner; no information is kept confidential. The salesperson may represent other buyers or sellers interested in the same property.

Customer service often applies when someone is interested in buying a property that is not listed for sale. The buyer salesperson approaches the seller, who may be willing to sell the property but does not wish to become a client of the brokerage company. They agree to customer service. The seller signs a form called "Confirmation of Co-operation and Representation" to acknowledge he or she will be receiving customer service, and not client services, from the salesperson. Customer service clients are often advised to consult a lawyer before signing an agreement to sell their property, as they are not provided any advice by the salesperson.

Multiple representation, also called dual agency, is a harder concept to understand. In a multiple representation, the real estate brokerage company represents both the buyer and the seller and thus must treat each party with the same level of loyalty. Sometimes the same salesperson represents both the buyer and the seller; sometimes two salespeople in the same brokerage company represent the buyer and the seller. Both the listing agreement (for the seller) and the representation agreement (for the buyer) state that a brokerage can provide multiple representation only if it has the written consent of both buyer and seller.

Sometimes clients think having one salesperson for both buyer and seller will mean less commission. Warning: the negative implications of multiple representation far outweigh any financial benefits.

Salespersons acting in multiple representations are not permitted to disclose any financial details to either party. For example, a salesperson who knows a buyer is willing to offer more money for the property cannot tell the seller. If the salesperson knows the seller has already bought a new home and is desperate to sell, the salesperson cannot tell the buyer. Ideally, you want your salesperson to find out the maximum a buyer will pay, or the minimum a seller will accept. They can't do this when they're acting for both buyer and seller. There is one exception: when salespersons are providing only customer service to one of the parties, for example the seller, they can then disclose financial information to their client, the buyer. As you can see, it's better to be a client than to receive customer services.

A second example: sellers have legal obligations to disclose *major* hidden defects to buyers, but they don't always have to disclose *minor* hidden defects. When a salesperson acts for both seller and buyer, he or she must disclose *all* defects they know about. This obligation could put the seller at a disadvantage. (More about physical defects in Chapter 2.)

In my review of the case law, I found many more legal disputes between sellers and buyers who were represented by the same real estate salesperson or brokerage. It's almost impossible to be fair to both buyer and seller in the same transaction. Buyers and sellers should always consider hiring their own real estate salesperson on every transaction, so that they have the comfort of knowing that the salesperson is always acting solely in their best interests. And make sure you ask to be treated as a client, not as a customer, so you'll benefit from all the advice and protection the salesperson can provide.

Some provinces use a concept called limited dual agency or designated agency. This concept is very similar to multiple representation. The limited dual agency forms use disclosure in advance to overcome some of the difficulties of representing buyers and sellers at the same time. I still strongly recommend having your own salesperson, one who is loyal to your interests only.

Some buyers want to approach a listing salesperson at an open house, without calling their own salesperson. This is extremely risky. Remember, until you sign a buyer representation agreement, a listing salesperson has a duty to tell his or her seller everything you say at the open house. You may inadvertently disclose information that will compromise your bargaining position later. Your salesperson can teach you just what to look for at an open house and, more important, what not to say. Your salesperson also knows how to protect you when you're drafting an agreement of purchase and sale. Remember, substantial legal obligations arise as soon as you sign the agreement.

Do your homework: hire the right salesperson before you start looking for a home, and relax! Your salesperson will show you the properties that are right for your family and your budget. And you'll be completely protected when you sign the agreement of purchase and sale.

THE LISTING AGREEMENT

The listing agreement governs rights and obligations of a seller and a real estate brokerage company. In some provinces, the document is called the listing contract or the selling brokerage agreement; the main principles, duties, and responsibilities of the listing salesperson and seller are for the most part the same. I'll refer to the current Ontario listing agreement as a guide; the explanations of each clause have similar application across Canada.

This is a Multiple Listing Service Agreement®
OR Exclusive Listing Agreement

              (Seller's Initials)   (Seller's Initials)

BETWEEN:
BROKERAGE: _____ (the "Listing Brokerage") Tel. No. (_____)_____

SELLER(S): _____ (the "Seller")
In consideration of the Listing Brokerage listing the real property **for sale** known as _____(the "Property") the Seller hereby gives the Listing Brokerage the **exclusive and irrevocable** right to act as the Seller's agent, **commencing** at 12:01 a.m. on the _____ day of _____, 20_____, **until**

11:59 p.m. on the _____ day of _____, 20_____ (the "Listing Period"), Seller acknowledges that the length of the Listing Period is negotiable between the Seller and the Listing Brokerage and, if an MLS® listing, may be subject to minimum requirements of the real estate board, however, in accordance with the Real Estate and Business Brokers Act (2002),

if the Listing Period exceeds six months, the Listing Brokerage must obtain the Seller's initials.

Sellers Initials

to offer the property **for sale** at a price of: Dollars (CDN$) _____. and upon the terms particularly set out herein, or at such other price and/or terms acceptable to the Seller. It is understood that the price and/or terms set out herein are at the Seller's personal request, after full discussion with the Listing Brokerage's representative regarding potential market value of the Property.

The Seller hereby represents and warrants that the Seller is not a party to any other listing agreement for the Property or agreement to pay commission to any other real estate brokerage for the sale of the property.

The Listing Agreement is a contract between the seller and the real estate brokerage company. The real estate salesperson who signs the document is a representative of a brokerage company. All salespeople who work for that brokerage owe duties to the seller.

The first key words are "exclusive and irrevocable." When you, the seller, sign the listing agreement, you are giving the listing brokerage the exclusive right to market your property for the time period noted in the agreement. The word "irrevocable" means that once you've signed the document, you can't change your mind. If you do need to change any terms of the listing agreement, you must sign a separate amending agreement with the brokerage company.

The "listing period" is the time you, as the seller, give the real estate salesperson to exclusively market your property. The "exclusively" part means no one else can try to sell your house during the specified period. Many real estate boards state that a property must be listed for a minimum of sixty days so they can place the property on their local MLS® system. There is nothing wrong with making the period shorter or longer, as your situation may warrant.

When the market is slow and the average time for a property to sell is more than sixty days, many salespeople will ask for a longer listing period because they'll have to invest more time and money in advertising your property. And sometimes sellers sign a twenty-four-hour listing agreement, for example if a salesperson has a buyer interested in a property but the seller will pay a commission on that transaction only. The twenty-four-hour agreement protects the salesperson for any offer he or she may bring from any buyer during the twenty-four hours.

In Ontario, if a listing will be for more than six months, a seller signs a separate acknowledgement. You'll see this acknowledgement in bold type in the listing agreement, and the requirement for a separate seller initial.

The listing agreement then states the seller may not sign any other listing agreement with any other salespeople. This clause protects the salesperson and the seller from having to pay two separate commissions to two different brokerage companies on a single sale.

If you, the seller, wish to terminate the agreement before the agreed-upon time period, you'll have to get the real estate brokerage company to agree to terminate the listing. If you believe the real estate brokerage or salesperson has materially breached the obligations stated in the listing agreement, you can also ask to terminate the agreement. If the brokerage refuses, you will need to obtain legal advice before proceeding further.

1. DEFINITIONS AND INTERPRETATIONS: For the purposes of this Listing Agreement ("Authority" or "Agreement"), "Seller" includes vendor, a "Buyer" includes a purchaser, or a prospective purchaser and a "real estate board" includes a real estate association. A purchase shall be deemed to include the entering into of any agreement to exchange, or the obtaining of an option to purchase which is subsequently exercised. This Agreement shall be read with all changes of gender or number required by the context. For purposes of this Agreement, anyone introduced or shown the property shall be deemed to include any spouse, heirs, executors, administrators, successors, assigns, related corporations and affiliated corporations. Related corporations or affiliated corporations shall include any corporation where one half or a majority of the shareholders, directors or officers of the related or affiliated corporation are the same person(s) as the shareholders, directors, or officers of the corporation introduced to or shown the property.

This means if anyone who is introduced to the property eventually signs an offer to buy the property, during the listing period or during the holdover period described in clause 2, the seller has to pay a commission. This protects the brokerage when a buyer introduced to the property attempts to buy it from the seller using a different name, or a company name, or asks for an option to buy and exercises it after the listing period, all for the purpose of avoiding real estate commissions. Do not attempt any secret deals to try to avoid the payment of real estate commission. Not only will you likely face legal proceedings, you will also not have the benefit of the advice you need when negotiating the agreement of purchase and sale.

2. COMMISSION: In consideration of the Listing Brokerage listing the Property, the Seller agrees to pay the Listing Brokerage a commission of _____% of the sale price of the Property _____ or _____ for any valid offer to purchase the Property from any source whatsoever obtained during the Listing Period and on the terms and conditions set out in this Agreement **OR** such other terms and conditions as the seller may accept.

The Seller further agrees to pay such commission as calculated above if an agreement to purchase is agreed to or accepted by the Seller or anyone on the Seller's behalf within _____ days after the expiration of the Listing Period **(Holdover Period)**, so long as such agreement is with anyone who was introduced to the property from any source whatsoever during the Listing Period or shown the property during the Listing Period.

If, however, the offer for the purchase of the Property is pursuant to a new agreement in writing to pay commission to another registered real estate brokerage, the Seller's liability for commission shall be reduced by the amount paid by the Seller under the new agreement.

The Seller further agrees to pay such commission as calculated above even if the transaction contemplated by an agreement to purchase agreed to or accepted by the Seller or anyone on the Seller's behalf is not completed, if such non-completion is owing or attributable to the Seller's default or neglect, said commission to be payable on the date set for completion of the purchase of the Property.

Any deposit in respect of any agreement where the transaction has been completed shall first be applied to reduce the commission payable. Should such amounts paid to the Listing Brokerage from the deposit or by the Seller's solicitor not be sufficient, the

> Seller shall be liable to pay to the Listing Brokerage on demand, any deficiency in commission and taxes owing on such commission.
>
> All amounts set out as commission are to be paid plus applicable federal Goods and Services Tax (GST) on such commission.

In the first blank, you, the seller, can choose whether you'll pay your commission as a percentage of the sale price or as a fixed fee. Typically, sellers agree to a percentage, which is shared by the listing salesperson and the buyer salesperson. There is nothing wrong with suggesting an alternative commission arrangement, for example five percent for the first $200,000 of the sale price and then three percent on the balance. It's important thing to make your choice very clear in writing.

One clause in this section has always caused confusion:

> for any valid offer to purchase the Property from any source whatsoever obtained during the Listing Period and on the terms and conditions set out in this Agreement **OR** such other terms and conditions as the seller may accept.

Some sellers think this means if they accept an offer and the buyer fails to complete the transaction, the sellers are still obligated to pay the real estate commission. This phrase was reviewed by the Supreme Court of Canada, which ruled that if the salesperson brings an offer "capable of closing," the seller must pay commission. But if the buyer fails to close the transaction for any reason, the seller pays no commission. (Typically, buyers have to back out because they don't have financing.) However, according to the Supreme Court, if the seller prevents the transaction from closing, the seller *does* have to pay the commission. (The usual reason is that, after signing the agreement, the seller decides it's not time to move, or finds out that there is another buyer out there who will pay more.) This is expressed in the following language:

> The Seller further agrees to pay such commission as calculated above even if the transaction contemplated by an agreement to purchase agreed to or accepted by the Seller or anyone on the Seller's behalf is not completed, if such non-completion is owing or attributable to the Seller's default or neglect, said commission to be payable on the date set for completion of the purchase of the Property.

What happens if you, as the seller, get an offer that fulfills the terms you agreed to in the listing agreement but you decide not to accept the offer? In some provinces, you have to pay the commission anyway. The clause is sometimes written as follows:

> The seller will pay commission if during the term of this agreement, an unconditional offer to purchase the property upon the terms specified in this listing agreement is presented to the seller which the seller refuses to accept.

I would advise you, as the seller, not to accept such a clause and just cross it out of any listing agreement. When you list a property for sale, you base your asking price on the market conditions and your personal circumstances at that time. But things can change. For example, you may lose your job and feel unable to sell your home. Beware of this provision.

The holdover period protects the real estate brokerage when a buyer and seller are introduced during the listing period, then agree to sell the property after the listing period expires. Typically, the holdover period is sixty days. Let's say a seller signs a new listing agreement with a new brokerage after the first listing agreement expires. Then a buyer who saw the property during the first listing makes an offer, and the seller accepts it. The seller subtracts the commission paid to the second listing brokerage from the amount he or she owes to the first brokerage.

For example, the first listing was for 5% on a property listed for $200,000. The commission payable is $10,000 and, because we're in Canada, we pay GST. A buyer purchases the property during the second listing, but within the first listing's holdover period. The second brokerage asked for a 4% commission — $8,000, again plus GST. The seller owes the first brokerage $2,000 plus GST — the difference between the first brokerage's commission and the second brokerage's commission.

If you know of several people who have expressed a private interest in your property, you may ask your brokerage to add them to a schedule to the listing agreement. In the schedule, you agree to a reduced commission or no commission at all if one of the people you know buys your home when it's put onto the market.

And, because we're in Canada, we need to pay the GST, as well. So, how do the commissions get paid? Once the transaction is completed, the buyer's deposit is applied to the payment of commission plus GST. If the deposit is too small to pay the full commission plus GST, the seller agrees to pay the balance immediately. (Typically, the seller's lawyer pays immediately after closing, using proceeds of the sale.) People in New Brunswick, Newfoundland and Labrador, and Nova Scotia pay Harmonized Sales Tax (HST) instead of GST, the amount of tax calculated on the full real estate commission. Ontario is scheduled to apply HST to real estate commissions by July 1, 2010.

3. FINDER'S FEES: The Seller consents to the Listing Brokerage or co-operating brokerage receiving and retaining, in addition to the commission provided for in this Agreement, a finder's fee for any financing of the property.

Real estate salespeople can recommend bankers or mortgage brokers to their buyer clients. These financial professionals can help buyers find the right mortgage loan at the best rates. Some mortgage brokers and financial institutions send a finder's fee to the listing or buyer brokerage for arranging this referral. In this clause the seller agrees to let the brokerage receive any finder's fee.

4. REPRESENTATION: The Seller acknowledges that the Listing Brokerage has provided the Seller with information explaining agency relationships, including information on Seller Representation, Sub-agency, Buyer Representation, Multiple Representation and Customer Service.

The Seller authorizes the Listing Brokerage to co-operate with any other registered real estate brokerage (co-operating brokerage), and to offer to pay the co-operating brokerage a commission of _____% of the sale price of the Property or _____ out of the commission the Seller pays the Listing Brokerage.

The Seller understands that unless the Seller is otherwise informed, the co-operating brokerage is representing the interests of the Buyer in the transaction. The Seller further acknowledges that the Listing Brokerage may be listing other properties that may be similar to the Seller's Property and the Seller hereby consents to the Listing Brokerage listing other properties that may be similar to the Seller's Property without any claim by the Seller of conflict of interest. The Seller hereby appoints the Listing Brokerage as the Seller's agent for the purpose of giving and receiving notices pursuant to any offer or agreement to purchase the Property. Any commission payable to any other brokerage shall be paid out of the commission the Seller pays the Listing Brokerage, said commission to be disbursed in accordance with the Commission Trust Agreement.

MULTIPLE REPRESENTATION: The Seller hereby acknowledges that the Listing Brokerage may be entering into Buyer representation agreements with Buyers who may be interested in purchasing the Seller's Property. In the event that the Listing Brokerage has entered into or enters into a Buyer representation agreement with a prospective Buyer for the Seller's Property, the Listing Brokerage will obtain the Seller's written consent to represent both the Seller and the Buyer for the transaction at the earliest practicable opportunity and in all cases prior to any offer to purchase being submitted or presented.

The Seller understands and acknowledges that the Listing Brokerage must be impartial when representing both the Seller and the Buyer and equally protect the interests of the Seller and Buyer. The Seller understands and acknowledges that when representing both the Seller and the Buyer, the Listing Brokerage shall have a duty of full disclosure to both the Seller and the Buyer, including a requirement to disclose all factual information about the property known to the Listing Brokerage.

However, the Seller further understands and acknowledges that the Listing Brokerage shall not disclose:

• that the Seller may or will accept less than the listed price, unless otherwise instructed in writing by the Seller;

• that the Buyer may or will pay more than the offered price, unless otherwise instructed in writing by the Buyer;

• the motivation of or personal information about the Seller or Buyer, unless otherwise instructed in writing by the party to which the information applies or unless failure to disclose would constitute fraudulent, unlawful or unethical practice;

• the price the Buyer should offer or the price the Seller should accept; and

• the Listing Brokerage shall not disclose to the Buyer the terms of any other offer.

However, it is understood that factual market information about comparable properties and information known to the Listing

Brokerage concerning potential uses for the Property will be disclosed to both Seller and Buyer to assist them to come to their own conclusions.

MULTIPLE REPRESENTATION AND CUSTOMER SERVICE:
The Seller understands and agrees that the Listing Brokerage also provides representation and customer service to other Sellers and Buyers. If the Listing Brokerage represents or provides customer service to more than one Seller or Buyer for the same trade, the Listing Brokerage shall, in writing, at the earliest practicable opportunity and before any offer is made, inform all Sellers and Buyers of the nature of the Listing Brokerage's relationship to each Seller and Buyer.

In clause 4, the listing salesperson reviews with the seller the duties of agency that may take place during the course of the transaction. Duties depend on whether the buyer is a client, is receiving customer service from another buyer brokerage, or is a client of the seller's listing brokerage. (If the buyer's salesperson is with the same brokerage, you'll have multiple representation, which we read about in the section on working with a REALTOR®, earlier in this chapter.) Or the seller's listing brokerage may be providing customer service to the buyer.

The first paragraph of clause 4 confirms that the listing salesperson has explained the different concepts of agency to you, especially the concepts of agency duties and the difference between a client and a customer. In most cases, buyers are represented by their own buyer real estate salesperson or brokerage, which owe the buyer similar duties of loyalty. As the seller, in this section you agree to pay the buyer broker typically half the commission. But remember, even though you're paying them a commission, the buyer salesperson is representing the interests of the buyer, not you.

In clause 4 you also acknowledge that your listing broker-age may be offering other similar properties for sale, either through your salesperson or other salespeople who work for the listing brokerage. You also acknowledge that you under-stand that the other listings may compete with your listing, and you agree that this shall not constitute any conflict of interest by the listing brokerage.

In this clause, you also appoint the listing brokerage as your agent for the purpose of receiving notices on your behalf. What it means is that, for example, a buyer can notify the bro-kerage that they've satisfied or waived a condition; the buyer does not need to notify the seller directly. (This is designed to make sure all parties have a written record of all important documents, and is explained in more detail in Chapter 3, clause 6 of the standard agreement of purchase and sale.)

You also agree that the buyer brokerage will be paid out of the commission you've agreed to pay the listing brokerage once the sale is closed. Terms for paying the commission are described in the commission trust agreement, printed on the back of the standard agreement of purchase and sale form. The commission trust agreement is explained in Chapter 3, in the analysis of the agreement of purchase and sale form.

The next paragraph deals with complications that arise if your listing brokerage also acts for the people who want to buy your home. This can occur when the buyer is a client of your listing salesperson; the buyer could be a client of another salesperson in the same brokerage firm. In both cases, multi-ple representation arises. As the seller, you agree in advance that your listing brokerage must be impartial in representing both buyer and seller, and therefore cannot disclose anything about price or motivation to either party. As indicated above, this means that if the listing salesperson knows that the buyer has already sold their home and is desperate to buy a home quickly, they cannot disclose this important information to the seller.

The listing brokerage can also offer customer service duties to a potential buyer and to other sellers during the time your house is listed. Don't worry: your salesperson can still disclose anything they know about the buyer's price and motivation if they are only providing that buyer with customer service duties.

5. REFERRAL OF ENQUIRIES: The Seller agrees that during the Listing Period, the Seller shall advise the Listing Brokerage immediately of all enquiries from any source whatsoever, and all offers to purchase submitted to the Seller shall be immediately submitted to the Listing Brokerage before the Seller accepts or rejects the same. If the Seller fails to advise the Listing Brokerage of any enquiry during the Listing Period and said enquiry results in the Seller accepting a valid offer to purchase during the Listing Period or within the Holdover Period after the expiration of the Listing Period, the Seller agrees to pay the Listing Brokerage the amount of commission set out above, payable within five (5) days following the Listing Brokerage's written demand therefor.

The listing brokerage will advertise the seller's property for sale in many different mediums, including over the Internet. As a result of these marketing efforts, some buyers may try to contact a seller directly about buying the property. In this clause the seller agrees to refer all enquiries to the listing salesperson. If you, the seller, secretly accept an offer during the listing period or the holdover period, you still have to pay commissions, and you'll probably become involved in unnecessary legal proceedings. And finally, you won't have the benefit of your salesperson's professional advice about your potential buyer, and you won't be protected in any negotiation of the agreement of purchase and sale.

6. MARKETING: The Seller agrees to allow the Listing Brokerage to show and permit prospective Buyers to fully inspect the Property during reasonable hours and the Seller gives the Listing Brokerage the sole and exclusive right to place "For Sale" and "Sold" sign(s) upon the Property. The Seller consents to the Listing Brokerage including information in advertising that may identify the property. The Seller further agrees that the Listing Brokerage shall have sole and exclusive authority to make all advertising decisions relating to the marketing of the Property for sale during the Listing Period. The Seller agrees that the Listing Brokerage will not be held liable in any manner whatsoever for any acts or omissions with respect to advertising by the Listing Brokerage or any other party, other than by the Listing Brokerage's gross negligence or wilful act.

This section gives the listing salesperson the right to put a "For Sale" or "Sold" sign on your property, and it also gives the salesperson the exclusive right to make decisions about the advertising of your property during the listing period. Make sure you talk to potential salespeople about their plans for advertising. Ask for a sample of flyers they've sent out on other deals, and ask what Internet advertising they'll do. After closing, you may not want your salesperson to advertise the price your property sold for, even though it's public information. Salespeople and brokerages must have your express permission before they can advertise the price your property sold for. If you are not comfortable with the purchase price being advertised after closing, then be careful when you sign any other documents. There's more information about the privacy rights of sellers and buyers in Chapter 10.

7. WARRANTY: The Seller represents and warrants that the Seller has the exclusive authority and power to execute this Authority to offer the Property for sale and that the Seller has informed the Listing Brokerage of any third party interests or claims on the property such as rights of first refusal, options, easements, mortgages, encumbrances or otherwise concerning the property, which may affect the sale of the Property.

In this clause, you state that you have the sole right to sell the property and that no one else has any rights in the property. If you inherit a property only for your use during your lifetime, other people will have rights to the property, and you may need their consent to sell. Make sure you have your original deed ready to present to the listing salesperson. You should also provide the report you received from your lawyer when you bought the property; the lawyer's report describes any mortgages or easements that may affect your title to the property, and which may have to be disclosed to any buyer.

8. INDEMNIFICATION: The Seller will not hold the Listing Brokerage responsible for any loss or damage to the Property or contents occurring during the term of this Agreement caused by the Listing Brokerage or anyone else by any means, including theft, fire or vandalism, other than by the Listing Brokerage's gross negligence or wilful act. The Seller agrees to indemnify and save harmless the Listing Brokerage and any co-operating brokerage from any liability, claim, loss, cost, damage or injury, including but not limited to loss of the commission payable under this Agreement, caused or contributed to by the breach of any warranty or representation made by the Seller in this Agreement or the accompanying data form.

In this clause, you agree that your listing brokerage will not be liable for any theft or vandalism that may occur on the property during the listing period, unless it was caused by the gross negligence of the listing brokerage or their salespeople. You also agree to indemnify (compensate) the listing salesperson if you misrepresent anything, and your action affects the sale.

Theft or damage to a property is always a potential problem, especially during open houses or other showings, when many people may be wandering around your home unsupervised. It is important to understand how open houses are conducted, so you can prepare for them in advance, by securing all cash, jewelry, CDs, computer discs, and other personal items before anyone comes into your home. Make sure to give explicit instructions about whether buyers are permitted to wear their shoes in your home, and place signs on the front door or in the vestibule to alert anyone coming in to look at your home. Instruct your salesperson that any buyer couple should not be permitted to separate and look at different parts of the home during an open house as it becomes difficult to monitor.

When you're selling, don't lie about your house; lying can lead to damage claims from unhappy buyers who have relied upon your statements. If you're not sure about anything, say so, and let the buyer do some research if it's important to them. There is more discussion about this topic in Chapter 3; see the section on representations and warranties, and how they affect the agreement of purchase and sale.

9. FAMILY LAW ACT: The Seller hereby warrants that spousal consent is not necessary under the provisions of the Family Law Act, R.S.O. 1990, unless the Seller's spouse has executed the consent hereinafter provided.

In Chapter 7, we discuss the rights of married spouses when a matrimonial home is being sold, even if both spouses' names are not on title. In this clause, you, the seller, indicate that unless your married spouse has also signed the listing agreement, you are not married or the property you're selling is not being used as a family residence.

10. VERIFICATION OF INFORMATION: The Seller authorizes the Listing Brokerage to obtain any information affecting the Property from any regulatory authorities, governments, mortgagees or others and the Seller agrees to execute and deliver such further authorizations in this regard as may be reasonably required. The Seller hereby appoints the Listing Brokerage or the Listing Brokerage's authorized representative as the Seller's attorney to execute such documentation as may be necessary to effect obtaining any information as aforesaid. The Seller hereby authorizes, instructs and directs the above noted regulatory authorities, governments, mortgagees or others to release any and all information to the Listing Brokerage.

In this clause, you authorize your salesperson to look for any information that they may need to effectively sell your property. Salespeople may wish to contact your mortgage provider, an assessment office, or a registry office. The clause also authorizes anyone with information about your home to provide it to your salesperson. The clause protects both buyers and sellers, to make sure that all relevant matters about the property are disclosed in a timely manner.

11. USE AND DISTRIBUTION OF INFORMATION: The Seller consents to the collection, use and disclosure of personal information by the Brokerage for the purpose of listing and marketing the Property including, but not limited to: listing and advertising the Property using any medium including the Internet; disclosing property information to prospective Buyers, brokerages, salespersons and others who may assist in the sale of the Property; such other use of the Seller's personal information as is consistent with listing and marketing of the Property. The Seller consents, if this is an MLS® Listing, to placement of the listing information and sales information by the Brokerage into the database(s) of the appropriate MLS® system(s), and to the posting of any documents and other information provided by or on behalf of the Seller into the database(s) of the appropriate MLS® system(s). The Seller acknowledges that the MLS® database is the property of the real estate board(s) and can be licensed, resold, or otherwise dealt with by the board(s). The Seller further acknowledges that the real estate board(s) may: distribute the information to any persons authorized to use such service which may include other brokerages, government departments, appraisers, municipal organizations and others; market the Property, at its option, in any medium, including electronic media; compile, retain and publish any statistics including historical MLS® data which may be used by board members to conduct comparative market analyses; and make such other use of the information as the Brokerage and/or real estate board deems appropriate in connection with the listing, marketing and selling of real estate.

In the event that this Agreement expires or is cancelled or otherwise terminated and the Property is not sold, the Seller, by initialling:

Does   **Does Not**

consent to allow other real estate board members to contact the Seller after expiration or other termination of this Agreement to discuss listing or otherwise marketing the Property.

Under the provisions of federal privacy legislation, more fully discussed in Chapter 10, all information about a property, including the residential address, is personal information and as such cannot be advertised without the express written consent of the owner. With this clause, you agree to permit the listing brokerage to advertise, to anyone and through any medium, all information about your property, including some information that may in fact be personal under the federal privacy act. You're also giving your salesperson permission to place information about your property — for example, a completed seller property information statement or a property condition statement — on the MLS® system so any buyer can see it. This clause also authorizes the real estate board to make use of any information about the sale of the property in any way they see fit — for example, handing it to a government department such as the provincial assessment department. You're also agreeing that other salespeople may use the final sale price of your property to compile comparative market analyses for future buyers and sellers in your area.

At the end of this section, you state whether you wish to be contacted by other salespeople if the listing expires before the property is sold. If you do not wish to be called, then just initial the circle where it states "Does Not."

12. SUCCESSORS AND ASSIGNS: The heirs, executors, administrators, successors and assigns of the undersigned are bound by the terms of this Agreement.

If you pass away during the course of the listing, your estate is still be bound to pay any commission should the sale be completed by the estate.

13. CONFLICT OR DISCREPANCY: If there is any conflict or discrepancy between any provision added to this Agreement (including any Schedule attached hereto) and any provision in the standard pre-set portion hereof, the added provision shall supersede the standard pre-set provision to the extent of such conflict or discrepancy. This Agreement, including any Schedule attached hereto, shall constitute the entire Agreement between the Seller and the Listing Brokerage. There is no representation, warranty, collateral agreement or condition, which affects this Agreement other than as expressed herein.

If you and your listing salesperson include a provision in any schedule to the agreement, and your provision is in conflict with anything in the printed clauses, the schedule will take precedence. For example, say you write in a schedule that the brokerage won't receive any commission if your cousin buys your home. Your added provision takes precedence over clause 2, which is about the seller's obligation to pay commission.

14. ELECTRONIC COMMUNICATION: This Listing Agreement and any agreements, notices or other communications contemplated thereby may be transmitted by means of electronic systems, in which case signatures shall be deemed to be original. The transmission of this Agreement by the Seller by electronic means shall be deemed to confirm the Seller has retained a true copy of the Agreement.

Clause 14 permits this agreement to be signed via fax machine or other form of electronic transmission. This is in the event that the parties need to have the form signed in order to place it on the local board MLS® system but the seller may be out of town. It is still advisable for the parties to sign original agreements later for their files and records. A true copy means that you have kept an identical copy of what you have signed.

15. SCHEDULE(S) _____ and data form attached hereto form(s) part of this Agreement.

This clause allows you to add schedules. After clause 15, there are some unnumbered sections of the listing agreement:

THE LISTING BROKERAGE AGREES TO MARKET THE PROPERTY ON BEHALF OF THE SELLER AND REPRESENT THE SELLER IN AN ENDEAVOUR TO OBTAIN A VALID OFFER TO PURCHASE THE PROPERTY ON THE

TERMS SET OUT IN THIS AGREEMENT OR ON SUCH OTHER TERMS SATISFACTORY TO THE SELLER.

_____ DATE _____

_____

(Authorized to bind the Listing Brokerage) (Name of Person Signing)

THIS AGREEMENT HAS BEEN READ AND FULLY UNDER-STOOD BY ME AND I ACKNOWLEDGE THIS DATE I HAVE SIGNED UNDER SEAL AND HAVE RECEIVED A TRUE COPY OF THIS AGREEMENT. Any representations contained herein or as shown on the accompanying data form respecting the Property are true to the best of my knowledge, information and belief.

SIGNED, SEALED AND DELIVERED I have hereunto set my hand and seal:

_____✳ DATE _____

(Signature of Seller)   (Seal) _____

_____✳ DATE _____

(Signature of Seller)   (Seal) _____

Here the listing salesperson and the seller sign the listing agreement. The salesperson is signing on behalf of the brokerage; the seller must be the person named on the property deed. Also in this clause, the listing brokerage agrees to market the property in accordance with the listing agreement. When you sign, you are indicating that you understand the terms of the listing agreement and that any information you provide about your property is true, to the best of your knowledge, information, and belief.

SPOUSAL CONSENT: The undersigned spouse of the Seller hereby consents to the listing of the Property herein pursuant to the provisions of the Family Law Act, R.S.O. 1990 and hereby agrees that he/she will execute all necessary or incidental documents to further any transaction provided for herein.

_____ ✳ DATE _____
(Spouse)   (Seal) _____

If the property is a matrimonial home (see Chapter 7), your spouse signs the listing agreement here.

DECLARATION OF INSURANCE
The
broker/salesperson _____
                              (Name of Broker/Salesperson)
hereby declares that he/she is insured as required by the Real Estate and Business Brokers Act (REBBA) and Regulations.

_____

Signature of Broker/Salesperson

In Ontario, under the _Real Estate and Business Brokers Act_, and in other provinces and the territories under similar statutes, all brokerages and salespeople must carry errors and omissions insurance, in case they make any errors while they're representing you. They also must carry insurance to protect any deposit that may be paid by any buyer under any agreement of purchase and sale. (This is in case the brokerage goes bankrupt.)

**Weisleder's Wisdom on the listing agreement**

1. As a seller, you should understand the differences between a client relationship and a customer relationship.

2. When you're selling your home, avoid multiple representation; make sure your salesperson is always working for you and not for possible buyers.
3. If you don't want your salesperson to advertise the price your property sells for, or if you don't wish to be contacted by other salespeople after the listing expires, make sure you say so in the listing agreement.
4. Check your deed and any letters from the lawyer who helped you buy your house to be sure you have the right to sell it. Also look for information about easements and mortgages.

THE BUYER REPRESENTATION AGREEMENT

The buyer representation agreement, also called the buyer brokerage agreement or the buyer agency agreement, is the main agreement between buyers and their real estate brokerage company. This agreement governs your rights and obligations when you're buying a property. This document establishes an exclusive relationship between you, the buyer, and your real estate brokerage. Most people know that when you sign a listing agreement and sell your house, your listing brokerage gets a commission. But a lot of people don't understand exactly what a buyer salesperson does. So I'll begin by telling you the buyer representation agreement says that when you sign, even if your buyer salesperson does not introduce you to the property you end up buying, you still owe that buyer salesperson a commission.

This is a difficult concept for many buyers to accept. But remember, your buyer salesperson spends many hours researching, searching, and networking to find you the right property; your buyer salesperson gives you advice about how to qualify for a mortgage; your buyer salesperson talks to a professional team and gets referrals so your buying decision is simple. And your buyer salesperson protects you when he or she is preparing the agreement of purchase and sale. You don't pay anything for the salesperson's time, and the salesperson gets paid only if you buy a house. And yet buyers expect a buyer salesperson to provide the best and most loyal service. No wonder buyer salespeople deserve a commission!

Before you sign a buyer representation agreement, take the time to interview several buyer salespeople. Make sure you're comfortable with the salesperson you choose. (This chapter will give you information about how to choose your buyer salesperson.) Once you've chosen a buyer salesperson, you should give the same commitment to your salesperson that your salesperson gives to you.

The buyer representation agreement clearly sets out the duties and responsibilities of both parties, and includes details about paying commissions. I will review each clause in detail in this section, using the Ontario agreement as a guide. Similar provisions are found in other provincial buyer representation agreements and buyer agency agreements.

Buyer Representation Agreement

This is an Exclusive Buyer Representation Agreement

BETWEEN:

BROKERAGE: _____,
Tel. No. (_____)_____
ADDRESS: _____
_____
_____

Fax. No. (_____)_____ hereinafter referred to as the Brokerage.

AND:

BUYER(S)_____
_____, hereinafter referred to as the Buyer,

ADDRESS: _____
_____
_____

The Buyer hereby gives the Brokerage the **exclusive and irrevocable authority** to act as the Buyer's agent **commencing**

at _____ a.m./p.m. on the _____ day of _____, 20_____,

and expiring at 11:59 p.m. on the _____ day of _____, 20_____ (Expiry Date).

Buyer acknowledges that the time period for this Agreement is negotiable between the Buyer and the Brokerage, however, in accordance with the Real Estate and Business Brokers Act of Ontario (2002),

If the time period for this Agreement exceeds six months, the Brokerage must obtain the Buyer's initials.
                                                        (Buyer's Initials)
for the purpose of locating a real property meeting the following general description:

Property Type
(Use) _____

_____

_____

Geographic Location _____

_____

_____

The Buyer hereby warrants that the Buyer is not a party to a buyer representation agreement with any other registered real estate brokerage for the purchase or lease of a real property of the general description indicated above.

The buyer representation agreement is a contract between a buyer and a real estate brokerage company. The real estate salesperson who signs the document is acting as a representative of the brokerage company. All salespeople who work for the brokerage company owe duties to the buyer, and this can get complicated when another salesperson in the brokerage acts for a seller or another buyer of the same property.

Notice the words "exclusive and irrevocable," in bold type. When you, the buyer, sign a buyer representation agreement, you are giving the buyer brokerage the exclusive right to find you a property that meets your specific needs during the time period noted in the agreement. The word "irrevocable" means that once you sign the document, you can't change your mind. You should also know that only a separate amending agreement with the brokerage can change any of the terms of your agreement.

The agreement comes into effect on the date you sign, and stays in effect until the expiry date, usually sixty days after you've signed. However, there is nothing wrong with making this time period shorter or longer, as the situation may warrant.

In Ontario, if your buyer representation agreement is for longer than six months, you need to sign a separate acknowledgement. You'll see this in bold type in the agreement.

Then you and your buying salesperson describe the general type of property you're looking for, as well as the general geographic location. Your salesperson uses this information to narrow the search — on MLS®, by physically visiting properties, or through networking contacts — for the most suitable property in your price range.

For example, you may want to look at only resale homes with your buyer salesperson; if you decide to buy a new home from a builder, you won't have to pay a commission to the buyer brokerage. (But be careful. In Chapter 9, I tell you about the many advantages to using a buyer salesperson even if you're looking at new homes or new condominium buildings.)

Next, you sign to show you're not a party to any other buyer representation agreement with any other salespeople. This protects both you and the salesperson from having to pay two separate commissions to two different brokerage companies for a single purchase. If you become unhappy with your buyer salesperson, both you and the buyer brokerage must be mutually released from the agreement. Only after that can you sign a new buyer representation agreement with another brokerage. If your salesperson refuses to agree to terminate your agreement, you should obtain legal advice before proceeding any further.

1. DEFINITIONS AND INTERPRETATIONS: For the purposes of this Buyer Representation Agreement ("Authority" or "Agreement"), "Buyer" includes purchaser and tenant, a "seller" includes a vendor, a landlord or a prospective seller, vendor or landlord and a "real estate board" includes a real estate association. A purchase shall be deemed to include the entering into of any agreement to exchange, or the obtaining of an option to purchase which is subsequently exercised, and a lease includes any rental agreement, sub-lease or renewal of a lease. This Agreement shall be read with all changes of gender or number required by the context. For purposes of this Agreement, anyone shown or introduced to the property shall be deemed to include any spouse, heirs, executors, administrators, successors, assigns, related corporations and affiliated corporations. Related corporations or affiliated corporations shall include any corporation where one half or a majority of the shareholders, directors or officers of the related or affiliated corporation are the same person(s) as the shareholders, directors, or officers of the corporation introduced to or shown the property.

This section explains that if your buyer salesperson shows you a property and you eventually sign an offer to buy the property, either during the buyer representation period or during the holdover period (clause 2), you have to pay your buyer salesperson a commission. This section protects the brokerage if a client attempts to buy the property later, using a different name, or tries in some other way to avoid paying the commission. Buyers who attempt such trickery usually end up in court.

2. COMMISSION: In consideration of the Brokerage undertaking to assist the Buyer, the Buyer agrees to pay commission to the Brokerage as follows: If, during the currency of this Agreement, the Buyer enters into an agreement to purchase or lease a real property of the general description indicated above, the Buyer agrees the Brokerage is entitled to receive and retain any commission offered by a listing brokerage or by the seller. The Buyer understands that the amount of commission offered by a listing brokerage or by the seller may be greater or less than the commission stated below. The Buyer understands that the Brokerage will inform the Buyer of the amount of commission to be paid to the Brokerage by the listing brokerage or the seller at the earliest practical opportunity. The Buyer acknowledges that the payment of any commission by the listing brokerage or the seller will not make the Brokerage either the agent or sub-agent of the listing brokerage or the seller.

If, during the currency of this Agreement, the Buyer enters into an agreement to purchase or lease any property of the general description indicated above, the Buyer agrees that the Brokerage is entitled to be paid a commission of _____% of the sale price of the property

or _____

The Buyer agrees to pay directly to the Brokerage any deficiency between this amount and the amount, if any, to be paid to the Brokerage by a listing brokerage or by the seller. The Buyer understands that if the Brokerage is not to be paid any commission by a listing brokerage or by the seller, the Buyer will pay the Brokerage the full amount of commission indicated above.

The Buyer agrees to pay the Brokerage such commission if the Buyer enters into an agreement within _____ days after the expiration of this Agreement **(Holdover Period)** to purchase or lease any real property shown or introduced to the Buyer from any source whatsoever during the term of this Agreement, provided, however, that if the Buyer enters into a new buyer representation agreement with another registered real estate brokerage after the expiration of this Agreement, the Buyer's liability to pay commission to the Brokerage shall be reduced by the amount paid to the other brokerage under the new agreement.

The Buyer agrees to pay such commission as described above even if a transaction contemplated by an agreement to purchase or lease agreed to or accepted by the Buyer or anyone on the Buyer's behalf is not completed, if such non-completion is owing or attributable to the Buyers default or neglect. Said commission, plus any applicable taxes, shall be payable on the date set for completion of the purchase of the property or, in the case of a lease or tenancy, the earlier of the date of occupancy by the tenant or the date set for commencement of the lease or tenancy.

All amounts set out as commission are to be paid plus applicable federal Goods and Services Tax (GST) on such commission.

As a buyer, you have a legal obligation to pay your buyer salesperson the commission. If the listing brokerage does not pay the buyer representative commission in the amount stated in the buyer representative agreement, then you pay any deficiency directly to your buyer representative. In practical terms, when you're interested in a property, your buyer representative will ask the listing brokerage if it will pay the traditional split of commission. If the answer is yes, there is little likelihood you'll have to pay anything to your buyer representative. As an example, let's say a home is selling for $200,000 with a 5% commission from the seller, which is $10,000, plus GST. It is understood by everyone that half of this 5% commission, or $5,000, will be paid to the buyer salesperson. But let's say the listing salesperson is only charging 2.5% commission to the seller, or $5,000, and indicates on the listing that they will not pay anything to the buyer salesperson. If the buyer, in the buyer representation agreement has agreed to pay the buyer salesperson 2.5% commission, or $5,000, then they will reduce their offer from $200,000, to $195,000, knowing that they are responsible for the buyer commission of $5,000. In this way, the buyer gets the property at the total price that they expected to pay in the first place and still enjoys the benefit of complete representation and protection from their buyer representative.

There is one more commission provision: sometimes a buyer representative finds a property for the buyer, and the buyer puts in an offer but then fails to complete the transaction for some reason. (Usually it's because the buyer doesn't have the financing.) The buyer still has to pay the commission to the buyer representative, who has completed what he or she set out to do. In other words, the buyer has to pay the commission to the buyer salesperson if the buyer is responsible for the transaction not closing. This is shown in the following language:

> The Buyer further agrees to pay such commission as calculated above even if the transaction contemplated by an agreement to purchase agreed to or accepted by the Buyer or anyone on the Buyer's behalf is not completed, if such non-completion is owing or attributable to the Buyer's default or neglect, said commission to be payable on the date set for completion of the purchase of the Property.

The holdover period (from paragraph three) provides additional protection for the real estate brokerage when a buyer sees a property during the listing period and then tries to buy it secretly from the seller after the buyer representation period expires. The holdover period is usually sixty days. Buyers and sellers who try this usually end up in serious legal trouble. But let's say a buyer is shown a house by a buyer salesperson, then signs a new buyer representation agreement with a second brokerage after the first buyer representation agreement expires, and then buys the property. The buyer is liable for commission, but the amount will be reduced by any amount the buyer pays the second buyer brokerage.

As a buyer, you may also consider adding a schedule to the buyer representation agreement if you already know of several properties you would like to buy. If your buyer brokerage agrees, you can add a schedule that reduces the buyer commission, or waives it, if you buy one of the properties you name in the schedule.

3. REPRESENTATION: The Buyer acknowledges that the Brokerage has provided the Buyer with written information explaining agency relationships, including information on Seller Representation, Sub-Agency, Buyer Representation, Multiple Representation and Customer Service. The Brokerage shall assist the Buyer in locating a real property of the general description indicated above and shall represent the Buyer in an endeavour to procure the acceptance of an agreement to purchase or lease such a property.

The buyer acknowledges that the buyer may not be shown or offered all properties that may be of interest to the buyer.

The buyer hereby agrees that the terms of any buyer's offer or agreement to purchase or lease the property will not be disclosed to any other buyer.

The buyer further acknowledges that the Brokerage may be entering into buyer representation agreements with other buyers who may be interested in the same or similar properties that the buyer may be interested in buying or leasing and the buyer hereby consents to the Brokerage entering into buyer representation agreements with other buyers who may be interested in the same or similar properties without any claim by the buyer of conflict of interest.

The Buyer hereby appoints the Brokerage as agent for the purpose of giving and receiving notices pursuant to any offer or agreement to purchase or lease a property negotiated by the Brokerage.

MULTIPLE REPRESENTATION: The Buyer hereby acknowledges that the Brokerage may be entering into listing agreements with sellers of properties the Buyer may be interested in buying or leasing. In the event that the Brokerage has entered into or enters into a listing agreement with the seller of a property the Buyer may be interested in buying or leasing, the Brokerage will obtain the Buyer's written consent to represent both the Buyer and the seller for the transaction at the earliest practicable opportunity and in all cases prior to any offer to purchase or lease being submitted or presented.

The Buyer understands and acknowledges that the Brokerage must be impartial when representing both the Buyer and the seller and equally protect the interests of the Buyer and the seller in the transaction. The Buyer understands and acknowledges that when representing both the Buyer and the seller, the Brokerage shall have a duty of full disclosure to both the Buyer and the seller, including a requirement to disclose all factual information about the property known to the Brokerage.

However, The Buyer further understands and acknowledges that the Brokerage shall not disclose:
- that the seller may or will accept less than the listed price, unless otherwise instructed in writing by the seller;
- that the Buyer may or will pay more than the offered price, unless otherwise instructed in writing by the Buyer;
- the motivation of or personal information about the Buyer or seller, unless otherwise instructed in writing by the party to which the information applies or unless failure to disclose would constitute fraudulent, unlawful or unethical practice;
- the price the Buyer should offer or the price the seller should accept; and
- the Brokerage shall not disclose to the Buyer the terms of any other offer.

However, it is understood that factual market information about comparable properties and information known to the Brokerage concerning potential uses for the property will be disclosed to both Buyer and seller to assist them to come to their own conclusions.

MULTIPLE REPRESENTATION AND CUSTOMER SERVICE:
The Buyer understands and agrees that the Brokerage also pro-vides representation and customer service to other buyers and sellers. If the Brokerage represents or provides customer service

to more than one seller or buyer for the same trade, the Brokerage shall, in writing, at the earliest practicable opportunity and before any offer is made, inform all sellers and buyers of the nature of the Brokerage's relationship to each seller and buyer.

In clause 3, the buyer salesperson reviews the duties of agency when the seller is a client of or is receiving customer service from another buyer brokerage, and also the duties of agency when the seller is a client of the buyer brokerage you are using (this is called multiple representation). And sometimes the buyer's brokerage is providing customer service to the seller. As a buyer, you should understand all the legal obligations that can arise in these circumstances.

In the second paragraph of clause 3, the buyer brokerage makes a commitment to find a property that will suit you, and to represent you in preparing and negotiating any offer to purchase. Then you acknowledge that given the general nature of the property description, the buyer representative may not be able to show you every property that might interest you.

The next paragraph reminds you that the buyer brokerage and the buyer salespeople who work for that brokerage may also represent other buyers, who may be interested in a property you want to buy. This usually happens when there are multiple offers. In many cases, you and your buyer salesperson may not know there are multiple offers, submitted by two different buyer salespeople who work for the same office but represent different buyers. The brokerage is not in a conflict of interest: both salespeople will do their best to represent the interests of their buyer clients.

The buyer also appoints the buyer brokerage as their own agent for the purpose of giving or receiving any notices under any offer or agreement that may be prepared on their behalf. This is done so that a written record of all documents that have to be exchanged during the agreement are properly given to your buyer salesperson.

What happens if your buyer brokerage also acts for the seller of the home you want to buy? Your buyer salesperson may have a seller client, or another salesperson in the same firm may have a seller client with a property that would interest you. This situation is referred to as "multiple representation." As the buyer, you acknowledge in writing that the buyer brokerage must be impartial when representing both buyer and seller, and cannot disclose information about price or motivation to either party. The buyer salesperson can't tell you the seller will take less for the property.

Sometimes a buyer brokerage provides customer service duties to a seller or other buyers during the time of your buyer representation agreement. In this situation, the salesperson providing customer service can disclose information about price or motivation. The salesperson may be receiving the commission for the sale but owes minimal loyalty duties to the seller in the customer service agreement.

In my view, it's not a good idea to agree to multiple representation. Buyers and sellers should each have their own brokerage company, working solely for them, so they'll get the best price and the best property. Don't be fooled: you may save a small amount on commission, but you won't get a better deal when there is multiple representation. Take the time to engage the right salesperson to represent you, whether you are buying or selling a property. Get the maximum protection available to you.

4. REFERRAL OF PROPERTIES: The Buyer agrees that during the currency of this Buyer Representation Agreement the Buyer will act in good faith and work exclusively with the Brokerage for the purchase or lease of a real property of the general description indicated above. The Buyer agrees that, during the currency of this

Agreement, the Buyer shall advise the Brokerage immediately of any property of interest to the Buyer that came to the Buyer's attention from any source whatsoever, and all offers to purchase or lease submitted by the Buyer shall be submitted through the Brokerage to the seller. If the Buyer fails to advise the Brokerage of any property of interest to the Buyer that came to the Buyer's attention during the currency of this Agreement and the Buyer arranges a valid offer to purchase or lease the property during the currency of this Agreement or within the Holdover Period after expiration of this agreement, the Buyer agrees to pay the Brokerage the amount of commission set out above, payable within five (5) days following the Brokerage's written demand therefor.

In this clause, you agree to work exclusively with your buyer brokerage during the term of your buyer brokerage agreement, and you agree to inform your buyer salesperson of any property that interests you, including any property you see that has a "For Sale" sign on it. If there is an open house and you want to see inside, call your own buyer salesperson. If you do go in, you must inform the salesperson showing the home that you're working with a buyer salesperson. If you say anything directly to the listing salesperson running an open house, that salesperson has a duty to disclose what you've said to the seller. You may inadvertently jeopardize your bargaining position by saying too much to the listing salesperson. If you go ahead and prepare an offer on the property without notifying your own buyer salesperson, you forfeit the advantage of separate professional advice during the negotiations, and you may still end up having to pay an extra commission to your buyer salesperson, in accordance with clause 2 of the buyer representation agreement.

This clause also makes it clear that if you find a property during the term of your buyer representation agreement and then secretly enter into an agreement with the seller, either during the term of your buyer representation agreement or during the holdover period, you still have to pay the commission to your buyer brokerage.

I cannot stress enough that when buyers engage in secret activities to avoid paying commission to their buyer salespeople, they'll become involved in unnecessary legal proceedings. As well, these buyers won't have professional advice that would protect them from the many potential pitfalls of buying a home. In my experience, most of these buyers regret their actions later, especially when they discover undisclosed problems with their home after closing.

> **5. INDEMNIFICATION:** The Brokerage and representatives of the Brokerage are trained in dealing in real estate but are not qualified in determining the physical condition of the land or any improvements thereon. The Buyer agrees that the Brokerage will not be liable for any defects, whether latent or patent, to the land or improvements thereon. All information supplied by the seller or landlord or the listing brokerage may not have been verified and is not warranted by the Brokerage as being accurate and will be relied on by the Buyer at the Buyer's own risk. The Buyer acknowledges having been advised to make their own enquiries to confirm the condition of the property.

In this clause, the buyer brokerage is making it clear that they are not qualified to provide any opinion regarding the physical condition of a home, and you are acknowledging that you can't hold them responsible for any hidden defects. In my opinion, every property purchase agreement should include a home inspection condition; as a buyer, you can hire a professional home inspector, who will give you a complete report on the house you want to buy. You can also talk to the seller as well as the neighbours to find out if there are neighbourhood conditions, such as a grow house on the street or nearby that may affect the value of the home you want to buy. For more information about "patent and latent defects," and home inspections in general, see Chapter 2.

6. FINDER'S FEE: The Buyer acknowledges that the Brokerage may be receiving a finder's fee from a lender in the event that a new mortgage or an increase in financing is required for a transaction contemplated by this Agreement, and the Buyer consents to any such fee being retained by the Brokerage in addition to the commission as described above.

One of the services real estate salespeople provide to buyers is their ability to recommend bankers and mortgage brokers who can help you find the right mortgage loan for your property, at the best rates available. Sometimes these mortgage brokers and financial institutions may send a finder's fee to the buyer brokerage for arranging this referral. In this clause you agree to the buyer brokerage receiving any finder's fee.

7. CONSUMER REPORTS: The Buyer is hereby notified that a Consumer Report containing credit and/or personal information may be referred to in connection with this Agreement and any subsequent transaction.

The first thing people notice about this section is that it is written in bold type. This section advises you, the buyer, that a seller may conduct a credit check on you when the agreement of purchase and sale is being negotiated. The Consumer Reporting Act governs how credit bureaus may use information they collect about consumers in the province of Ontario. Similar legislation applies in all provinces and in the territories.

A seller may want a credit check when the buyer asks the seller to take back a mortgage as part of the purchase price. A poor credit history tells the seller that the buyer may be unable to make the payments.

Sellers who refuse to complete the transaction because of the credit report are obligated to inform the buyer; if the buyer asks where they got their credit information, the sellers will provide where the information came from.

8. USE AND DISTRIBUTION OF INFORMATION: The Buyer consents to the collection, use and disclosure of personal information by the Brokerage for such purposes that relate to the real estate services provided by the Brokerage to the Buyer including, but not limited to: locating, assessing and qualifying properties for the Buyer; advertising on behalf of the Buyer; providing information as needed to third parties retained by the Buyer to assist in a transaction (e.g. financial institutions, building inspectors, etc.); and such other use of the Buyer's information as is consistent with the services provided by the Brokerage in connection with the purchase or prospective purchase of the property.

The Buyer agrees that the sale and related information regarding any property purchased by the Buyer through the Brokerage may be retained and disclosed by the Brokerage and/or real estate board(s) (if the property is an MLS® Listing) for reporting, appraisal and statistical purposes and for such other use of the information as the Brokerage and/or board deems appropriate in connection with the listing, marketing and selling of real estate, including conducting comparative market analyses.

Under the provisions of federal privacy legislation all information about a property, including the residential address, is personal information, and therefore cannot be advertised without the express written consent of the owner. This clause authorizes the real estate board to make use of any information about the sale of the property as they see fit, including providing the information to any other government department, such as the provincial assessment department. This also permits other salespeople to use the final purchase price of your property in order to compile a comparative market analysis for future buyers and sellers of homes in your area. (I discuss privacy more fully in Chapter 10.)

9. CONFLICT OR DISCREPANCY: If there is any conflict or discrepancy between any provision added to this Agreement and any provision in the standard pre-set portion hereof, the added provision shall supersede the standard pre-set provision to the extent of such conflict or discrepancy. This Agreement, including any provisions added to this Agreement, shall constitute the entire Agreement between the Buyer and the Brokerage. There is no representation, warranty, collateral agreement or condition, which affects this Agreement other than as expressed herein.

Clause 9 indicates says that if you and your buyer salesperson add a provision in any schedule to the agreement that is in conflict with anything in the preprinted clauses, your provision in the schedule will take precedence. For example, say you add a schedule in clause 2, that the brokerage will not receive any commission if you purchase a home owned by your brother during the term of your buyer representation agreement. Your schedule takes precedence over anything indicated in clause 2 about your obligation to pay commission.

10. ELECTRONIC COMMUNICATION: This Buyer Representation Agreement and any agreements, notices or other communications contemplated thereby may be transmitted by means of electronic systems, in which case signatures shall be deemed to be original. The transmission of this Agreement by the Buyer by electronic means shall be deemed to confirm the Buyer has retained a true copy of the Agreement.

This clause permits your buyer representation agreement to be signed via fax machine or other form of electronic transmission. You use this clause if you're out of town and you want your buyer salesperson to start looking for properties immediately, or to prepare an offer for you. In my opinion, it's a good idea to sign original agreements later, for the files and records. True copy means you have kept an identical copy of what you have signed.

11. SCHEDULE(S) _____ hereto form(s) part of this Agreement.

This clause 11 contemplates adding additional schedules when required.

THE BROKERAGE AGREES TO REPRESENT THE BUYER IN LOCATING A REAL PROPERTY OF THE GENERAL DESCRIPTION INDICATED ABOVE IN AN ENDEAVOUR TO OBTAIN THE ACCEPTANCE OF AN AGREEMENT TO PURCHASE OR LEASE A PROPERTY ON TERMS SATISFACTORY TO THE BUYER.

_____ DATE _____

_____
(Authorized to bind the Brokerage) (Name of Person Signing)

THIS AGREEMENT HAS BEEN READ AND FULLY UNDERSTOOD BY ME AND I ACKNOWLEDGE THIS DATE I HAVE SIGNED UNDERSEAL AND HAVE RECEIVED A TRUE COPY OF THIS AGREEMENT. Any representations contained herein are true to the best of my knowledge, information and belief.

SIGNED, SEALED AND DELIVERED I have hereunto set my hand and seal:

_____ ✳ DATE _____

(Signature of Buyer) (Seal) (Tel. No.)

_____ ✳ DATE _____

(Signature of Buyer) (Seal)

Here is where the buyer salesperson, on behalf of the brokerage, and you, the buyer, sign the buyer representation agreement. The buyer brokerage is agreeing to help you find a property and represent you in the preparation of any agreement of purchase and sale for any property you're interested in. You're indicating that you understand the terms of the buyer representation agreement.

DECLARATION OF INSURANCE

The broker/
salesperson _____

(Name of Broker/Salesperson)

hereby declares that he/she is insured as required by the Real Estate and Business Brokers Act (REBBA) and Regulations.

_____

(Signature of Broker/Salesperson)

Under the Real Estate and Business Brokers Act (in Ontario) and similar legislation across the country, all brokerages and salespeople must carry errors and omissions insurance. This protects them if they make any errors while representing you. It also protects any deposit you provide under any agreement of purchase and sale, should a brokerage go bankrupt.

Weisleder's Wisdom on
the buyer representation agreement

1. Buyer brokerages can give you a huge advantage. All you have to do is sign a buyer representation agreement.
2. When you sign the buyer representation agreement, you also agree to pay the buyer brokerage commission if you sign a purchase and sale agreement during the term of the buyer representation agreement; yes, you pay the commission even if you find a property on your own.
3. Try and avoid multiple representation; make sure your salesperson is always working in your sole best interests and has no similar duties to sellers.

Whether you are a buyer or a seller, much of your success in finding the right property, negotiating your agreement, and avoiding problems after closing will depend on your ability to find the right REALTOR® to represent your interests. If you do your homework and select the right salesperson, you'll have maximum protection when you're looking to buy or sell a home.

Weisleder's Wisdom on
how to find the right REALTOR®

1. Real estate agents are also referred to as real estate salespeople.
2. When you're looking for a real estate salesperson, ask for referrals from your friends, relatives, and co-workers.
3. When you find a salesperson you're interested in, check their websites.
4. Ask the salesperson for testimonials from previous clients.
5. Look at samples of the salesperson's marketing material, so you'll know how your home will be marketed.

6. Be wary of any For Sale By Owner systems. If you're selling, you probably won't save any money, and you'll have little protection during the negotiating process. And there may be legal liability after closing.

7. Lawyers are not substitutes for REALTORS®; they do not have the same experience in marketing or negotiating agreements of purchase and sale.

8. Before you sign a listing or buyer representation agreement, consider the importance of being a client of the brokerage. Customer service gives you fewer benefits and less protection.

9. It is important to understand the fine print in any listing or buyer representation agreement – especially your obligation to pay commission.

10. If you secretly avoid paying commission by making private deals with a buyer or seller, you won't have professional advice during the negotiation process, and you may end up in litigation.

CHAPTER 2

Preparing to Sell or Buy a Home

Property rights in Ontario and the rest of Canada have been established since Canada was first settled in 1795. Some historical distinctions affect the rights of landowners even today. Although the provinces were settled at different times, many of these principles have similar application across the country.

HOW PROPERTY IS REGISTERED

In Ontario, there are currently two systems of land registration: the land registry system and the land titles system. (The land titles system is also called the Torrens system; the land registry system is sometimes referred to as the Registry System.) The land titles system was not accepted in parts of Canada until 1885, so almost all the land that was settled in Ontario and the rest of Canada from 1795 until 1885 was registered in the land registry system.

In Ontario, there are currently fifty-four counties. Every county has its own registry office, which holds the records of land ownership. In the registry system, all counties are subdivided into villages, townships, or cities. These are then subdivided into concessions. Early settlers used chains to measure the land; each piece of chain was 66 feet long. They made each concession 100 chains wide; that's 6,600 feet, or one and a quarter miles. In between each concession they built a concession road, which was 66 feet long. Even today, most concessions are 6,600 feet wide. In many cities, major streets are one and a quarter miles apart. For example, in the City of Toronto, as you travel south, the distance between Steeles, Finch, Sheppard, York Mills, Lawrence, Eglinton, and St. Clair avenues is one and a quarter miles. These avenues were all originally concession roads. As you drive into more rural areas, many of these roads are given only a number, for example, Concession 6.

Later, concessions were divided into farm lots. Each lot was about two hundred acres. An acre is 43,560 square feet. If you own a piece of land that was divided using the registry system, it may still be referred to as part of a farm lot, in a concession, in a city, in a county. Every farm lot has a registration book dedicated to it in the Registry Office. This book is called the "Abstract Book." Because a farm lot is so large, there may be hundreds of documents registered in each abstract book. To find a title to a property in the registry system is a time-consuming process. Buyer lawyers are required to search back forty years into the abstract book to find any easement, mortgage, lease, lien, or other encumbrance that might affect the seller's title.

A piece of property may be right in the middle of a two-hundred-acre farm lot, so the legal description often reads like a treasure map from a children's game. For example:

Commencing at the Northeast corner of Farm lot 2, Concession 3 in the Township of King, County of Simcoe. Then west 2000 feet to a tree stump. Then south 400 feet to a marker, which is the POINT of Commencement ["Point of commencement" is where the actual legal description begins]. Then south 100 feet, then west 40 feet, then north 100 feet and then east 40 feet.

When you try and find the points yourself, you may notice that the tree stump disappeared, possibly many years ago, so there is no real way to visually determine whether your boundaries are in fact correct. In Ontario, only a registered land surveyor is licensed to review the history of title and visit the property to identify the legal boundaries. You may have seen steel or iron markers in the ground with coloured paint at the top. These are typical boundary marker planted by surveyors. It is a criminal offence under the laws of Canada to remove such markers.

Most land in the registry system has not been marked by surveyors. Sometimes boundary lines have shifted because of a legal principle called "adverse possession." These shifts are recognized in the land registry system. For practical purposes, if someone at some time constructed a fence or other structure over your property line and your neighbour can prove he or she has had uninterrupted possession of the property that is now on their side of that fence for more than ten years, they may obtain possessory title over your land, even though it may be contrary to what is registered on title. Adverse possession is the main drawback of the registry system. Lawyers may be unable to find claims of adverse possession registered against the title in the registry system, but the claims will still bind the land.

If you don't have a current or up-to-date survey of your property and the property turns out to be located in the registry system, you may be subject to adverse possession claims; they're usually disputed in court and can lead to very expensive litigation between neighbours. There is an expression that good fences make for good neighbours. That may be true, but only when the fences are on the correct property lines.

In the registry system, all deeds and other documents offer evidence of ownership, with no absolute guarantee.

Most properties in southern Ontario remain in the registry system. If your property is in the registry system in Ontario, consider hiring an Ontario land surveyor to prepare an up-to-date survey. This is especially important if you're selling your home. With the survey, you can with confidence disclose to any buyer that the quality of your title is secure and not in dispute. Having the survey could increase your sale price. Or, if the survey shows some problems, you can disclose the problems immediately to any buyers and thus minimize potential problems. If you don't tell buyers, and they discover the problems, they could refuse to close the transaction. (More about that in Chapter 3.)

PROPERTY LINE, FENCES, TREES, AND OVERHANGING BRANCHES

Owners have rights and obligations regarding maintenance and repair of fences and care of trees that are on their side of the property line. The *Forestry Act of Ontario* and similar statutes across the country indicate that if a tree trunk is on the boundary line between two adjoining properties, then it is jointly owned by both owners, and both owners have an obligation to maintain the tree. Under the *Line Fences Act* and similar legislation, owners are encouraged to work together to build fences between their properties. The general rule is that each owner is responsible for half the cost to erect a simple fence between their properties. If one of the owners wants a much more elaborate fence, the owner who does not want a fancy fence pays half the cost of a simple fence; the other owner pays the costs to make the fence more elaborate.

What if a tree or hedge is on your neighbour's land and the branches are overhanging onto your land? Do you have a right to trim these branches or hedges? The answer is that yes, you have the right to trim the branches or hedges back to the property line, but as a courtesy, you should notify your neighbour that you will be doing this.

What if a tree on your neighbour's land is right up against the fence on the boundary line, and over time, the tree trunk pushes the fence into your yard? If the tree nudged the fence at least ten years ago, does the neighbour acquire title to the land under the tree by the principle of adverse possession? The answer is, conceivably, yes.

It's important for owners across Canada, especially those whose land is registered in the registry system, to have an up-to-date survey. With the survey, you'll know for certain where your boundary lines are. And you can be more vigilant in observing any fence, tree, or hedge that may be sitting on or adjacent to your boundary line.

There are other issues with the registry system. Say you use part of your neighbour's land to get to your land without permission. If this goes on for more than twenty years, you may be able to claim an "easement by prescription," which gives you the right to continue walking or driving over your neighbour's property, even if nothing is registered against title to the property. The registry system is used in other provinces, and brings with it the same principles and problems.

The land titles system, also called the Torrens system, was created in 1858 by Sir Robert Torrens, Prime Minister of Australia. His system was accepted in Canada in 1885 and was called the land titles system here. At that time, many parts of northern Ontario had not yet been settled, so much of the land in northern Ontario was registered in the land titles system. Many parts of western Canada, also settled later than 1795, use the land titles system. The land titles system is a register of ownership; each piece of land is separately surveyed, and ownership is guaranteed by the provincial or territorial government. If an error is made on the title, there is a government insurance policy to assist the owner in correcting the error.

In the land titles system, each piece of land has a separate dedicated "parcel unit" in a land registry office. Title searches are extremely simple: a lawyer reviews the parcel register, which identifies the current owner and lists any mortgages, easements, covenants, or other restrictions against title. In the land titles system, if it's not on the parcel register, it does not exist. If your neighbour moves the fence on your boundary line into your property, no matter how many years ago, you can legally demand your neighbour to move the fence back to the position as stated in your deed. (If he does not, you can get a court order to force him to do it.) And there are no easements acquired by prescription in the land titles system, no matter how many years the land was used by someone else.

Even if a tree trunk moved a boundary fence, the owner could never claim ownership of your land.

To find out if your property is registered in the land titles system, look at the plan number on your deed. If the plan number has the letter "M" in it, your property is in land titles. If you live in Ontario in a subdivision that was created after April 1, 1971, your home is registered in the land titles system.

It is possible to move your property from the registry system to the land titles system, but this can be an expensive and lengthy process. First, a lawyer completes a full forty-year search to find all documents registered in the abstract book. Those documents are then captured on a new parcel unit. Then you hire a registered land surveyor, who makes a new survey. Next, every owner whose land physically touches your land receives a copy of the survey. All these owners have the right to dispute the boundaries on the new survey. If no dispute arises, the land is registered in the land titles system and immediately acquires the "protections of Land Titles," the land is protected by the government insurance policy.

If your land is registered in the land titles system, use it as a selling feature. Your buyer can be certain the quality of the title is secure and guaranteed by the provincial government.

No matter where your property is registered, there may be other issues affecting property rights. Most owners do not own the timber or mineral rights on their properties, so it's possible someone could acquire these rights. This can be a real issue for rural or cottage properties. There may also be environmental regulations that affect properties, or conservation legislation that restricts land from further development. And governments have the power to expropriate some or all of your land for the benefit of the public. All properties are subject to local zoning bylaws; some historical buildings may have heritage designations, making it very difficult to renovate or demolish the building. Sellers and buyers should be aware of all issues that may affect the sale or purchase of the property.

Weisleder's Wisdom on the registry system and the land titles system

1. Most lands in Canada that were settled between 1795 and 1885 are still registered under the land registry system.
2. Lands settled after 1885 are typically found in the land titles system.
3. Lands in the registry system are not guaranteed, and are subject to claims of adverse possession and prescription.
4. Lands in the land titles system are guaranteed and are not subject to any claim of adverse possession or prescription.
5. Sellers and buyer should obtain an up-to-date survey of a property, no matter how the land is registered.

6. Be mindful of things that can affect property rights, such as fence lines, trees, overhanging branches, hedges, environmental issues, zoning, and heritage legislation; disclose everything to any buyer.

ESTABLISHING A SALE PRICE

It's the market that dictates the sale price of a home, and the market usually depends on supply and demand, as in most businesses. In a seller's market, when there are more buyers than available homes for sale, prices will increase and there will typically be multiple offers on a property. In a buyer's market, when there are more homes for sale than available buyers, sales will decrease, and sellers' salespeople must prepare them to "handle the truth" about the real value of their home. A real estate professional can assist you in finding the right price in any buyer's or seller's market.

12 QUESTIONS TO ASK BEFORE SELLING OR BUYING A HOME

Sellers think the home they are selling is special. Buyers want to fall in love with a home before they buy. Yet remember, when you are looking at the real value of a home, it is still going to be about supply and demand. Here are some questions to help buyers and sellers determine whether the area they're looking at will be in demand.

1. Is your area's average income increasing faster than the provincial average?

2. Is your area's population growing faster than the provincial average?

3. Is your area creating jobs faster than the provincial average?

4. Does your area have more than one major employer? Think of the troubles in the auto industry. Real estate values in entire towns and cities devalue overnight because a major automobile plant or parts supplier closes.

5. Are real estate values rising faster in regions far away from you?

6. Have the local political leaders created an environment that is assisting growth? Look at the land transfer tax policy change in the City of Toronto, introduced on January 1, 2008; it had a negative effect on real estate values all over the city.

7. Are you expecting a new major development? Development often brings an increase in property values.

8. Is your area considering a major transportation improvement? Better roads make it easier for people to commute to and from your area.

9. Is the area attractive for baby boomers as well as young families?

10. Is your town experiencing short-term layoffs?

11. What are the demographics in your area?

12. What is the crime rate, and how does it compare to the provincial average?

You can find answers to many of these questions by searching the Internet and by reading the statistics published by your municipality and local police departments. Good real estate salespeople who market in your area may include a lot of this information on their own websites. The more information you have at your fingertips about a neighbourhood you are interested in, the less likely you'll have an unpleasant surprise after you purchase your property.

SELLER DISCLOSURE OBLIGATIONS

As a seller, you should understand that potential buyers have more access to information than ever before, so they'll be very informed when they come to look at your property. The principle successful sellers have come to realize is that the more you disclose to your potential buyers about your property, the better your chance of obtaining your desired sale price. And you are much less likely to have any legal complications after closing.

The principle of disclosure applies to three major areas of property "defects" that should be disclosed in advance to buyers. They are:

1. Legal or title defects
2. Physical defects
3. Psychological defects

As a general principle, if you disclose everything, the chances of a claim being made against you after closing of the sale are slim. If you do not disclose the defect, there is always the chance of a lawsuit. The question each of you must ponder is this: "Do I really want to risk a lawsuit or become the next legal precedent?"

The best advice a lawyer will give you on this issue is your chances of success if you are sued. For example, your lawyer may say:

If you do not disclose the problem, you will still have a ninety percent chance of success in any lawsuit as a result of the current
case law.

Unfortunately, what lawyers do not often explain is what
you'll go through in a court case if your buyer makes a claim
against you. Most people who have experienced a legal proceeding will tell you it was never worth it, no matter who was
successful in the end. There is more information about the
legal process in Chapter 11.

I have a test to help me decide whether to disclose any
information: "Would it matter to me if I was buying the property?" If the answer is yes, then take the safe route and disclose
the problem to your buyer.

LEGAL OR TITLE DEFECTS

People who buy a property are not expecting title "surprises."
Some sample surprises: fence lines that are not on the property line; easements that may prevent a buyer from
constructing additions or interfere with their in-ground
swimming pool plans; a neighbour's garage that encroaches
over the property line. When a buyer's lawyer finds any undisclosed issue with your title, the buyer in most cases has the
right to cancel the agreement to buy your home.

An up-to-date survey of your property will indicate all
these issues, and make it easy for you to disclose everything to
any buyer. Make sure a copy of the survey is given to every
potential buyer, and ask the buyer to acknowledge, in the offer
to purchase, every "defect" on the survey. Get an up-to-date
survey, and advertise it as a selling feature when you list your
home. With a current survey, a buyer will know that the

quality of the title, including the location of all structures and fence lines, is undisputed. No unwanted surprises for the buyer; no disputes later from any adjacent owners.

The next-best thing to a current survey is the reporting letter you received from your lawyer when you bought the property in the first place. Your lawyer would have conducted a search of title, and most lawyers include a summary of the search of title in the reporting letter. Look for an underlined paragraph headed "Title."

The reporting letter usually provides the lawyer's opinion about the title conveyed to you, and includes a discussion about easements and restrictive covenants that may affect the property. Reporting letters also discuss any issues that may have arisen at your closing, such as any dispute about fence lines or a neighbour's garage partially on your property. You can use the reporting letter to disclose all easements, covenants, and other title defects to any potential buyer, and you can put the information right in the agreement of purchase and sale.

PHYSICAL DEFECTS

When it comes to physical defects, the growing practice across Canada is for sellers to sign a property condition statement (pcs). In Ontario, the document is called a "Seller Property Information Statement." In the pcs, sellers can provide a representation, to the best of their knowledge and belief, of the physical condition of their property. If there is any physical defect, the pcs informs the buyer.

There has been much debate about whether a seller should sign a pcs. Some real estate boards in Canada require a disclosure form from all sellers, to be delivered to buyers before an offer is presented. In other boards the PCS is not required, but if you don't provide it, there is a suspicion that you must have something to hide. The PCS is not a warranty, but allows you to disclose any property defects you know about.

The PCS includes a series of questions; the seller can initial either Yes, No, Does Not Know, or Does Not Apply.

An example: "Does the seller know of any water leakage problems in the roof or the basement?" If you know you have a leak, initial the "Yes" box.

Should you complete the PCS and make it available? There is much discussion about this. Some legal decisions have relied on this statement as evidence against sellers who did not disclose problems on the PCS statement.

The courts in general are not turning the PCS into a seller warranty. The language on the form makes it abundantly clear that sellers provide the statement for information purposes only, and that the form cannot be relied on by a buyer as a warranty. Buyers have a responsibility to make their own inquiries: this is why most transactions are conditional on the buyer being satisfied with the results of an inspection conducted by a qualified home inspector. Sellers who don't know the answer to a question are not obliged to find an answer; they can initial the "Does Not Know" box. Sellers are legally obliged to disclose all material latent defects they know about, especially when the defects may render a property uninhabitable. If you know of a defect and you don't disclose your knowledge, you will likely be found liable for negligent or fraudulent misrepresentation, which could lead to a legal claim for damages. You're liable with or without the PCS.

If a buyer raises a concern about a potential defect during the negotiations, and if you can provide an answer, write the information in the property condition statement. There is nothing wrong with adding explanations or qualifications to any item on the form. It's a good idea to bring all potential problems to the attention of buyers before they sign the agreement of purchase and sale form.

Do you need to disclose problems you have already rectified? The case law indicates that yes, these problems should be disclosed. The buyer's home inspector will then have the opportunity to examine the area that was rectified, and the buyer will have a better idea as to whether the problem will or will not reoccur.

PATENT VERSUS LATENT DEFECTS

The legal principles regarding physical defects are similar across Canada, but for the most part the case law is confusing. There have been many legal arguments and debates about the definitions of "latent defect" and "patent defect," and whether a defect makes a property uninhabitable, and whether sellers should disclose defects. There is also the concept of "caveat emptor," or "buyer beware." I'll try and make these concepts easy for you to understand, whether you're buying or selling a property.

A patent defect is one that's obvious and can be readily observed during a normal home visit by a buyer, for example, a broken window. Because they can see the problem, buyers are legally deemed to have accepted patent defects under the principle of caveat emptor. In other words, if you can see the defect when you view the home, you can't complain later that you were cheated by the seller.

A latent defect is a problem that's hidden from view and cannot be observed in a home inspection. If the seller knows about it, he or she is legally obliged to disclose the latent defect to any buyer. Examples from the case laws and from real estate statutes across the country tell us that a material latent defect is one that:

a. renders a property uninhabitable by the buyer;
b. renders a property dangerous or potentially dangerous;
c. renders a property unfit for the buyer's purpose, if that purpose is known to the seller or salesperson;
d. will cost a substantial sum of money to repair;
e. has engendered a municipal or governmental work order or similar deficiency notice against the property; or
f. causes any concern about lack of proper building, occupancy, or final inspection permits.

Some examples of material latent defects are:

a. mould or other environmental contaminants on the property;
b. basement apartments that do not meet zoning, building, or fire-code regulations;
c. structural problems; and
d. major leaks in the roof or basement.

Some latent defects may not be deemed material, such as:

a. insufficient insulation that doesn't render a property uninhabitable and doesn't violate any building or fire code, but results in increased energy costs;
b. aluminum wiring that is acceptable but will probably cost a lot of money to repair or upgrade;
c. certain kinds of wood-burning stoves or knob-and-tube wiring that may cause an increase in insurance premiums; and
d. some dampness in areas of the basement.

In all cases, it makes sense to disclose everything and avoid argument.

Some legal practitioners argue that completing a property condition statement puts the seller at risk of litigation; they instruct their seller clients not to complete the form. Some sellers have been successfully sued because of something written on the property condition statement. But in these cases, it was demonstrated that these sellers deliberately lied or concealed something when they completed the statement. It's not the disclosure statement that will get you into trouble; it's what you say when you fill it out. If you complete the statement carefully and honestly, there is little likelihood you'll become involved in a legal proceeding.

The case of *Gibb v. Sprague* was tried in Edmonton in December 2008. The buyers purchased the property and hired a home inspector; the inspection revealed no defects. The sellers did not complete a property condition statement. The buyers asked the sellers if they ever had flooding in the basement, and the sellers said no. Several months after closing, the buyers noticed a bad smell in the basement, and discovered a serious mould problem. The sellers said they didn't know anything about this problem.

The mould problem was classified as a latent or hidden defect; it was labeled as a material latent defect that should have been disclosed if the sellers knew about it. At trial, the sellers admitted that the basement had indeed flooded seven years previously. The court said the sellers should have known to check for possible mould after flood damage. There was evidence that the sellers were actively deodorizing the basement when the property was shown to the buyers. The sellers must have known something smelled in the basement. During the showing, the sellers said they were only trying to get rid of a smoky smell.

The sellers were held liable for not disclosing the latent defect to the buyers. The lawsuit could have been avoided if the sellers had disclosed the flood and the possible mould problem.

In the case of *Dupere v. Evans*, decided January 9, 2006 in Halifax, the sellers disclosed to the buyers that there had been two minor leaks involving their oil tank during their twenty-five years of ownership. Before the closing, the buyers hired an environmental consultant to test the land. The test revealed that the property was very close to violating the Nova Scotia guidelines for contaminated soil. The buyers were able to terminate the transaction by demonstrating that the sellers' disclosure did not go far enough in explaining the actual condition of the soil on the property.

In the case of *Lunney v. Kuntova*, which was decided on February 24, 2009, in Ottawa, the seller's home was ninety years old. The seller signed a seller's property information statement indicating that she had no knowledge of any structural problems. A buyer put in an offer conditional on a satisfactory home inspection report. The seller and the seller's salesperson were not present when the home inspection was done for the buyer. The home inspection report indicated that the foundation needed major repairs; the buyer then told the seller he would not waive the home inspection condition. The buyer did not tell the seller the reason, and did not show her the home inspection report. A second buyer put in an offer with a home inspection clause, and the second inspector did not find any problem with the foundation. The second buyer waived the condition and closed the transaction. Three years later, the problem with the foundation came to light, and the home had to be completely rebuilt.

The buyer sued the seller, claiming she must have known about the problem with the foundation. The court found that the buyers did not prove the seller knew about the problem, because she never saw the first home inspection report. Had the buyer been able to prove that the seller knew about the foundation problem, then the seller would have been liable for the buyer's damages.

There are some instances when it is not appropriate for a seller to complete the PCS form, especially when a seller doesn't have first-hand information about the property. For example:

1. The seller is in a retirement home, or is infirm and cannot accurately recollect the condition of his or her home;
2. The seller has not occupied the home, but has rented it to tenants; or
3. The seller has passed away, and the executor or trustee of the estate doesn't have any actual knowledge about the physical condition of the house.

There is a temptation in all these situations to tell prospective buyers they're purchasing the home "as is," then let them protect themselves. (I discuss the phrase "as is" and its legal effect later on in this chapter.) If you were looking for a home and the seller told you to accept the physical condition of the property "as is," would you put in a full price offer? Could you trust the physical integrity of the house or the personal integrity of the seller? Most buyers would view the statement as a warning, and presume there's something physically wrong with the house. This presumption will be reflected in the price the buyer offers for the house.

As a seller, you can see that using the words "as is" is not a very smart business decision. You won't attract the right buyer and the highest price for your home. Remember, the lawyers who warn you against completing a property condition statement are not business or marketing people — they're lawyers.

If you can't complete a PCS form, you can still provide reassurance to potential buyers about the physical condition of the home by obtaining a pre-listing home inspection, from a reputable local inspection company. You give this report to any potential buyer. If the inspectors discover any defects, you can repair them or not, at your discretion. You'll have to disclose the problems to buyers. For years, this is how disclosure has been dealt with in commercial transactions. Owners prepare a "book" that includes an engineering report, an environmental assessment, and a full lease audit for serious potential buyers. The book seems to attract a more sophisticated buyer and to generate a better price for the seller, because there are no surprises. Sellers of residential property may notice the same reaction when they provide a home inspection report. In multiple offer situations, the PCS could also save buyers from having to pay for a pre-offer inspection. (See Chapter 4 for a discussion of multiple offers.) If the seller hires a recognized reputable inspection company, buyers can for the most part rely on the report, when participating in a multiple offer.

The principle remains the same for residential and commercial transactions: make complete disclosure as soon as possible. You'll give reassurance to proposed buyers and protect yourself from unwanted legal proceedings. I encourage buyers to always obtain their own home inspection report even when a seller provides a PCS, for additional protection, before deciding to purchase any home.

If you disclose fairly the physical condition of your property, there are fewer unknowns for both buyer and seller, and buyers can decide with confidence whether to accept the property as outlined in the inspection report before they sign the agreement of purchase and sale.

I still encourage buyers to always hire your own home inspection company, and make your offer to purchase conditional on that inspection.

PSYCHOLOGICAL DEFECTS AND STIGMAS

Is there any difference between disclosing a physical defect in a property, such as moisture leaking into a basement, and disclosing a psychological defect, such as a suicide on the property? There should be no distinction whatsoever. Psychological defects or stigmas are matters most people like to know about if they're buying a property.

Some salespeople and lawyers have attempted to draft a clause to try to deal with the difficult issue of potential psychological defects in a home:

> The seller warrants, to the best of their knowledge and belief, that the said property does not contain any hidden defects and that there have been no deaths, suicides, illegal activities, or murders on this property at any time, and that there are no neighbourhood conditions that could affect the buyer's use, enjoyment, or perceived value of the property.

The clause, however, is very subjective. What are "neighbourhood conditions"? Do they include a group home, a halfway house, a home for mentally challenged people, or subsidized housing? What if there are rumours that the house is haunted? What if there was a suicide on the property, but it happened four years ago and there have been two ownership changes since then? Does "neighbourhood" mean down the street or on the next block?

The clause illustrates that buyers are concerned about psychological issues, which, unlike a leaky roof, have no direct physical effect on a property. We can find out how much it costs to fix a leaky roof. It is much more difficult to determine how much, if any, value is lost when a property is associated with a psychological stigma. Here's a court case, as an example.

Summach v. Allen

This was a case in Kelowna, British Columbia, in 2003, in which buyers signed an offer to purchase a beachfront property. The buyers inquired about the park next door and were told by the seller that it was a "public beach." Before moving in, the buyers found out it was a nude public beach, and they refused to close. The seller sued. I know what you are thinking: "Wouldn't a nude beach next door increase the value of the property?" Well, the buyers didn't think so. And it was clear that the sellers knew there was a nude beach and didn't disclose this to the buyer.

The result, after three years of proceedings, including an appeal to the British Columbia Court of Appeal, was that the seller did not have to disclose information about the nude beach to the buyer. The court of appeal in B.C. wrote:

> The presence of nude bodies next door or parading in front of one's house may or may not be a defect. This requires a subjective test. To allow defects to be determined by individual preferences would open the floodgates of litigation by remorseful buyers and create an impossible standard of disclosure for sellers. In this case, the alleged defect was occurring outside the boundaries of the property purchased.

> The presence of a nude beach next door is not a defect, latent or patent. There is no duty on the seller to disclose the existence of the nude beach.

Will this court decision become an iron-clad precedent for any future situation involving a stigma defect? What about a suicide on a property? In a Quebec decision in 2006, the court held that a suicide was not a significant fact that needed to be disclosed to a buyer. Yet in many parts of the United States, the law says a seller must disclose any murder or suicide on their property to any potential buyer. Police forces are making grow-house registries publicly available across the country. Will Canadian sellers have to disclose the existence of a grow house down the street?

If you know there's a registered sex offender living next door, should you disclose it to any buyer, based on the Summach decision? Lawyers may give you different answers, as the law is not clear. A lawyer for a buyer could make a good argument that a sex offender neighbour is a material latent defect, which makes the property uninhabitable by buyers who would fear for the safety of their family. Will this logic apply to a halfway house four doors down from your property? Do you want to be involved in the next court case to find out the answer?

There's a simple way to check for psychological stigmas: conduct a Google search on the municipal address you're interested in. Google searches can reveal a home invasion, for example, since most newspaper articles can be found on the Internet.

Buyers can and should walk the neighbourhood and talk to people who live there. Eventually, the truth about psychological "secrets" will come out. It's a good bet that most buyers care deeply about who is living on the street they're thinking of moving to.

Buyers can also ask sellers and listing salespersons if they know of any hidden defects or adverse neighbourhood condition. If you ask the question, sellers have a legal obligation to respond truthfully.

To reduce any possibility of legal claims against you as a seller, disclose everything you know to be true, including any psychological stigmas. You can't publish the information on any MLS® system, because of privacy laws, but you can note that all buyers or buyer salespersons should contact the listing salesperson before submitting an offer. The listing salesperson can then inform them about the psychological defect, in writing, before the buyer submits an offer.

With proper disclosure, sellers can achieve a successful closing of their transaction, and they won't have to worry about surprise lawsuits.

WALKING THE PROPERTY

As a seller or buyer, take the time to walk the property and look for any issues that need to be clarified, for example, boundary lines and encroachments. Also consider environmental concerns: perhaps there is or was a gas station or dry-cleaning business on or near the property, and perhaps there is soil contamination. If there is a septic bed, do you see any dampness in the area that was not caused by a recent rainfall? Is the wiring knob and tube or aluminum? Is there a buried oil tank on the property? Have all abandoned or unused wells on the property been properly closed? Is there a wood stove in the house? Will you have year-round access to the property, or are there private rights-of-way issues?

Remember that there are surveyors, environmental experts, and insurance experts who can help you avoid problems with the transaction. As an example, many standard agreements of purchase and sale forms state if a building is not insurable, the buyer can cancel the agreement. Lots of problems — with the wiring, wood stove, or insulation — can make a building uninsurable, or make the insurance unaffordable. Sellers, identify and rectify all such problems. Buyers, consider adding a condition to the agreement of purchase and sale, stating that you must be able to obtain affordable insurance coverage. You'll find examples of such clauses in Appendix 1.4.

Engage an environmental consultant if you have any concerns about the property, for example a buried oil tank.

Investigate any boundary dispute; obtain an up-to-date survey. In Figure 1, the swimming pool is encroaching onto the neighbour's land. After the buyer moves in, the neighbour could demand that the pool be moved; the buyer would have to pay for the relocation of the pool.

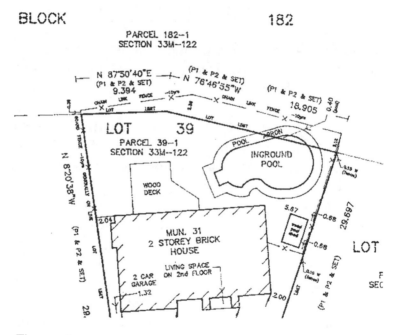

Figure 1

Many buyers and sellers think title insurance will protect them from all boundary issues. This is not the case. Yes, title insurance protects against losses related to title issues, but it does not completely solve the problem of the swimming pool. Title insurance may pay for relocating the pool, but cannot compensate for the substantial inconvenience to the buyer.

And the buyer may never be able to use the backyard as initially intended.

An up-to-date survey can provide information about any encroachments, rights of way, and overhead wires that could affect the property. Sellers can market the up-to-date survey as a positive selling feature.

DISCLAIMER CLAUSES – ARE THEY WORTH IT?

There has been much discussion about whether a seller can or should use the words "as is," or use disclaimer clauses to avoid liability. There are disclaimers for measurements on a property and for defects.

"As is" clause

Buyers acknowledge they are purchasing the property 'as is', sellers make no warranties or representations regarding electrical, plumbing, and heating systems, as well as any appliances.

Disclaimer clause

Here's an example of such a clause, used by salespeople across the country:

The square footage or lot dimensions have been calculated using the standards developed by the provincial real estate association, which in some instances may differ from measurement guidelines used by other sources. The measurement figure noted is believed to be accurate (but not guaranteed) within a discrepancy of 5%. If the buyer is relying on the calculation of square footage or lot dimensions they should attend to their own verification, with either an up-to-date survey or further inspection.

When I review the case law, I can see that a disclaimer or "as is" clause can reduce a seller's risk of liability but does not completely protect a seller who has knowledge about a survey or physical defect in a property and doesn't disclose it. Disclaimer clauses are good if a seller is not familiar with the property; the disclaimer clause will alert buyers that a detailed inspection is needed before they make any purchase decisions.

In Chapter 9, we will look at some of the issues that arise if you buy a property from a bank when a mortgage has gone into default. One of the main issues is that banks will typically insert an "as is" clause because they have no actual knowledge of the condition of the property. The result always is that buyers lower their purchase price offer; they know that they may have to budget for problems later. (See Chapter 9 for more information about buying a house from a bank.)

Weisleder's Wisdom on disclosure of defects

1. There are three types of defects in a property: legal or title defects, physical defects, and psychological defects.
2. By disclosing all defects, you add certainty to any transaction and protect yourself from legal proceedings after closing.
3. Check the lawyer's reporting letter for any legal or title defects.
4. Don't be afraid to complete any SPIS or PCS disclosure forms; when you complete them, be careful and accurate.
5. Buyers, carefully review any PCS form a seller gives you, and still make your agreements conditional on a satisfactory home inspection.

6. Sellers, if you can't complete a PCS form, conduct a pre-listing inspection, and deliver a copy of the report to potential buyers.

7. Sellers, walk the property and identify any boundary and environmental issues and disclose them.

8. Buyers, google the address of any property you are interested in to check for psychological defects.

9. "As is" and other disclaimer clauses may reduce liability, but they will likely lead to lower purchase price offers.

10. The main principle for sellers is, "If it would matter to you if you were buying the property yourself, then just disclose it."

WHAT TO DO BEFORE BUYING A HOME

When you're buying, there is no substitute for driving and walking through neighbourhoods you're interested in. Do it at different periods of the week. For example, early Monday morning will tell you how many school buses are in the area and the makeup of the children on the street. How long does it take you to get to work at 7:30 a.m.? Don't be afraid to knock on doors and talk to people to get a sense of how open and friendly they are. Most people prefer talking to people in person, rather than on the phone, and people are often proud of the area they live in. If you find the people living in the area are not very friendly, ask yourself whether this is really the neighbourhood you want to move into.

Check the condition of the front landscaping on the street. If the neighbours care about their front lawns, you'll know they take pride in their homes and in the neighbourhood.

As you walk through the neighbourhood, be aware of noises and smells. Can you hear passing cars on a nearby highway? Are there odours from a nearby factory? Sellers may be less than candid about neighbourhood conditions.

You may also want to visit the local planning department at city hall to ask whether there are any plans for new developments in the area. "Developments" can include a brand new shopping mall or a large condominium tower and can have both a positive and negative effect on the neighbourhood. The developments may increase the overall market value of the properties in the area, but the increased traffic could disrupt the peaceful nature of the area.

Consider the possibility of your neighbour's home being demolished and replaced with a much larger home that changes your view and blocks sunlight. In Canada, your view, also called the "right to light," is not guaranteed in planning legislation. Keep this in mind when you're looking for a new home.

Research the schools in the area. Is there a waiting list to get in? Do they offer extracurricular activities your children are interested in? Do they publish the test scores of the school? If yes, how do the scores compare to the provincial averages?

Does the neighbourhood have sidewalks so your children can ride their bicycles safely? Are the streets well lit at night? If front porches are closer to the sidewalk, it also makes the area safer as there are more eyes watching the street at any given time.

Are you close to churches, synagogues, doctors' offices, and libraries? Are there parks, golf courses, or skating rinks?

Use the Internet as a primary information-gathering tool when you answer the twelve key questions at the beginning of this chapter. Look at the websites of real estate salespeople with signs in the area; often their websites summarize key local data.

Salespeople can also help you understand governmental programs for buyers; the government will assist with your purchase if you qualify. For example, you may be able to borrow money from your RRSP to make the down payment, or you may be able to use a mortgage program if you don't have a lot of money available for a down payment. There are also land transfer tax programs and federal income tax credits for first-time home buyers.

Here's another simple technique: list the top three things you like about your current location. This could include your proximity to schools, parks, and public transit. Then list the top three things that would be on your wish list, perhaps a large backyard for your children, a home office, or four bedrooms instead of three. Show your lists to the real estate salesperson you decide to work with. The lists will help you focus on what is really important to you; it will keep you from getting carried away by the in-ground pool that may turn out to be more bother to maintain than it's worth. Try not to focus too much on the "features" of a particular home, such as granite countertops and fancy doors. Think about the space you need, both inside the home and in the yard. When you have space, you can add the features that appeal to you. If you have features and no space, you may need to move again. And don't buy a home just because you can fit all your existing furniture into it. It is better to buy the house that fits your budget, and get rid of the furniture.

Weisleder's Wisdom on what to do before buying a home

1. Check the Internet to find demographic information about the area.
2. Look at the websites of local real estate salespeople for information about the neighbourhood.
3. Walk the neighbourhood you're interested in.
4. Talk to the people who live there.
5. Go at different times of day and different days of the week.

6. Check for noise and smells.
7. Check the landscaping on the front lawns.
8. Ask at city hall about any planned new developments.
9. If you see a house you like, try to envision it after the neighbours replace their existing home with a larger new home.
10. List what you like best about your current location; write a wish list for your new location.
11. Don't focus on your existing furniture, or on the features of a house you might buy; make sure your new home is the right size for your needs.

THE PROCESS

The process of buying a home usually involves five elements:

1. The mortgage loan
2. The home inspection
3. The survey
4. Home insurance
5. Title insurance

The mortgage loan

Before you even think about applying for a mortgage loan, check your credit score. It's the first thing a bank will look at when you ask for the loan. You want your credit information to be accurate and up to date, and you want your credit score to look good. One simple way to improve your credit score is to reduce the number of credit cards you have, and make all your payments on time. Every credit card application affects your credit score. If you're thinking of changing jobs, finalize the mortgage loan first.

It's your right to check what your credit score is. The higher your score, the better your ability to obtain credit. Go to www.fcac.gc.ca/eng/publications/CreditReportScore/CreditRepo rtScoreTOC-eng.asp, which is a website run by the Financial Consumer Agency of Canada, to learn what credit reports look like and how your own credit score compares with other Canadians. Usually you provide identification and pay a small fee to get your credit history. Sometimes your score can be affected by things beyond your control. Let's say you apply for a cell phone and the sales associate inadvertently presses the "check" button twice when checking your credit. One factor that hurts your score is the number of times your credit gets checked.

Or maybe your bank didn't transfer funds from one of your accounts to the other when you asked them to, and a cheque bounced. Get a letter from your bank and send it to the credit reporting company (also called a credit bureau), and you'll improve your credit rating. Get your credit status worked out before you approach your bank for a mortgage loan.

The number-one expense after you buy your new home is the monthly mortgage payment. How much can you realistically afford to borrow for your home purchase?

Historically, real estate ownership has been a safe long-term-growth investment, but there are always downturns in the market. Make your buying decision for the long term, not for a quick profit.

Ideally, you should have 25% of the down payment on the property plus all closing costs in cash; for the balance, you borrow from a bank. You'll need money for property taxes and home maintenance costs. Do you want your home to be a place where you give up everything just to have a roof over your head? Better if your home is a place where you create happy memories for you and your family.

If you cannot afford 25% or more of the down payment, you may be able to get an insured high-ratio mortgage with a minimum 5% of the down payment. If you get the high-ratio mortgage, you also need mortgage loan insurance. (The policy protects the lender if you default.) Fees for the policy range from $75 to $250, and the premium cost ranges from 0.5 to 3.75% of your total loan. The premiums depend on the size of your loan and the value of your home. You can pay the insurance policy premium when you purchase the home, or you can add it to the principal of your mortgage loan. Be careful when you apply for a high-ratio mortgage: make sure you understand exactly what your costs will be, so you can make informed budget decisions. In other words, be sure you can afford to carry the home using this kind of financing.

Be careful when you qualify yourself for a home. Can you cut your expenses to afford more on the mortgage, in order to move up to a better home? Maybe you need to be looking for a home with a downstairs rental, to help you with the monthly payments. (Refer to Chapter 6 to learn some of the pitfalls owners suffer when renting to tenants who have not been properly qualified.) Make your offer conditional on the basement apartment being legal in accordance with the local zoning laws and the local fire code regulations.

The first step: approach a mortgage broker or financial institution with all your employment and financial information, and ask how much you can safely borrow, still maintain your standard of living, and handle all maintenance and real estate taxes. With this information, you can tell your buyer salesperson your price range.

Being prequalified for a loan amount doesn't guarantee that you'll get the loan. Banks can change their lending practices, as we have witnessed during the credit crisis in 2008 and 2009. It's the reason all real estate transactions should still be made conditional on being approved for the mortgage loan. (An example of the clause is in Appendix 1.6.) Before your bankers give approval, they do an independent appraisal on the property to satisfy themselves that it's worth at least as much as you have offered to pay. You can expect the banks to be extra vigilant because the credit crisis in the U.S. started when lenders were not checking the underlying value of real estate before approving loans.

If the bank completes an appraisal just before closing and decides the home is not as valuable as your offer, they may require you to make a larger down payment. This will reduce your loan amount. Or they may refuse to complete the loan altogether. This could be disastrous because buyers often are required to waive their financing condition within three to seven days of signing their purchase agreement, and some buyers waive the condition before they have written approval from the bank. If the bank rejects the loan at the last minute, you may not be able to come up with the necessary closing proceeds. When this happens, you forfeit your deposit and may be subject to legal action from the seller.

Talk to your financial institution when you are prequalified for a mortgage. Ask them about their appraisal requirements. You want to be certain you can waive your financing condition with confidence once you get the approval from your financial institution.

Try to satisfy all your conditions in good faith, or you could be subject to legal action by the seller. If you understand the mortgage loan application process before you start to look for a property, you'll be prepared and well informed.

Weisleder's wisdom on the mortgage loan process

1. Check your credit score. Make sure you correct any inaccuracies.
2. Approach your mortgage broker or bank to find out what amount of money you can borrow before you start looking for a home to buy.

3. Do not overextend yourself when buying a home; make sure you can maintain your existing standard of living.
4. Confirm the bank's appraisal policy, so you'll know when it's safe to waive any financing condition on your purchase.

The Home Inspection

The most important and reliable way to check the physical condition of a home is by getting a home inspection. The inspection has benefits and some restrictions.

Ontario has an association for home inspectors: the Ontario Association of Home Inspectors, or OAHI. Your buyer salesperson can probably provide you with the names of three qualified home inspectors in your area. Once you have the names, go to www.oahi.com to make sure the inspectors are in fact registered. There are similar associations across Canada.

All home buyers have the right to make their offer to purchase conditional on a satisfactory home inspection report. Even when there are multiple offers, buyers may hire an inspector to conduct a pre-offer inspection. (There is an example of a home inspection clause in Appendix 1.3.)

Here are some questions to consider when choosing a home inspector or a home-inspection company:

1. Does the inspector have experience with the type of home you want to buy?
2. Does the inspector have insurance? What happens if there is an error in the report that costs the buyer substantial money in repairs after closing? Is there any language in the home-inspection contract that limits the liability of the inspector?

In some regions in Ontario and the rest of Canada home inspectors have had difficulty obtaining insurance protection.

Many inspectors have express language in their agreements that any liability will be limited to the amount of money the buyer paid for the inspection report, which is usually three to four hundred dollars. In most cases, this amount doesn't pay to repair the problem the inspector didn't notice.

If you get a home inspection, have you negated any representations made by the seller in any property condition statement? The principles regarding patent, latent, and material latent defects that must be disclosed by sellers discussed earlier in this chapter will continue to apply. Your seller must still be truthful in disclosing and not concealing defects on the property. Always conduct a home inspection.

Some real estate brokerage companies have arranged a different kind of home inspection, based on a "committee" of professionals to assess the roof, the wiring, the plumbing, the furnace, and the dampness levels in the basement. For each area of the house they hire a specialist: a basement waterproof expert, an electrician, a plumber, and a representative from the local gas utility company who checks the furnace. The committee may take a little longer and may require a longer condition period; however, the committee may give a buyer more because the experts are looking at the elements of the home that cost the most to repair or replace. Ask your salesperson about committees as they may be a very good alternative for you to consider when choosing a home inspector.

Sellers warrant that major appliances and electrical, plumbing, and heating systems will be working only on the closing date. If problems occur even one or two weeks after closing, it's unlikely you'll be able to obtain compensation from the sellers. There is a solution available for buyers (and for existing homeowners). Some companies that operate across Canada, such as Direct Energy, will arrange after-closing warranties. Buyers can get coverage for problems with the wiring, plumbing, furnace, air conditioner, and even major appliances for one year after closing. Do your research and set up the warranties immediately upon closing. I can speak from personal experience as a customer of this warranty that it works and is an effective protection for buyers.

Your home inspector will tell you what the inspection revealed, but you should be an active participant in the inspection. When we first see a home, we often focus on things like closet space and landscaping. Pay attention: you don't want any unwelcome surprises later.

Here are some things to look for during a home inspection:

1. Take a boom box with you to the inspection, and play music in all the rooms. Does the sound go right through the entire house? Are all the walls well insulated?
2. Run some water – turn on the shower and the toilets – and listen. Can you hear the plumbing throughout the house?
3. Check the water pressure in the shower. How long does it take to get hot?
4. What happens if you flush the toilet while the shower is on? Does the pressure or temperature change? What if two showers are on at the same time?
5. Does running the dishwasher affect the water pressure in the rest of the house?
6. Turn on every single appliance; make sure they're all working.
7. Check every electrical outlet, both inside and outside the house.
8. If the seller says there's hardwood under the carpet, lift corners of the carpeting to make sure the hardware flooring is there.
9. Check the utility bills carefully. Is the home energy efficient?

10. Walk the entire property and ask the inspector if there are any signs of underground oil tanks or other environmental hazards.

11. Ask the seller or the seller's salesperson if there has been any recent improvement made to the house and whether there are any existing warranties on the home that can be transferred to you.

It's best if the seller is not with you during the home inspection. You may not be able to have a candid conversation with your home inspector. If the seller's real estate salesperson is in attendance, remember that whatever you say can be communicated to the seller. Don't say anything you wouldn't want the seller to hear.

If there are any disclaimer clauses in the listing or in the agreement, be even more careful during your home inspection. Disclaimer clauses tell you there may be something wrong somewhere on the property, and that you'll be the one with responsibility for it. If there is a disclaimer about the lot measurements, make your offer conditional on your satisfaction with a new survey.

There is no such thing as a perfect home. There will always be some issues that concern you. But make yourself well informed about the physical condition of the home before you decide to purchase. Your goal is to minimize surprises later.

Weisleder's Wisdom on the home inspection process

1. Get references for your home inspector, and make sure that he or she is registered with a provincial association.

2. Make every home purchase conditional on your satisfaction with the home inspection report.

3. Remember that most home inspection reports have limitation-of-liability clauses.
4. Look into obtaining after-closing warranty protection for the plumbing, electrical, and heating systems and the major appliances.
5. Attend the home inspection.
6. Participate in the home inspection. Check all plumbing and wiring in the home.
7. Turn on all of the appliances to make sure they work.
8. Be extra vigilant in your inspection if the seller has added any disclaimer clauses to the agreement.
9. Watch what you say during the home inspection if the seller or the seller's salesperson is in attendance.

The importance of a survey for buyers

Many buyers think that if they have title insurance, they don't need a survey. Title insurance does not protect buyers against all problems that may have been disclosed by an up-to-date survey of the property.

Buyers have faced all kinds of difficulties over the years because they purchased a property without a survey done by a licensed surveyor, such as:

a. building a house on the wrong lot;
b. building a swimming pool on part of a neighbour's property;
c. building a cottage on land someone else owned; and
d. discovering major easements after closing.

It is always preferable to have a current survey before you buy a property: you'll know about fence lines, encroachments, and easements before you complete the transaction. It is true that title insurance will pay to correct many of the problems, but if you discover them after closing, you have to make the corrections, which may cost more than the title insurance will pay. As well, your corrections may affect views and other desirable features.

Surveyors carry their own errors and omissions insurance coverage. If they make a mistake, their insurance may provide more protection than the title insurance.

Sellers can provide different types of surveys to buyers. The most desirable is a survey plan and report signed and sealed by a registered land surveyor. You can compare this survey to the title described in the deeds and other documents registered against title, to make sure all is in order. Most sellers don't have this type of survey, but they may have other types of surveys that can provide a similar level of comfort. This would include an older survey that still shows the current location of all structures, fence lines, and easements located on the property.

Whatever type of survey you receive, be sure to walk the property and compare what you see with your own eyes to what is on the survey. For example, are all fences and backyard sheds you see included on the survey? Are all hedges that separate the boundary lines accurately represented? Sometimes an older survey plan does not show all this information.

Look for survey monuments — metal or iron stakes that are found on many boundary lines, sometimes with orange or red paint at the top to help you find them. The monuments clearly identify the boundary lines between neighbours, as well as cities, municipalities, and counties, and indicate that a surveyor has conducted a historical review of the title to your property. You can be assured that the monuments are in accordance with the title as shown in your deed. It is a criminal offence in Canada to knowingly remove a survey monument.

Take a measuring tape with you. If the survey states that the distance from one fence line to the other is forty feet, measure it yourself. If the survey says there are forty feet from fence to fence, and you look at the fence lines and the area between the

fences, you can't complain later about a one- or two-foot difference between survey and reality. Case law is not on your
side. (In Chapter 3, you'll find more information in the section
called "Legal Description and the words 'more or less' in the
Agreement of Purchase and Sale.") Take the time to measure
as you walk the property.

The date on the survey is less important than the information it contains. For example, if a survey was prepared six
months ago but the seller built an addition onto the home
three months ago, the survey is not up to date. Often a ten-
year-old survey will show all current structures and boundary
lines. You can rely on that ten-year-old survey to demonstrate
the soundness of your title.

You'll find examples of different types of survey clauses in
Appendix 1.9.

Weisleder's Wisdom on the survey

1. Having a proper survey adds certainty to your quality of
   title.
2. Request a proper survey from the seller every time you
   buy a house.
3. Always walk the property with the survey plan, and
   compare what is written with what you can see.
4. Measure distances to make sure they are accurate.
5. Look for metal stakes, which are a sign that the seller
   should have a signed and sealed registered land
   surveyor's report available.

Home insurance coverage

The financial crisis that is affecting buyers looking for mortgage financing is also adversely affecting insurance companies,
which are being much more careful in assessing risk. It's not as

easy as it used to be to secure fire insurance coverage for your new home.

Every bank mortgage requires that the buyer secure adequate home insurance coverage and demonstrate that they have it before the transaction closes. Insurance companies require a separate inspection of the property before they approve the coverage. Start working with your insurance agent before you buy a home: ask what the insurance requirements will be, and ask how soon the inspection can be done. Your record with your insurance company may affect your ability to obtain insurance coverage. For example, let's say you made two home insurance claims in the past two years. When you now ask about insuring a new house, you may notice that a significant premium has been added. Insurance companies also raise their premiums if they notice any risks associated with the home you're buying, such as asbestos insulation, knob-and-tube wiring, or a wood-burning stove.

As discussed in Chapter 3, your lawyer is given time to search to find out if the principal building on the property can be insured against risk of fire. If it cannot, you can terminate the transaction. Uninsurable buildings include a grow house that was not properly repaired, or an environmental damage, such as an oil spill that was not properly cleaned up. If the home can be insured — even if the premium is significant — you have to close the transaction. The good news is that you may add a condition to your agreement: if you can't obtain home insurance coverage at a reasonable premium, you may terminate the transaction. (There's more information in Chapter 3, under "Title Search, clause 8," and there are examples in Appendix 1.4.)

Don't leave the insurance question to the last minute. Make sure your insurance agent is involved early and that the insurance inspections are completed before you have to waive your conditions. You don't want insurance "surprises" just before closing.

1. Start working with an insurance agent before you start looking for a property.
2. Find out if any claims you've made in the past will affect your ability to obtain home insurance coverage.
3. Consider adding a condition to your agreement that you can terminate a transaction if you can't obtain home insurance coverage at a reasonable premium.
4. Do not leave insurance coverage to the last minute.

Title insurance

I recommend title insurance for every buyer of real estate. Title insurance protects you against certain title defects, problems with zoning setbacks, unpaid property taxes, and — perhaps most important — it gives you complete protection if someone tries to steal your property through what is called a "fraudulent conveyance."

We have seen an alarming increase in fraud artists attempting to steal the registered title of unwary owners by forgeries that have been registered on title. If you have title insurance, you are protected against this kind of fraud, and all the legal costs of correcting the error are included in the title insurance coverage.

Across Canada, anyone who owns property can obtain title insurance through a lawyer. I highly recommend title insurance for anyone who owns property.

Title insurance won't fix every problem. For example, it may not help when there are errors in legal descriptions or lot areas. If you think you bought a fifty-foot lot, and a more recent survey says you have a forty-eight-foot lot, you're protected only for what was registered on title. If you had the opportunity to walk the property and didn't measure, the title insurance policy won't help you.

Always make your home purchase conditional on being satisfied with the contents of an up-to-date survey of the property before closing. The up-to-date survey will immediately clarify any dispute regarding lot dimensions and square footage; it can identify any potential zoning setback violations; and it can guide you if you want to add another room or a swimming pool by telling you if your upgrades will encroach on any neighbouring property or right of way.

Weisleder's Wisdom on title insurance

1. Always purchase title insurance when you're buying a home.
2. Title insurance protects against many title and survey defects, as well as any fraudulent attempt to steal your title.
3. Title insurance is still not a substitute for the peace of mind you can get from an up-to-date survey for your property.

PROFESSIONAL ADVISERS

I encourage buyers and sellers to get professional advice about all aspects of the real estate process. If you don't already have advisers, ask friends, relatives, and work colleagues for referrals; you can also ask your real estate salesperson.

Buyers can discuss their purchase ability with mortgage loan brokers and insurance specialists. Buyers and sellers need legal advisers, should there be anything in the agreement of purchase and sale they don't understand or need clarified. Before you hire a lawyer, ask what the fee will be; also ask about the cost of all anticipated disbursements, so you'll know how much the closing will cost. If you are buying a specialized property, such as a cottage, I recommend that you use a local lawyer who may be more familiar with the way the town or city works and can provide relevant local knowledge. Cottage properties will also typically require separate conditions and inspections of wells and septic systems. (For examples of these conditions, see Appendix 1.8.a and 1.8.b.)

Sellers, especially those of you in the seniors category who want to downsize or change their lifestyle, talk to your families and financial advisers before you decide to sell your home. Maybe you could install ramps or an elevator to your home, or hire a live-in caregiver, instead of moving into a retirement home. I recommend that seniors find out in advance if the net proceeds of the sale of their home will cover all the costs of living in a retirement home or other facility.

Buyers, consider hiring a private planner to assist you with any zoning, parking, and permit issue, especially if you're contemplating improvements to the property you want to buy.

Doing your homework and research in advance and working with competent professionals will give you maximum protection when you're buying or selling a home.

Weisleder's Wisdom on preparing to sell or buy a home

1. Understand the two land registration systems so you can anticipate the effects of a boundary dispute on your property.
2. Know the twelve questions to ask so you can determine the market value of the area you are interested in.
3. Sellers, protect yourself against liability after closing by revealing all legal, physical, and psychological defects on the property in advance.

4. Complete any sellers property information statement or property condition statement form carefully, and consider conducting pre-listing inspections when the form can't be completed for any reason.

5. Sellers, stage your home effectively before offering it for sale.

6. Buyers, research a neighbourhood by walking it at different times, speaking to the neighbours, checking at city hall, and using the Internet.

7. Buyers and sellers, understand the process and importance of obtaining the mortgage loan, home inspection, survey, home insurance, and title insurance before you enter into any agreement to buy or sell a home.

Always have professionals — REALTORS®, mortgage brokers, lawyers, planners, and financial advisers — to help you buy or sell a home successfully.

CHAPTER 3

The Agreement of Purchase and Sale

For most buyers and sellers, the standard real estate agreement of purchase and sale is one of the largest contractual obligations they ever enter into, yet it constantly amazes me how little they know about what the clauses in the agreement mean. Not understanding the contract can lead to very dangerous consequences, especially when you add in all the emotional stress that comes into play when you're negotiating the agreement, usually at 11:00 p.m. At that point, the negotiation usually involves only price, as buyers struggle with how much they can afford and sellers try to get as much as they can so they can afford *their* new house.

Yet there are so many other consequences and concerns that can have a dramatic effect on what happens after the deal is closed. Your new home could be problem free, or you may end up in legal proceedings because of something you didn't understand, or because of misrepresentations when the agreement was entered into.

Whether you're a buyer or a seller, you can prepare for this stressful process by understanding in detail what all the clauses in the agreement mean, so you'll know which rights and obligations you can live with, and which need to be changed to satisfy your needs.

As I explain the clauses, I will be using the standard "Agreement of Purchase and Sale form," which has been adopted for use by most real estate boards in Ontario and across Canada. In some provinces, the clauses may be in different order or under different categories; the main principles and terminology are essentially the same. This agreement is designed for the sale of residential resale homes only; there is a different form for resale condominiums (I discuss it in Chapter 8). Builders generally prepare their own standard forms, one for new homes and one for new condominiums. If you're buying a newly built home or condominium, it's a good idea to have legal counsel before you enter into the agreements. Or you can add a condition to your offer, giving you time to consult with your legal advisers before you close the purchase. (There is more information about buying new homes or condominiums in Chapter 9.)

A great deal of thought and effort has gone into preparing the residential standard form. It has evolved over the years, partially as a result of lawsuits that resulted from confusion or vagueness in prior versions. Changes were made to the form to clear up these ambiguities. Still, if you do not understand exactly what the clauses mean, you may be disappointed, especially if you want to make changes to your home after you buy it. More on that later. There is also room in the agreement to add in additional clauses, depending on your own particular circumstances. These can include clauses related to conditions, the survey, chattels and fixtures, assignment rights, limitations of liability, and other representations or warranties about a subject matter that may be important to buyers or sellers. We will look at each of these possible additional clauses, so you understand their legal consequences.

In British Columbia, for example, before they sign the agreement, buyers and sellers are given an information sheet that explains some of the important clauses, including the deposit, title, closing date, insurance obligations, and other fees that they will be responsible for. A careful salesperson will take the time to make sure buyer and seller clients understand all the fine print.

In this chapter, we'll look at the "Residential Resale Agreement" clause by clause. I'll explain the background of each clause, as well as its intended meaning and its effect on buyers and sellers. I'll also give you relevant case law that interprets the actual wording.

OREA Ontario
Real Estate
Association

This Agreement of Purchase and Sale dated this _____ day of _____ 20_____

BUYER, _____, agrees to purchase from
(Full legal names of all Buyers)

SELLER, _____, the following
(Full legal names of all Sellers)

When you buy property, use your full legal name. In some cases, only one buyer signs the offer but title will be placed in the name of two or more owners. And sometimes the buyer who signs the offer does not take title to the property. Every person who signs the offer as a buyer will have a legal obligation to perform everything in the offer, unless there is a clause that limits his or her liability. (The concept of liability is discussed in detail in Chapter 5.) What this means is that once you put your name on the agreement as a buyer, you obligate yourself to be legally responsible to complete any promise you make in the offer, which means paying a certain amount of money to buy a property. If your agreement is accepted and you don't complete the agreement for any reason, you may forfeit your deposit and also may be liable for any other losses the seller suffers because the house didn't sell for the stated price.

If you're not married but living with a partner and you both put an offer on a house, I recommend that you both sign the agreement of purchase and sale, and that you both take title to the property together, to ensure that your ownership interests are protected if you later break up. Unmarried couples are not generally afforded the same kind of protections as married spouses when it comes to real property in Canada; make sure your name always goes on title to any property you purchase with your partner.

Often a seller who gets an offer from a married couple will usually insist that both husband's and wife's names are shown as the buyers for the property. The reason is that sometimes a couple decides to make the offer in the name of the spouse who has no assets, so if anything goes wrong, the couple can limit their liability — the seller may not bother to get damages from someone who has few assets. Or a couple may decide to insert the name of a corporation as the buyer. The reason is that the corporation also has no assets other than the deposit that is being submitted. If the corporation doesn't complete the deal, again there is no further liability on the couple. Sellers who see these maneuvers on an agreement usually insist on a substantial deposit, so that the buyers don't walk away from their commitment.

The agreement should only be signed and submitted when you are seriously interested in purchasing a property. This is also one of the advantages of using a qualified REALTOR®. A buyer salesperson usually qualifies the buyer clients before they make an offer; this invariably gives confidence to the sellers and the sellers' salesperson that the buyers are serious.

When you're the seller, check your title deed, which you received when you purchased the property, and use the exact names and spellings registered on title when you fill in the agreement to sell. If the property is registered in the names of husband and wife, then both must sign the agreement as the sellers. If the seller is a corporation, make sure the person signing for the corporation has the authority to bind the corporation to the agreement. If one of the sellers named on the deed has passed away, the will of the deceased owner must first be probated by the estate trustees (formerly referred to as the executors) named in the will. If no dispute arises during the probate, the estate trustees will sign the agreement on behalf of the selling estate. There is an old expression, "Where there's a will . . . there's a relative." Don't assume any probate will proceed smoothly. A disgruntled relative may object to the provisions of a will, and it may take years to resolve the objection. If you are acting as the trustee for an estate, don't enter into agreements for the estate to sell any real estate until you're sure the probate has been completed and you have the authority to deal with the property.

What happens if the property is registered in only one married spouse's name, but it's a matrimonial home — a home that is ordinarily occupied by the spouses and their children as a family residence? In this situation, both spouses have an interest in the home, so the registered owner signs the agreement on the "seller" line and the partner signs in the "spousal consent" section, which is shown on page 174. If a couple has separated but have not signed a separation agreement, and only one spouse is on title and is living in the matrimonial home, both spouses will still have to sign the agreement of purchase and sale, again on the seller line and the spousal consent section. Did you know that couples can have more than one matrimonial home? They can, so the same rules apply for the family cottage or ski chalet that's ordinarily used by the family. If you are buying from a couple going through a divorce, make sure both spouses have accepted the agreement. You don't want to deal with either spouse trying to cancel the agreement later.

1. Buyers, submit your offers in your full legal names, especially when two or more people are involved.
2. Sellers, demand a higher deposit if an offer is signed by only one of two spouses, or if an offer is submitted in the name of a corporation that may have no assets except the deposit.
3. Look at your original deed and make sure the person listed on title to the property signs in the seller line.
4. If the property is owned by a corporation, make sure the person signing for the corporation has the authority to sign for the corporation.
5. When you're acting as a trustee for an estate, be sure that the probate application has been completed before you sign any agreement to sell the property.
6. If a matrimonial home is involved, a non-registered spouse signs the agreement in the spousal consent section.
7. If you are not married and buying a property with your partner, make sure your name is registered on title, to adequately protect your interests.

REAL PROPERTY:

Address _____ fronting on the _____ side of _____ in the _____ and having a frontage of _____ more or less by a depth of _____ more or less and legally described as _____ _____ (the "property"). (Legal description of land including easements not described elsewhere)

Great care must be taken to ensure that the property being offered for sale is in fact correctly described. When there are issues with fence lines, encroachments, easements, or

covenants that may affect a property, the best advice is to disclose all these issues in advance, up front, to any potential
buyer, to avoid problems with closing. To make this information as clear as possible, the form provides four different ways
to describe a property.

1. Street address. Here we write in the municipal address of
   the property, for example, 1000 Green Lane. This can be
   challenging in rural areas where there is only a rural route
   number. When there is no clear identifiable number, take
   great care in completing the remaining three ways to
   describe the property.
2. Fronting on. An example might be "fronting on the west
   side of Green Lane." Include the north, south, east, or
   west side of the applicable street. This is done for greater
   clarity, as many corner properties have a municipal
   address on one street yet front onto a different street.
3. Frontage and Depth. For these lines, be exact: provide
   the actual frontage of the property, usually in feet, and the
   actual depth of the property, also using feet. Here you
   must be very careful to examine the legal documents that
   relate to the title of the property – the deed, the survey,
   and, to a lesser extent, the municipal tax bill. The words
   "more or less" are included to cover only minor
   discrepancies. In legal decisions, if an error is made in the
   description of "Frontage and Depth," but the error is not
   greater than five percent of the total area of the property,
   the seller is usually protected by the words "more or less."
   But it could be dangerous to rely on these words. A court
   will look at other factors in making its determination:
   whether there are fences surrounding the property and
   whether the buyers had the opportunity to "walk the
   property" before submitting an offer. If you say that the
   property has a frontage of fifty feet, and the actual

> footage between the fences is forty-eight feet, the buyers
> are essentially getting the land they thought they were
> getting, which is the land between the two fences. If there
> are no fences on the property, the buyers may be able to
> claim they were deceived or that the seller
> misrepresented the frontage.

When a seller makes an error of more than ten percent, the courts have permitted some buyers to claim a reduction — or "abatement" — in the purchase price. This can be disastrous for a seller, who must complete the sale at a reduced price.

When anything is not clear, and you know the buyer will be relying on the accuracy of the information you provide, include a disclaimer clause. (I discuss disclaimer clauses in Chapter 2.) The clause will tell buyers they may want to make their offer conditional on the preparation and approval of an up-to-date survey of the property.

If you are a buyer and the square footage area is important to you, make it clear that the purchase price is in fact being based on an expected square footage or acreage, so that everyone is making sure that the total area of the property is accurately described. Buyers, include square footage conditions in your offer to purchase if the size of the lot is particularly important to you.

Let's say you want to buy a fifty-foot lot so you can demolish the existing house on the property and build two semi-detached homes. Let's also say the zoning bylaw requires a minimum twenty-five-foot frontage for each of the semi-detached houses. Here even a one-foot discrepancy in the frontage can be a problem. You may have to apply to the local committee of adjustments for a variance to the zoning bylaw. Your neighbours will be given the opportunity to challenge, defeat, or delay your application. The one-foot discrepancy can cause you extreme hardship.

Sellers, examine the survey, deed, and tax bill carefully to make sure you've been precise in describing the frontage and depth. Buyers, insert a condition that if the property does not contain the necessary frontage, you have the right to terminate the transaction.

Sellers, if there are any conflicts or discrepancies between your measurements and your documents, ask for legal advice before you list the property, to avoid problems later. Let's say you are having a dispute with one of your neighbours about the location of a fence, and the survey doesn't resolve the dispute. The best advice for any seller is to disclose this dispute and all its particulars to any potential buyer before the buyer submits an offer. As I indicate throughout this book, full disclosure is the best protection against unwanted legal proceedings. In this example, it also demonstrates the seller's overall integrity, and may earn the seller the benefit of the doubt should any other matter arise during the course of a transaction.

If the property has an irregular shape and it is difficult to note the actual frontage and depth measurements, attach a copy of the survey to the offer, so there is no confusion; insert the words "as per the attached survey" in the line "Frontage and Depth."

4. Legal Description. The legal description is the lot and plan number listed on the deed to the property. Sellers, once again examine the source documents, such as the deed and survey, so the legal description is correct. Most properties are legally described as a specific lot or part of a lot or parcel unit on a plan, in a city and county. (See the section on the Registry and Land Titles systems in Chapter 2.) Also examine another source document: the reporting letter you received from your lawyer when you purchased the property. If there were any issues affecting title, such as easements or restrictive covenants, they

would most likely have been discussed before closing and included in the report. A buyer may accept a seller's minor easements for utilities and restrictive covenants, but does not accept any major easements, encroachments, or other issues on title to the property. If you know of any easement or right of way affecting the property — say, a mutual driveway or lane at the back of the property — disclose them. Attach another page or a schedule if you need more room. Your goal is to clearly identify anything that may affect title to the property. A title insurance policy does not in most circumstances correct legal issues such as fence-line disputes, easements, or encroachments that affect a property. Let any potential buyers know about all title or legal defect issues before they make you an offer. (See clause 10 for more about easements and restrictive covenants; title insurance is discussed in Chapter 2.)

If you're buying, make sure there's an up-to-date survey. If a current survey is not available, and the seller refuses to pay for one, there may be a problem that both buyer and seller are unaware of — a problem that may not be repaired by title insurance. A current survey tells a buyer immediately if there are any encroachments or easements or problems with the boundary lines. It may not be a bad idea to have a casual conversation with some of the neighbours to determine if there are disputes about the property lines. Ask the neighbours if they have a survey; a current survey of a neighbour's property may show you some potential problems on the property you're buying. As discussed in Chapter 2 on the Land Registry Systems, if the land you're buying is registered in the land titles system, you can usually take comfort in the fact that whatever is mentioned on the deed is absolute and correct.

> ### Weisleder's Wisdom on
> ### real property and legal descriptions

1. Examine all source documents, including the deed, survey, tax bill, and lawyer's reporting letter, to determine the exact legal description as well as the frontage and depth measurements of a property.
2. Disclose any title defect, such as major easements, rights of way, encroachments, and fence-line disputes, to your buyers before they submit an offer.
3. Always obtain or make your transaction conditional on obtaining an up-to-date survey of a property before making an offer; you'll avoid surprises later about boundaries or quality of title.
4. Attach a copy of the survey to any offer to sell, so all buyers and sellers have the up-to-date information.

PURCHASE PRICE:
Dollars (CDN$) _____

"Purchase Price" means the total money the seller will receive in exchange for transferring the property to the buyer. Use both words and numbers, the same as when you write a cheque, to avoid any confusion. Often salespeople prepare four copies of the agreement for signature by the buyers and sellers, one each for the buyer, seller, buyer's lawyer, and seller's lawyer. Make sure all copies are identical; double check the total purchase price. There was a case where the purchase price was changed from $419,000 to $499,000 on the fourth copy of the offer by an unscrupulous buyer, who never intended to pay $499,000. The buyer used the phony copy to obtain a high-ratio mortgage for $450,000. The buyer used the mortgage proceeds to pay the seller $419,000, then disappeared with the rest of the money. The sellers and salespeople were accused of fraud and had to answer questions when the mortgage company investigated. Be careful: even though you're innocent, you may be investigated by police and read about yourself in the local paper. Review every copy of the agreement before you sign.

If the purchase price is based on the total number of acres you're buying, make sure the wording clearly describes what you expect to get, and get a survey before closing. If you do all this and don't receive the number of acres you expected, your purchase price will be adjusted so you only pay for the acres you receive.

DEPOSIT: Buyer submits _____
(Herewith/Upon Acceptance/as otherwise described in this Agreement)

_____ Dollars (CDN$) by negotiable cheque payable to _____ "Deposit Holder" to be held in trust pending completion or other termination of this Agreement and to be credited toward the Purchase Price on completion. For the purposes of this Agreement, "Upon Acceptance" shall mean that the Buyer is required to deliver the deposit to the Deposit Holder within 24 hours of the acceptance of this Agreement. The parties to this Agreement hereby acknowledge that, unless otherwise provided for in this Agreement, the Deposit Holder shall place the deposit in trust in the Deposit Holder's non-interest bearing Real Estate Trust Account and no interest shall be earned, received or paid on the deposit.

Buyer agrees to pay the balance as more particularly set out in Schedule A attached.

For clarity, the deposit should also be listed in both words and numbers, the same as when you're writing a cheque. And you will be writing a cheque: the cheque for the deposit is usually made payable to the listing brokerage and used to pay the commission to the listing brokerage after the transaction is completed. If there is any money left after the commission and the GST are paid, the balance is forwarded to the seller. If the commission plus GST was $12,600 and there was only $10,000 paid as a deposit, then after closing, the lawyer for the seller will pay the balance of $2,600 to the listing broker out of the closing funds received from the buyer.

In most provinces, the deposit monies are paid to the seller "herewith," which means the seller gets the cheque and the signed offer from the buyer at the same time. Or the deposit can be paid "upon acceptance," which means within twenty-four hours of the seller accepting the offer.

In Ontario, though, most salespeople use the words "upon acceptance." Under the *Real Estate and Business Brokers' Act* in Ontario, all listing brokerages must place any deposits they receive into their trust accounts within five days of receipt. If a buyer hands over an offer with a cheque attached, the cheque usually goes immediately into the listing broker's trust account even if the seller hasn't yet accepted the offer. The difficulty occurs if the seller does not accept the offer and the deposit now has to be paid back to the buyer. In order to remove the funds from the listing broker's trust account, both the buyer and seller must agree by signing a mutual release, to confirm that both parties are in agreement to return the deposit. This process can take several days and the buyers will be prevented from using these deposit monies to make an offer on a different property. Since most buyers cannot afford to wait to get their deposit money back, they use the words "upon acceptance" so that they do not have to hand over the deposit unless and until the seller actually accepts their offer.

When the offer is made "upon acceptance," it states further that buyers have twenty-four hours from acceptance to actually pay the deposit. The twenty-four-hour requirement was recently added to the standard form in Ontario to resolve confusion about the meaning of the words "upon acceptance." On the last page of the agreement, in the "Confirmation of Acceptance" section, there is a place to note the date and time the acceptance is completed, so that we can figure out when the twenty-four-hour time period starts. The logical question is then: "What happens if you are late in paying the deposit?" Can the seller sue the buyer? Can either of them get out of the deal?

In the decision of *1473587 Ontario Inc. v. Jackson*, decided in 2005, an offer was prepared by Loblaws to purchase property. The agreement provided that the deposit was due and payable within five days of acceptance. It turned out that, because of an administrative error, the deposit was not delivered until seven days after the date stipulated in the agreement. The seller refused to accept the deposit and took the position that the agreement was over; the seller then sold the property to a different buyer. Loblaws sued and lost. The judge focused on the standard form clause 19 (now clause 20), "Time Limits," in the agreement. Clause 19 stated, "Time shall be of the essence of this Agreement," meaning time limits are significant and must be followed. The judge ruled that the delay by Loblaws constituted a fundamental breach of the contract, so the seller could take the position that the agreement was at an end.

As a postscript, the second buyer eventually also failed to close the deal, and Loblaws acquired the property after all. Unfortunately, they incurred thousands of dollars in legal fees before it was all over.

How will this decision affect a buyer who takes more than twenty-four hours to pay a deposit? Could a seller take the position that the deal is over? In a seller's market, where prices are rising, many sellers may say a transaction is over if they know there is another buyer willing to pay more for the property. I don't like litigation. If I were the seller and I tried to cancel a deal, I would be running the risk of the buyer starting a lawsuit and tying up the property in court for several years. If your buyer doesn't get the deposit delivered in time, immediately contact your lawyer for advice. The best solution may be to obtain the deposit from your buyer and close the transaction quickly.

When you're a buyer, you can't predict how your seller is going to react. If you know you'll need two or three days to get the deposit together, then say so in the agreement, so that there is no confusion. Change the twenty-four hours to forty-eight or seventy-two hours, especially if you need to get a bank draft or certified funds, or arrange to courier the deposit to a location in another city. In other provinces, the agreement states that the deposit must be paid "on a certain date." Make sure you write that date in your diary, so the deposit is always paid on time. It's always a good idea to avoid litigation.

What if the deposit cheque bounces? Will the deal be cancelled? Based on the Loblaws decision, a bounced cheque could very well be grounds to cancel an agreement. However, I caution sellers from taking this position. Sometimes cheques bounce for reasons that are beyond the control of the buyer. What I would do is contact my lawyer for instructions. As a seller, for example, you may decide to continue with the deal, provided the buyer increases the amount of the deposit, to give you more assurance that the transaction will indeed close on time.

Sellers, be vigilant about who is writing the cheque for the deposit. A new fraudulent practice has emerged: unscrupulous buyers steal a company cheque from an organization that writes many cheques, then change the "payee" name to the seller's brokerage company. They submit the "deposit" with an agreement and a short home inspection conditional period. Then they cancel the deal, claiming they're not satisfied with the results of the home inspection, and they ask for their money back. The innocent brokerage company writes them a cheque; the buyers take the money and run. You never want to be connected in any way to a fraudulent transaction. When you're accepting an offer, ask where your deposit cheque will be coming from.

More and more sellers and brokerage companies are insisting on certified cheques or bank drafts for all deposits to eliminate bounced or forged cheques. This is perfectly legal; if you're a buyer, agree if you think it's appropriate.

Some buyers think they may sign an agreement, have it accepted by the seller, and then simply get out of the deal by not paying the deposit. Those buyers are wrong. The moment a buyer signs an agreement that is accepted by a seller, the buyer is bound to all the legal promises and obligations described in the offer to purchase, including the obligations to pay the deposit and also the balance due on closing. Suppose, as an example, you sign an agreement as a buyer and agree to pay $400,000 for a property, with a $20,000 deposit, and your offer is accepted by the seller. You then change your mind, decide to keep the $20,000 deposit, and cancel the transaction. If the seller sells the property to someone else for $375,000, you may have to make up for the seller's lost $25,000.

Buyers and sellers should know the legal significance of the deposit and a listing brokerage's trust account. A deposit cannot be disbursed from a brokerage's trust account until the transaction closes, or unless there is a mutual release signed by the buyer and seller, or there is a court order. If there is a dispute and the matter goes to court, the deposit is paid to the court or stays in the trust account until the legal matter is decided. If a buyer defaults on an agreement, the court usually determines that the deposit will be forfeited to the seller, even if the seller sells the property for more money later. By paying the deposit, a buyer is paying part of the total purchase price and is also showing good faith; in other words, they are indicating they intend to complete the transaction. A buyer who doesn't close violates this good faith obligation and thus forfeits the deposit.

If a deal falls apart and the seller is awarded the deposit, the listing brokerage can't keep any part of the deposit for themselves unless the seller promised to share it with the listing broker in the listing agreement under these circumstances. Sellers sometimes agree to such a provision in commercial listing agreements, but it's rare in residential listing agreements.

Weisleder's Wisdom on deposits

1. Buyers, all deposits must be paid when stated in the agreement; if you need more time, change the wording on the offer.
2. Sellers, if a deposit is not being paid directly by the buyer, ask where the money is coming from.
3. Consider asking for certified cheques for large deposits.
4. Get a lawyer's advice if a deposit cheque bounces, but avoid litigation, if possible.

The schedules attached to an agreement typically include provisions regarding payment of the balance due on closing, as well as clauses about the survey, conditions, representations, warranties, and any other matter important to buyers and sellers. These provisions and clauses are discussed in detail later on in this chapter.

1. IRREVOCABILITY: This Offer shall be irrevocable by _____ until _____ a.m./p.m. on (Seller/Buyer)
the _____ day of _____ 20_____, after which time, if not accepted, this Offer shall be null and void and the deposit shall be returned to the Buyer in full without interest.

Typically, the agreement process starts with a buyer making an offer to a seller. In some provinces, the section where you do this appears at the end of the agreement, just before the buyer signs. No matter where the section is located, the buyer agrees to leave the offer "open" for a specific time, so the seller may consider the offer and then either accept it, reject it, or sign it back with a counter-offer. If the seller signs a counter-offer, then the word "buyer," written in the first blank, is crossed out and replaced with the word "seller," because now it's the seller making an offer to the buyer. In some provinces, there is a separate section for a counter-offer, for greater clarity.

Let's try to understand this process a little more. Although the buyer has agreed to leave the offer "open" for acceptance for perhaps several hours, he or she has not received any money or other consideration for doing this. Therefore, you would think that the buyer could just change their mind and cancel their offer up to the time that the seller actually accepts it.

However, if you look at the back of the offer, beside the area where the buyer and seller sign, are the words, "I have hereunto set my hand and seal." The legal significance of the seal is that it means that the person signing cannot change their mind about anything contained in the offer until the irrevocable date expires. It means that they were so serious about making this offer that it must have been important enough to them that they did not need extra money to leave the offer open for a specific time period. But if an offer is not signed under seal, then a buyer has the right to change their mind and cancel the offer at any time before the seller actually accepts it. Once the seller accepts any offer, whether under seal or not, it is too late for the buyer to change their mind.

If you forget to indicate a time limit in the irrevocable clause, no one will think your offer is open "forever." The law says an untimed offer will remain open for "a reasonable time." So complete this clause very carefully: important legal obligations flow from it.

If you submit a deposit with the offer and the offer is not accepted, the deposit is returned to you. Once an offer is accepted, a deposit can be returned only when the buyer and seller agree by signing a mutual release.

Weisleder's Wisdom on irrevocability

1. When you sign "under seal," it means you can't change your mind.
2. Buyers and sellers, once you sign an agreement "under seal," legal liability ensues, even if the buyer never remits a deposit.
3. If the offer is left open indefinitely, through carelessness, the courts will infer that it is to be left open for only a reasonable period.

---

2. COMPLETION DATE: This Agreement shall be completed by no later than 6:00 p.m. on the _____ day of _____, 20_____. Upon completion, vacant possession of the property shall be given to the Buyer unless otherwise provided for in this Agreement.

Think carefully about your completion or closing date. Make sure the date you choose is a regular business day, from Monday to Friday, as title cannot be transferred on a weekend or statutory holiday.

Many buyers automatically choose the last day of a month because they have given notice that they'll be vacating their apartment, or are planning to close the sale of their house on the last day of the month. You may be adding an enormous amount of stress by choosing the same day.

It is always preferable to close the purchase of your home a few days before you have to leave your current location, if at all possible, so the entire move-out move-in process is not rushed. If you're living in an apartment, you have to be careful to provide the correct written notice before you leave. There's a thorough discussion of leaving your apartment and the required notices to be given in Chapter 6.

If you are moving out at the end of a month, try to schedule your purchase closing date at least a week before that. This will give you the time to inspect your new home, and you can paint, clean, or make minor repairs to get your new home ready for you to move into. If you don't rush the process, there is also less likelihood of things breaking or being damaged during the move.

If you're selling one house and buying another, you can still sell a few days after you purchase. Ask your bank and obtain interim financing, called a "bridge loan," so you can pay for your new home before you get the proceeds from selling your old house. You have to pay interest on the bridge loan, but the cost of the interest for a few days will be well worth it, and you'll be moving in a much more relaxed atmosphere.

If you're selling a home that's rented to tenants, and your buyer has asked for "vacant possession on closing," the tenants must be off the premises. (We will discuss this in Chapter 6.) Suffice to say that it may be easier to just pay your tenants an incentive to leave the home even before you put it up for sale, to avoid any potential problems on closing.

In Ontario, the clause indicates that the building must be vacant no later than 6:00 p.m. on the day of closing. In today's environment, lawyers can electronically transfer title from a seller to a buyer from the computers in their offices, and the transaction may be completed as early as 10:00 a.m. on the day of closing. Legally, once the title has been transferred and keys are exchanged, the buyer should have vacant possession. A time of 6:00 p.m. was specified in the agreement because the Ontario government registry offices close at 5:00 p.m., so it's possible to transfer title up to 5:00 p.m.; the extra hour is so the lawyers can still make arrangements if anything goes wrong at the last moment. It happens: the buyer's funds may not reach the seller's lawyer by five because the courier got stuck in traffic.

If the seller is late in leaving the home and granting the buyer vacant possession, and the buyer incurs extra moving expenses as a result, the seller is responsible for the costs. In one case, the seller was not out of the home until after 9:00 p.m. The movers would not wait, and the buyers had to pay to put their goods in storage until they could arrange a new moving time. The seller had to pay these costs. If you're a seller and you believe you'll need more time to move, protect yourself. Insert a clause into the agreement stating that vacant possession will not be granted until, for example, 9:00 p.m. on the date of completion. If you're a buyer, insist on an early time for vacant possession, so you don't incur extra moving expenses.

In other provinces, the agreement indicates the closing date, without reference to a specific time. In my view, the legal principle is still the same: vacant possession must be provided once title has been transferred, which typically occurs during the afternoon. Sellers, if you will require extra time to get everything out of the house, add that amount of time to the agreement. No confusion, and no unnecessary moving expenses.

What does the phrase "vacant possession" mean? Can sellers leave unwanted items in the basement? Can they leave you with a very messy home? In general, buyers expect an empty home, in a broom-swept condition. In most offers, buyers request this in a specific clause. (The clause is in the Appendix) Sellers, arrange to have all unwanted items, especially large items, such as old furniture or metal bed frames, removed before the closing. These days there are many companies that, for a reasonable fee, will attend at the seller's home and remove all unwanted items. If a seller does leave large items and other junk in the home or the garage after closing, a buyer can hire such a company and charge the costs to the seller.

If you're a buyer, don't wait for closing to be "surprised" by a seller's junk. Stay involved. Ask your salesperson to find out if the junk is being removed. Check the house during your pre-closing visit to see if the seller is cleaning up. If it's not being done, ask your salesperson to be a pest and offer to arrange a bin for the seller. If you are a seller, leave the house the way you want your new house to be left for you.

Weisleder's Wisdom on completion or closing date

1. Make sure the closing date is a regular weekday, not a Saturday or Sunday and not a holiday.
2. Schedule the closing of your home purchase to happen before your sale closes or your lease ends.
3. Provide adequate notice to your landlord.
4. Make a deal with your tenants so they'll leave before you put your home up for sale.
5. In the agreement, set a specific time vacant possession is to be granted to avoid unnecessary moving costs.
6. Hire a bin company to remove all junk before closing.

3. NOTICES: Seller hereby appoints the Listing Brokerage as Agent for the purpose of giving and receiving notices pursuant to this Agreement. **Only if the Co-operating Brokerage represents the interests of the Buyer in this transaction**, the Buyer hereby appoints the Co-operating Brokerage as Agent for the purpose of giving and receiving notices pursuant to this Agreement. Any notice relating hereto or provided for herein shall be in writing.

This offer, any counter offer, notice of acceptance thereof, or any notice shall be deemed given and received, when hand delivered to the address for service provided in the Acknowledgement below, or where a facsimile number is provided herein, when transmitted electronically to that facsimile number.

FAX No. _____ (For delivery of notices to Seller)

FAX No. _____ (For delivery of notices to Buyer)

The agreement of purchase and sale includes many important provisions, conditions, and obligations. To avoid vagueness, uncertainty, or misunderstanding, almost all notices under the agreement must be given in writing and should be signed by the sellers or the buyers. If buyers want to waive a condition, for example the home inspection condition, they have to sign a waiver, or a "notice of fulfillment of the condition," then hand it to the buyer representative. Clause 6 permits the buyer representative to deliver the notice directly to the listing salesperson or brokerage so the sellers know the condition has been waived. For matters that are fundamental to the validity of the agreement — for example whether the offer has been accepted — the signed agreement is sent directly to the seller or the buyer, as the case may be. There are also guidelines for delivering a notice: by hand to the buyer or seller's address, as shown on the back of the agreement in the acknowledgement section, or by fax to the fax number written into the acknowledgement section on the back of the agreement.

We sign the acknowledgement section on the back of the offer to provide confirmation from both seller and buyer that the final acceptance of the agreement has been communicated to both seller and buyer in a timely manner and there are instructions to deliver a copy to the buyer and seller lawyers.

Don't ask your salesperson to sign any notice on your behalf, or initial any changes to the agreement on your behalf. This is how lawsuits get started. Sometimes it's inconvenient to wait up late at night to make sure all signatures and changes are finalized by both parties, but this contract is too important to leave anything to chance.

Buyers and sellers ask whether real estate agreements can be accepted through other electronic means, such as e-mail. If any method of acceptance is not printed on the agreement form, you can't use it. No agreement of purchase and sale form in Canada allows notice to be given via e-mail, but the question is being reviewed, given the realities of the amount of business done over the Internet. Until changes are made in the forms, e-mail is not permitted.

Make sure you initial all changes and finalize everything before the irrevocable date and time noted in clause 1. Until you do, the agreement has not yet been accepted; buyers and sellers could take the position that there is no binding agreement. Be especially careful when there are multiple offers on a property. Work closely with your buyer or seller salesperson to make sure your agreement is signed, accepted, and delivered in a timely manner, and deal with all notices as soon as possible.

Weisleder's Wisdom on notices

1. Buyers and sellers, always personally sign any notice under the agreement.
2. Make sure all notices are signed and delivered to the address noted in the acknowledgement on the back of the offer.
3. Never ask your salesperson to initial any document on your behalf.

4. Electronic methods of giving notice are not yet available in the agreement of purchase and sale forms across Canada.

4. CHATTELS INCLUDED: _____

_____

_____

5. FIXTURES EXCLUDED: _____

_____

_____

6. RENTAL ITEMS: The following equipment is rented and not included in the Purchase Price. The Buyer agrees to assume the rental contract(s), if assumable: _____

_____

_____

One of the more problematic areas between buyers and sellers is the rights and obligations regarding chattels included with the purchase price and fixtures that will be removed or replaced before closing. First, what's a "chattel"? What's a "fixture"? Here's a simple principle to remember: "If it takes a tool, that's the rule."

In other words, if you require a tool to remove something from the house, it is most probably a fixture. If you can pull it out easily, like a plug from a wall, it's a chattel. But even with simple principles, it can be very confusing. A garage-door opener looks like a chattel because you can hold the remote in your hand, but it's a fixture because it's part of the built-in garage-door assembly. A front door key is also a fixture since it is a part of the front door lock. What about mirrors or sliding doors you can remove by lifting them out of their slots? What about carpets that are not tacked down, or a dishwasher that's connected by a simple valve you can remove with your hand? To avoid confusion later, educate yourself before you list your house for sale or put in an offer.

If you're a seller, it's a good idea to remove or replace any fixtures you intend on taking with you when you move. If you want to keep the dining room chandelier, the gold-plated faucets in your bathroom, your drapes, the broadloom, a built-in oven or stove, or any other items you may have an emotional attachment to, take them out of your house before you list it. Replace the chandelier with a cheaper version, or make it very clear in the agreement that you're taking the chandelier with you.

When you're a buyer, there is no such thing as too much detail regarding the chattels you expect to receive on closing. My best advice is to list the make and model (and serial numbers, if available) of all appliances that are being included, and also note the colour and location of all drapes, carpeting, pool equipment, satellite dishes, sheds, bushes, and anything else you expect to be on the property when you move in. Salespeople may have lengthy lists of chattels and fixtures to help buyers and sellers keep track of what's included and what's not. Leave nothing to chance. During any home inspection, take photographs of all of the chattels and fixtures so you'll know if they've been replaced before the closing. Arrange for a pre-closing visit so you can satisfy yourself that all the chattels and fixtures that are supposed to remain on the property are still there. (There's a clause for the pre-closing visit; see Appendix 1.3.c.) Some chattels and fixtures may contain a seller's personal information, such as family photographs on magnets placed on a fridge; get permission from the seller before you take photographs. Sellers, I encourage you to be co-operative in this regard. Most home inspectors take these pictures anyway, as part of their inspection duties.

I recall from my days in private practice that I always dreaded receiving a call from buyers on the day following closing. They never called to thank me for all the work I did on their behalf. It was always about problems with their new home, anything from damages caused during the moving process to the removal of fixtures from the property. It was as though they viewed me as a sheriff who somehow had the ability to pick up the phone and solve their problems in an hour.

One client complained that the mailbox had been removed. I asked him what name was on the mailbox. He told me it was the seller's name. When I asked why he needed a mailbox with the seller's name on it, he replied, "It's the principle." The same principle explained another buyer's anger at plastic light-switch plates being removed — plates that probably cost 50¢ at the hardware store.

I heard about an offer that said "existing washer and dryer." The seller left behind a washing machine with a hair dryer on top.

Once, a fellow lawyer in my law firm closed a deal for his own house and came into the office the next day saying the seller had removed all the light switches from the wall and left only a few wires sticking out. The seller had also taken all the toilets. Apparently, the seller had heard that the buyer was going to demolish the house. What the seller did not hear was that the buyer intended to live in the house for a year before demolishing it. After I almost fell down laughing, I thanked him. From then on, whenever a buyer called me after closing to complain about missing fixtures, I always answered, "Just be happy you have your toilets."

Chattels and fixtures are important to sellers and buyers alike. For sellers, remember to leave the home you're selling just the way you want to receive the home you are buying.

What about rental contracts? Some contracts are not transferable. So do your homework: ask about the hot water tank, the furnace, satellite receivers, air conditioning units, and the alarm system. If you're buying, you may not want to assume an alarm contract; you may prefer to install your own system. The seller may have to incur a penalty for cancelling the contract before it expires. Look at all contracts carefully; ask any rental suppliers if their contracts can be assumed and what costs may be involved. Again, the trick is to have no surprises.

What about the condition of the chattels and fixtures? In most agreements, the buyers typically request that the chattels and fixtures, including all heating, air conditioning, and plumbing, will be "in good working order," or "in working order," on closing (see Appendix 1.1.a and 1.1.b). There is no real difference between "working order" and "good working order." Both phrases mean that all chattels and systems will be working when the buyer takes possession of the property. They do not mean the seller warrants that everything will be working one month after closing. Sometimes buyers can't check all the chattels and fixtures on the date of closing; a clause deals with this:

> The seller represents and warrants that all chattels, the furnace and the heating, plumbing and air conditioning systems will be in good working order on closing. This warranty shall survive closing but only to the extent that the said chattels, fixtures and systems are in good working order on closing.

What this clause means is that if there is not enough time on the day you move in to check all the appliances and systems in your home, and you find out when you try them a few days later that they are not working, then you can still ask the seller to repair them, as they were likely also not working on the day of closing either.

When we say that a warranty survives closing for a month, it is like a warranty that you receive when you buy an electronic item, like an iPod. It means that if something breaks down during this one-month period, the seller is responsible to repair it. Sellers do not like to give these kinds of warranties on anything in the house after they move out because there is always the problem of deciding whose fault it was that the item broke down. That is why, for the most part, sellers only give a warranty that everything will be working on the day you move in and no longer.

Sometimes, however, it is not possible to check whether an item is working, even a few days after you move in. An example might be the condition of the swimming pool when the property is purchased in February and there is no way for a buyer to check to see whether the pool is in good operating condition. One way to deal with this problem would be for the seller to give a warranty about the condition of the pool that will extend until May 1, when the pool is normally opened for the season. If sellers are reluctant to provide this, an alternative would be for the sellers to provide the pool closing report typically completed by the maintenance company that looks after the pool, which should indicate the condition of the pool at the time it was closed for the season. Examples of special clauses for swimming pools can be found in Appendix 1.10.

If you know that some of your appliances are not working when a buyer submits an offer to buy the property, disclose the condition of the appliances immediately. If an appliance breaks down after the agreement has been signed but before closing, the seller has to conduct the repairs.

In a court decision in Ontario, a seller was caught switching appliances after the agreement was signed and before closing. The buyer had video evidence, taken during the home inspection, that clearly showed the appliances — but not the appliances in the house on closing. The sauna wasn't working; some other systems were also not working. The court ordered the seller to pay for replacing the appliances and to repair the sauna and the disabled systems. The seller also had to pay "punitive damages" — an extra $10,000 — for attempting to deceive the buyers. This case serves as a lesson to sellers that this type of behaviour will not be tolerated. It's also a lesson to buyers: make and keep a detailed list or photographs of any chattels or fixtures you expect to receive on closing, and conduct a pre-closing visit to make sure everything you expect to get is still on the property.

For buyers, as discussed in Chapter 2, you may be able to obtain warranty protection for appliances and home systems after closing, to give you peace of mind that you will not encounter unexpected repair bills during your first year of ownership.

Weisleder's Wisdom on chattels, fixtures, and rental items

1. If it takes a tool, that's the rule.
2. Sellers, before you show your home to any potential buyers, remove or replace any fixtures or chattels you want to retain after closing.
3. Describe all chattels and fixtures clearly, with make, model, and serial numbers, and photograph where possible.
4. Buyers, always include a pre-closing-visit clause in the agreement, so you can check that all chattels and fixtures are being left behind.
5. Buyers, quickly check all chattels, fixtures, and systems as soon as possible after you take possession, and bring up any problems or questions with the seller or the seller's salespeople as soon as possible after closing.
6. Contact all rental-contract suppliers to determine what contracts, if any, can be transferred to a buyer; clearly identify the transferrable contracts in the agreement.

7. Sellers, if you know a chattel, fixture, or system is not working on the day an offer is submitted by a buyer, and if you have no intention of repairing the item, provide full disclosure to the buyer before you accept any offer, to avoid any confusion on closing.

8. Sellers, don't switch any chattels or fixtures once the agreement is signed, or you may face legal liability and punitive damages.

9. Buyers, consider obtaining after-sale warranty protection for appliances and other home systems.

7. GST: If this transaction is subject to Goods and Services Tax (GST), then such tax shall be _____ the Purchase Price.
(included in/in addition to)
If this transaction is not subject to GST, seller agrees to certify on or before closing, that the transaction is not subject to GST.

Virtually all residential resale transactions, whether single-family dwellings or condominiums, are not normally subject to GST, so usually buyers will always insert the words "included in" for this clause, so they won't be subject to any additional payment of GST. For example, if your purchase price is $105,000 with GST included, and it later turns out that GST should have been collected on the transaction, the purchase price will be changed to $100,000, plus $5,000 GST. The seller remits the $5,000 to Revenue Canada, and the buyer's purchase price remains unchanged. This process can be very costly to sellers, who may not know whether GST is in fact payable. If you have run a business out of your home or are writing off any expenses related to your home against your business, you may have to charge GST on part or all of the purchase price, in which case you'll insert the words "in addition to" in this clause.

If you do run a home business, consult your accountant and find out your tax status before you place your home on the market. If you find out you have to charge GST, immediately advise your listing broker.

In Nova Scotia, New Brunswick, and Newfoundland and Labrador, there is already a harmonized sales tax (HST), which includes provincial sales tax on the sale of certain real estate. An example of an HST clause is:

All conveyances of real property are subject to the Harmonized Sales Tax ("HST"), unless the conveyance is specifically exempt pursuant to the Excise Tax Act. The facts required to determine exemption from HST are entirely dependent upon the use of the property by the seller and are therefore accordingly within the knowledge of the seller only. The conveyance contemplated by this Agreement shall be:
>   Exempt from HST
>   Not exempt from HST; included in the purchase price
>   Not exempt from HST; over and above the purchase price

The printed agreements in the HST provinces ask the seller to state if the property is exempt from HST; if the buyer will have to pay HST on closing; or if the HST is included in the purchase price. The HST can increase the cost of the home significantly. In its 2009 budget, the Ontario government announced a similar HST, scheduled to apply to new-home and new-condominium purchases with a value of more than $400,000, commencing July 1, 2010. Exemptions may be considered and passed by the Ontario government before July 1, 2010.

8. TITLE SEARCH: Buyer shall be allowed until 6:00 p.m. on the _____ day of _____, 20_____, (Requisition Date) to examine the title to the Property at Buyer's own expense and until the earlier of: (i) thirty days from the later of the Requisition Date or the date on which the conditions in this Agreement are fulfilled or otherwise waived or; (ii) five days prior to completion, to satisfy Buyer that there are no outstanding work orders or deficiency notices affecting the Property, and that its present use (_____ _____) may be lawfully continued and that the principal building may be insured against risk of fire. Seller hereby consents to the municipality or other governmental agencies releasing to Buyer details of all outstanding work orders affecting the property, and Seller agrees to execute and deliver such further authorizations in this regard as Buyer may reasonably require.

This clause gives the lawyer for the buyer permission and time to conduct various searches to determine the status of title and zoning of the property, and anything that may affect the principal building on the property.

The first question is: how much time should you give your lawyer to conduct these various searches? In Ontario, searches involve different amounts of time depending on whether the property is registered in the registry system or the land titles system (for information about the land registration systems in Ontario, see Chapter 2). You want to give your lawyer sufficient time to complete all the required searches, and also enough time before the closing for the seller's lawyer to correct any problems your lawyer finds. If there is a two-month closing date in the agreement, we normally provide three weeks to a month for the buyer's lawyer to search the title. If it's a very short closing, such as two weeks, we might give the buyer's lawyer until closing to complete the searches. The buyer and seller lawyers will have to work together to get the transaction completed on time.

If you are a buyer and you are inserting a condition into the agreement, then you must take this into account when filling in this search time period. For example, if the agreement is conditional for sixty days on the buyer selling their existing home, then the time period to be inserted should be thirty days after the condition is satisfied or waived by the buyer. You do not want your lawyer doing any searches until the deal is firm.

Problems with title include, for example, an encroachment of a neighbour's shed or garage onto your property, or a dispute over a fence-line boundary. Or maybe an easement covers more than ten percent of the total property. The easement could be a right-of-way over a lane at the rear of the property, or a utility easement in favour of Bell Canada, the electric company, or the city, for storm and drainage maintenance. Typically, these problems cannot be cured by title insurance. Or there may be work orders or deficiency notices because the principal building on the property doesn't comply with local bylaws relating to building codes, fire codes, or health requirements. A city inspector may have noticed these infractions during an inspection, or the neighbours may have complained. These infractions will typically be recorded in the local city hall offices.

The phrase "present use" refers to the zoning on the property. In this clause, the seller specifies exactly how he is currently using the property, which can be lawfully continued by the buyer. An example of a violation of the zoning bylaw is an illegal basement apartment, rented to a tenant, or a basement apartment that doesn't follow the specifications of the local building and fire departments. The seller is also stating that the building is insurable. Some properties may not be insurable, for example, a grow house, or a former grow house that has not been repaired; other environmental problems, for example an underground oil tank, may prevent a buyer from obtaining insurance on the property. Insurance can be costly if the property has asbestos insulation (the insulation would need to be removed) or knob-and-tube wiring (the wiring may require an upgrade). If you think it may be expensive to insure the property, consider inserting a separate condition clause describing the problem. The buyer will then have the right to get out of the deal if the insurance premium is too high.

If the buyer's lawyer finds any problems with any of the title, the zoning, work orders, or the insurability of the property, the lawyer tells the lawyer for the seller. The seller must attempt, in good faith, to correct the problems before the closing. If the problems can't be corrected, the buyer may either accept the defects and complete the transaction or refuse to complete the transaction and ask for the deposit to be refunded. (The buyer's choices are discussed in clause 10, Title, a few pages along.)

In some provinces, the only search referred to in the agreement is the title search. There is no mention of zoning, work orders, or insurance. In these provinces, buyers ask for a separate representation by the seller that the current use of the property can be continued by the buyer, that there are no work orders or deficiency notices registered against the property, and that the buyer can obtain insurance on the property at a reasonable premium.

9. FUTURE USE: Seller and Buyer agree that there is no representation or warranty of any kind that the future intended use of the property by Buyer is or will be lawful except as may be specifically provided for in this Agreement.

Most houses sold in Ontario are single-family homes. What the seller is saying here is that he or she is not making any promises that the home can be used for any other purpose by the buyer once the buyer moves in. For example, what if the buyer wants to change this home so he or she can use it as a triplex, or a small commercial building? To protect the buyer in this example, we insert a condition into the agreement to make the transaction conditional on the buyer's ability to rezone the property to the intended use.

Don't rely on a seller's verbal statements about how the property can be used. Either include the seller's statement in writing as a "seller's representation" in the agreement, or make your offer conditional on getting permission for your intended use.

10. TITLE: Provided that the title to the property is good and free from all registered restrictions, charges, liens, and encumbrances except as otherwise specifically provided in this Agreement and save and except for (a) any registered restrictions or covenants that run with the land providing that such are complied with; (b) any registered municipal agreements and registered agreements with publicly regulated utilities providing such have been complied with, or security has been posted to ensure compliance and completion, as evidenced by a letter from the relevant municipality or regulated utility; (c) any minor easements for the supply of domestic utility or telephone services to the property or adjacent properties; and (d) any easements for drainage, storm or sanitary sewers, public utility lines, telephone lines, cable television lines or other services which do not materially affect the use of the property. If within the specified times referred to in paragraph 8 any valid objection to title or to any outstanding work order or deficiency notice, or to the fact the said present use may not lawfully be continued, or that the principal building may not be insured against risk of fire is made in writing to Seller and which Seller is unable or unwilling to remove, remedy or satisfy or obtain insurance save and except against risk of fire in favour of the Buyer and any mortgagee, (with all related costs at the expense of the Seller), and which Buyer will not waive, this Agreement notwithstanding any intermediate acts or negotiations in respect of such objections, shall be at an end and all monies paid shall be returned without interest or deduction and Seller, Listing Brokerage and Co-operating Brokerage shall not be liable for any costs or damages. Save as to any valid objection so made by such day and except for any objection going to the root of the title, Buyer shall be conclusively deemed to have accepted Seller's title to the property.

In the first sentence, the buyer is asking the seller to convey a "good clean and marketable title" to the property, without any liens or encumbrances. A "clean title" means that there are no claims against the property that will affect the peaceful possession of the property by the buyer. However, the buyer does agree to accept certain title defects mentioned in subparagraphs 10(a) to (d) in this clause. It is important to understand what these subparagraphs include and what they do not include.

The first subparagraph (a) states that the buyer will accept "any registered restriction or covenant that runs with the land provided that such has been complied with."

First let's try and understand what a restrictive covenant means. A restrictive covenant is a promise given by one landowner to another landowner that restricts how the owner will use the property. The way these promises developed is that over time, landowners started dividing their properties and selling pieces to buyers. But since the sellers still retained land next door to the land they were selling, they demanded that the buyers agree to certain restrictions about how their land was going to be used, to preserve the value of the seller's remaining land.

For example, let's say an owner is dividing his land and he knows that the zoning bylaw permits duplexes and triplexes in his area. This owner believes that if the buyer builds a triplex next door, it will devalue his remaining land. So he gets the buyer to agree to insert a covenant, or promise, on title that the buyer and any future owner will not build anything except a single-family home on that land.

The words "complied with" mean that as long as the current seller is complying with, or following, any promises or restrictive covenants that are on the title, then the buyer has to accept them. This can have dramatic and sometimes disastrous consequences on unsuspecting buyers. In other words, if anyone who ever owned the property made a promise that limits the use of the property, and the promise is written on the property's title, the promise will continue forever. Let's say the property is zoned residential, a zoning that permits single-family dwellings, duplexes, and triplexes. You look at the property and find a single-family residence, and your intention is to buy the land so you can knock down the house and build a triplex for investment purposes. You check with the local zoning department, and find that you can do this. However, on title, there is a registered "covenant," or promise, that the owner will not build anything except a single-family dwelling on the property. Because the seller is complying with — or following — this promise, you'll also have to accept it, meaning you won't be able to build your triplex. In other words, restrictive covenants can override zoning bylaws.

Restrictive covenants cannot, however, override human rights. In the early 1900s, there were promises put into deeds in some parts of Ontario that prevented the sale of the property to certain races or religious groups. Thankfully we now live in a society that does not tolerate these types of covenants, and any owner can apply to a court to have these covenants removed from their title, as the covenants are not reasonable.

A reasonable "promise on title" will however apply to any buyer who wants to make changes to a property. So if you're a buyer and you want to make any change to the home you are buying, such as an addition to the home, building a pool, installing an antenna, or changing the type of structure on the property, choose one of three alternatives to make sure you're protected:

1. Have your salesperson or lawyer check the title to find out if there are restrictive covenants that prevent you from making your proposed changes.
2. Make the transaction conditional on finding nothing registered on title that prevents you from making your changes.
3. Ask the seller to inform you of any restrictive covenant on title. If there are none, ask the seller to tell you that in writing, and include it in the agreement.

In subparagraph (b), the buyer agrees to accept what is included in agreements between an original land developer and the city. For example, when developers decide to take a 100 acre piece of land and build 200 homes, they must first enter into agreements with the local city and utility companies about how services will be brought to these new homes, as well as other requirements by the city for the homes and the neighbourhood. The city and the developers enter into what is called a "subdivision agreement," which outlines these requirements. In Ontario, some common provisions in subdivision agreements which affect your property rights are, for example, restrictions against antennae and against clotheslines. What subparagraph (b) states is that as long as the seller is following any promise that might be contained in a subdivision agreement, then the buyer has to accept this as well.

You no longer have to worry about having a clothesline: given the concerns about energy conservation, the Ontario government passed a law in April 2008 saying that any restriction against clotheslines is now null and void. But if you do have plans to erect an antenna on your home after you move in, make sure that you indicate this in your agreement.

In subparagraphs (c) and (d), the buyer agrees to accept any minor easements for the supply of a public utility and of telephone and cable; there are also easements for storm sewers and drainage. These easements are typically found on the side, front, or rear of your property and allow service providers such as telephone, hydro, and cable access so they can repair and maintain their equipment, whether the equipment — usually wires — is on your property or your neighbours' properties. The key word here is "minor." Court decisions have said that so long as these easements make up less than five to seven percent of your property, and are found on the side, front, or rear of the property, a buyer must accept them. "Minor easements" do *not* include a mutual driveway you share with your neighbour, a laneway right-of-way on your property, or a major utility easement. These exceptions are major easements, because they would materially impact your intended use of your land. For example, an easement that runs right down the middle of your backyard could prevent you from installing an in-ground pool.

Ask whether there are any easements on the property and the exact location, as even minor easements may interfere with your landscaping plans or prevent you from building a garden shed.

If you're a seller and you're not sure if any easements affect your property, the first place to look is the legal description in your title deed. Also look at your survey, if you have one. And read the reporting letter you received from your lawyer when you bought the property; during the title search, the lawyer should have uncovered any registered easement on your property. The reporting letter will also discuss any issues that came up during your closing, for example a dispute about fence lines. To be safe, disclose all easements, covenants, and any other title defects right in the agreement of purchase and sale. When you practice full disclosure, you make sure the buyer can't use a title defect as a way to terminate the transaction.

The balance of the clause tells us the buyer's and seller's rights if the searches for title, work orders, zoning, or insurability show defects the seller can't correct before the closing. The buyer has two choices: accept the defect and complete the transaction, or refuse to accept the defect and terminate the transaction.

Let's examine a situation where a buyer used an undisclosed title defect to refuse to complete a transaction. In the case of *Ridgely v. Nielsen*, the buyer purchased an expensive property in central Toronto in 2007. On title to the eighty-foot-wide property was a twenty-foot-wide storm and drainage easement, which could interfere with the buyer's intended use of the backyard. This easement was not disclosed to the buyer. The buyer's lawyer discovered the easement, which covered twenty-five percent of the area of the property, and the buyer refused to accept it. The seller couldn't remove the easement. The judge agreed that the easement was not a minor easement, and stated that the buyer did not have to accept it. The buyer terminated the transaction without penalty.

In another case, an easement bisected an owner's backyard down the middle and covered ten percent of the total area of the property. The court determined that this was a major easement, because it prevented the buyer from using the backyard for his intended purposes. The buyer was permitted to terminate the transaction.

The message is clear: disclose legal title defects, and avoid any misunderstandings with your buyers.

If you know that there is a problem with your basement apartment — a zoning issue or an incorrect retrofit according to the local fire code or city bylaws — tell the buyer before the agreement is signed.

Clause 10 indicates that buyers can terminate a transaction if they find out the main building on the property is not insurable, for example if the property was used as a grow house and was not properly repaired. But what happens if the buyers find out the costs to insure the home is much greater than they anticipated? This could happen if, for example, there is asbestos insulation, knob-and-tube wiring, or a wood-burning stove in the main building. Buyers who made insurance claims on a previous home may have to pay a high premium to insure the house they want to buy. Let's say a typical insurance premium for a home in a given area is $1,500, but as a result of a wood stove in the new house or a claim in the old house, the buyer cannot obtain insurance coverage for less than $4,000. Could the buyer terminate the transaction?

The answer appears to be no, even if the buyer has to pay substantially more to obtain insurance coverage. It may be wise for buyers to insert a separate condition in their agreement of purchase and sale, saying that if they can't obtain insurance coverage at an acceptable cost, they may terminate the transaction. (There is an example of this condition in Appendix 1.4.)

In most other provinces, a more general statement says a buyer accepts any easement or restrictive covenant that may affect a property provided that it does not materially interfere with the buyer's enjoyment of the property. It's still very important that sellers disclose any title deficiency they may know about. You can fulfill this obligation by providing a copy of any deed or survey that describes easements or encroachments. Or check your lawyer's report, from when you purchased the property; it should include any matters affecting title that you agreed to accept when you bought the property. Buyers, always ask about easements and restrictive

covenants on title, so nothing will interfere with any changes
you may wish to make on a property after closing.

Weisleder's Wisdom on title

1. Sellers, check your deed, survey, and lawyer's reporting
   letter for any easements, covenants, encroachments, or
   other title defects, and disclose everything to your buyers.
2. Sellers, before entering into an agreement, disclose to
   buyers the existence of any zoning issue, such as illegal
   basement apartments or retrofits that do not comply with
   municipal bylaws.
3. Buyers, be sure to ask about any easements, covenants,
   or other title defects that could affect your intended use
   and enjoyment of the property.
4. Buyers, make your transaction conditional on being
   satisfied that you can obtain insurance coverage on the
   property at a reasonable premium.

11. CLOSING ARRANGEMENTS: Where each of the Seller and
Buyer retain a lawyer to complete the Agreement of Purchase and
Sale of the Property, and where the transaction will be completed
by electronic registration pursuant to Part III of the Land
Registration Reform Act, R.S.O. 1990, Chapter L4 and the
Electronic Registration Act, S.O. 1991, Chapter 44, and any
amendments thereto, the Seller and Buyer acknowledge and agree
that the exchange of closing funds, non-registrable documents and
other items (the "Requisite Deliveries") and the release thereof to
the Seller and Buyer will (a) not occur at the same time as the registration of the transfer/deed (and any other documents intended
to be registered in connection with the completion of this transaction) and (b) be subject to conditions whereby the lawyer(s)
receiving any of the Requisite Deliveries will be required to hold
same in trust and not release same except in accordance with the

terms of a document registration agreement between the said lawyers. The Seller and Buyer irrevocably instruct the said lawyers to be bound by the document registration agreement which is recommended from time to time by the Law Society of Upper Canada. Unless otherwise agreed to by the lawyers, such exchange of the Requisite Deliveries will occur in the applicable Land Titles Office or such other location agreeable to both lawyers.

There has been an increase in fraudulent activity relating to real estate in the past several years. Phony buyers forge certified cheques or bank drafts to buy a property, wait until the funds are paid out by lawyers or brokerage companies, then disappear. In this clause, sellers and buyers give their respective lawyers authority to complete the registration and closing of a real estate transaction via electronic means. Registration of the deed on the title register can be done electronically, and so can the wiring of funds directly from the buyer lawyer's bank account to the seller lawyer's bank account. Law firms and brokerage companies may require that all funds from a buyer are deposited by wire directly from the buyer bank to the brokerage or law firm trust account. This system will provide a clear electronic verification that funds are, in fact, on deposit and available for transfer on closing, and will protect against fraud.

12. DOCUMENTS AND DISCHARGE: Buyer shall not call for the production of any title deed, abstract, survey or other evidence of title to the property except such as are in the possession or control of Seller. If requested by Buyer, Seller will deliver any sketch or survey of the property within Seller's control to Buyer as soon as possible and prior to the Requisition Date. If a discharge of any Charge/Mortgage held by a corporation incorporated pursuant to the Trust And Loan Companies Act (Canada), Chartered Bank, Trust Company, Credit Union, Caisse Populaire or Insurance Company and which is not to be assumed by Buyer on completion, is not available in registrable form on completion, Buyer agrees to accept Seller's lawyer's personal undertaking to obtain, out of the closing funds, a discharge in registrable form and to register same, or cause same to be registered, on title within a reasonable period of time after completion, provided that on or before completion Seller shall provide to Buyer a mortgage statement prepared by the mortgagee setting out the balance required to obtain the discharge, and, where a real-time electronic cleared funds transfer system is not being used, a direction executed by Seller directing payment to the mortgagee of the amount required to obtain the discharge out of the balance due on completion.

This paragraph contains two separate topics. The first sentence discusses the seller's obligation regarding the survey and any other title document in his or her possession. The rest of the paragraph describes how a bank mortgage or a mortgage from another lending institution is discharged from title.

The survey clause

The first sentence says sellers must provide buyers with any survey or other title document, for example a sketch, that they have in their possession. The clause does not say the documents must be up to date, and for this reason, it is recommended that buyers add a separate clause to the agreement requesting an up-to-date survey of the property, showing the current locations of all fence lines, structures, and any improvements on the property. Let's say it turns out that the main building on the property is too close to the lot line. In some cities, zoning bylaws state that a home cannot be constructed less than six feet from the side lot line; in some cities, the distance is four feet. If your side wall is less than four feet from the lot line, you must apply for a variance to the local committee of adjustments, so your house can stay where it is. Title insurance will pay the costs of the application. But there is no guarantee that you'll get the variance; your neighbours can object to your request. It makes much more sense to look at an up-to-date survey *before* you buy than to repair problems *after* you buy. Look for metal stakes at the corners of the lot; they'll often have orange or red paint at the top. These stakes were likely planted by a registered land surveyor; it's a criminal offence to remove a property boundary stake. The presence of stakes is a clue that the property has been surveyed recently.

If you lose land through possession — that is, if you buy a home thinking that the distance between the fence lines was fifty feet and it turns out to be only forty-eight feet, title insurance may not pay for the loss that you may perceive to the value of your land. (See Chapter 2 for more information about the land registry system.) There is no substitute for a complete and up-to-date survey of the property you want to buy. If the seller doesn't have one, I strongly recommend that you obtain one on your own, and make your offer to purchase conditional on being satisfied with the contents of the new survey. The survey will reveal the location of any easement on the property; it will tell you if the fences are on the property lines. A survey will provide peace of mind. (There are examples of survey clauses buyers can use in Appendix 1.9.)

Weisleder's Wisdom on the survey clause

1. This clause obligates sellers to give buyers any survey they have in their possession.
2. When you are buying a property, include a separate clause stating that the seller will provide an up to date survey of the property.
3. If the seller has no survey and refuses to provide one, make your transaction conditional on obtaining and being satisfied with an up-to-date survey of the property.

4. Title insurance is a protection against certain problems associated with not having a survey, but is not a substitute for having an up to-date-survey of your property.

The mortgage discharge

Most sellers will have a mortgage on their property, and most of these mortgages will need to be discharged when the sale closes. Yet the practical reality is that it usually takes three to four weeks for a bank to process the discharge document that will be registered on title. When the buyer acquires title to the property from the seller, the seller's mortgage will still stay on title for a few weeks after closing, so the bank can process the discharge. This section of the agreement provides a mechanism so the lawyers can deal with the slowness of the banks. The seller's lawyer provides a discharge statement from the bank showing exactly how much money is required to discharge the mortgage on closing. The buyer writes a cheque for this amount as part of the closing proceeds. The seller's lawyer delivers the cheque directly to the bank that holds the mortgage. The seller's lawyer then agrees to register the discharge as soon as he or she receives it from the bank, and to notify the buyer's lawyer of the details. However, this process applies only for mortgages from banks, trust companies, credit unions, and insurance companies. If you have a private mortgage on your property, for example if a relative lent you money, you have to discharge your debt on or before closing, and get a written discharge. You will have to make arrangements with your relative to come in and sign the discharge paper at the lawyer's office before your deal closes, so that upon closing, your lawyer registers the discharge.

13. INSPECTION: Buyer acknowledges having had the opportunity to inspect the property and understands that upon acceptance of this Offer there shall be a binding agreement of purchase and sale between Buyer and Seller. **The Buyer acknowledges having the opportunity to include a requirement for a property inspection report in this Agreement and agrees that except as may be specifically provided for in this Agreement, the Buyer will not be obtaining a property inspection or property inspection report regarding the property.**

The first thing you notice about this paragraph is the bold print. Then you may notice that the first sentence appears to be unnecessary. Isn't it obvious that when the offer is accepted there will be a binding agreement between the seller and the buyer? But in fact, the first sentence says much more: it states that the buyer has had the opportunity to inspect the property. *Then* it states that the buyer's acceptance of the offer means there's no going back on the deal. In between the inspection and the acceptance, there are all those obvious defects in the property the buyer should have noticed and now has accepted. A "defect" would include a cracked window you can easily see. If you don't say in the agreement that the seller will repair the crack in the window, the legal doctrine of *caveat emptor* — buyer beware — applies. Unless you specify them and state that the seller will repair them, you must accept every patent defect that was in the property the day you signed the agreement. If, on the other hand, the window broke after you signed the agreement and before closing, the seller is responsible for making the repair. Insist on a pre-closing visit, to make sure the property is exactly as it was on the date you signed the agreement of purchase and sale.

"Latent," or hidden, defects are not easily observable during a routine inspection. These can include leaks from the roof or basement, cracks in the foundation, or the presence of asbestos or other potentially dangerous insulation. The law regarding latent defects is not clear-cut and has led to much legal debate over the years. The case law indicates that the seller must disclose major latent defects he knows about. Latent defects make a property:

   a. uninhabitable or dangerous;
   b. unfit for the buyer's purpose; or
   c. in violation of a city work order.

Sellers, be up front about all defects you're aware of. You don't want legal proceedings after closing. (There is more information about patent and latent defects as well as property condition statements in Chapter 2.)

In other provinces, the agreement says whether a seller will or will not provide a copy of a property condition statement. Buyers, make your agreements conditional on being satisfied with the results of a home inspection, no matter what you receive from a seller.

13. INSURANCE: All buildings on the property and all other things being purchased shall be and remain until completion at the risk of Seller. Pending completion, Seller shall hold all insurance policies, if any, and the proceeds thereof in trust for the parties as their interests may appear and in the event of substantial damage, Buyer may either terminate this Agreement and have all monies paid returned without interest or deduction or else take the proceeds of any insurance and complete the purchase. No insurance shall be transferred on completion. If Seller is taking back a Charge/Mortgage, or Buyer is assuming a Charge/Mortgage, Buyer shall supply Seller with reasonable evidence of adequate insurance to protect Seller's or other mortgagee's interest on completion.

This clause says it's the responsibility of the seller to maintain the property until closing. Say you're buying: there is a fire on the property and the house burns down or is substantially damaged. You have two choices: take the insurance proceeds and complete the transaction, or refuse to close. You have to decide by the closing date, even though you probably won't know by the closing date, if the insurance company will pay the claim, or how much they'll pay. If the insurer suspects the fire was deliberately set, or that the homeowner violated a provision of the policy, they may refuse coverage entirely. Most buyers who are put into this position refuse to complete the transaction. Only buyers who were planning to demolish the house anyway will typically close the deal.

There have been legal disputes about the meaning of "substantial damage." Things are clear if the house burns down completely. But what happens if only part of the house is damaged? What if the damage is $10,000? What if it's $50,000? Are there any guidelines for a buyer who has to decide whether to refuse the deal? In reality, no. Every instance is different, and must be considered carefully.

What happens if you find out about the fire after closing? Can you make a claim against your own insurance policy? It's probably too early for you to make a claim. And it may be too late for the sellers to make a claim on their policy, because technically they no longer own the home. A buyer may have no alternative but to make a claim against the sellers, because they didn't fulfill their obligation to maintain the property until closing.

If you're buying, always include a pre-closing site visit to the property to make sure there has been no damage since you signed the agreement. And ask your buyer salesperson to confirm that the seller has removed any junk that has accumulated in or on the property. It's much easier to conduct the final site inspection if you don't have to move any junk to get a good look at the place. And make sure the seller hasn't replaced any appliances with cheaper models.

No insurance is transferred on closing. Sellers cancel their policies on the day of closing; buyers obtain insurance that will become effective on the day of closing. These days it can be difficult to insure a property with a buried oil tank, a wood-burning stove, or inadequate knob-and-tube wiring. Consider making your purchase conditional on being able to find adequate insurance for a reasonable cost.

Weisleder's Wisdom on insurance

1. It is the seller's responsibility to maintain insurance on the property until closing.
2. If there is substantial damage to the property between the time of signing the offer and closing, the buyer must choose to take the insurance proceeds and complete the transaction, or refuse to close.
3. Buyers, make sure you have included at least one or two site visits in the agreement, so you can check for damage to the property between signing the agreement and closing the sale.
4. Buyers, make your transactions conditional on finding insurance coverage at a reasonable cost.

15. PLANNING ACT: This Agreement shall be effective to create an interest in the property only if Seller complies with the subdivision control provisions of the Planning Act by completion and Seller covenants to proceed diligently at his expense to obtain any necessary consent by completion.

This provision says that if the land for sale has to be subdivided in any way — for example, if you're buying an empty half-acre at the back of the seller's property — the seller needs permission from the local planning authorities before selling the land. Usually the seller makes an application before the local committee of adjustments. An application typically takes four to six weeks; the committee sends a notice of the application to all neighbours in the immediate area of the land the seller wants to divide. The neighbours and the local rate-payer group have the opportunity to support or oppose the application. Even after the application is approved by the committee, there are thirty days in which anyone can appeal the decision. If there are no appeals, you can buy the land you want, provided the seller satisfies any conditions imposed by the committee. If there is an appeal, you may have to wait six months to a year for the case to be decided by the provincial municipal board.

All these potential time periods must be accounted for in the agreement of purchase and sale, and both buyer and seller must understand the risks when applying for a severance.

It's better if the owner gets the severance before putting the property up for sale.

Weisleder's Wisdom on the Planning Act

1. To subdivide your property, you need the permission of the municipality in which your land is located, in accordance with the provisions of the provincial *Planning Act*.
2. The land-severance process usually takes four to six weeks, but neighbours and interested rate-payer groups can oppose the application.
3. After the severance is granted, the decision can be appealed, which may delay the process for months.
4. If your sale transaction is conditional on a successful land severance, include provisions to deal with the possibility of the severance being delayed.
5. It's better to sever the property before you put it up for sale.

16. DOCUMENT PREPARATION: The Transfer/Deed shall, save for the Land Transfer Tax Affidavit, be prepared in registrable form at the expense of Seller, and any Charge/Mortgage to be given back by the Buyer to Seller at the expense of the Buyer. If requested by Buyer, Seller covenants that the Transfer/Deed to be delivered on completion shall contain the statements contemplated by Section 50(22) of the Planning Act, R.S.O.1990.

It is the seller's responsibility to prepare the deed that will be delivered to the buyer on closing. It is the buyer's responsibility to prepare the land transfer tax affidavit and any mortgage documentation needed for the transaction. In Ontario, because most lawyers now use the electronic method of registration, the buyer's and seller's lawyers have the authority to complete this information on behalf of their clients.

This clause also requires that the buyer and the seller complete statements in the deed saying that, to the best of their knowledge and belief, the conveyance of the property does not violate the provisions of the *Planning Act*. The lawyer for the seller and the lawyer for the buyer also complete these statements. If there was any violation of the *Planning Act* in any prior conveyance affecting the property, these statements serve to correct the error from now on.

17. RESIDENCY: Buyer shall be credited toward the Purchase Price with the amount, if any, necessary for Buyer to pay to the Minister of National Revenue to satisfy Buyer's liability in respect of tax payable by Seller under the non-residency provisions of the Income Tax Act by reason of this sale. Buyer shall not claim such credit if Seller delivers on completion the prescribed certificate or a statutory declaration that Seller is not then a non-resident of Canada.

What if a person selling a house is not a resident of Canada? In this clause, sellers provide proof that they are residents of Canada, typically by a sworn statement. Sellers who are not residents of Canada must pay any income taxes owing on the property before closing, and they must obtain a certificate from the Canada Revenue Agency (CRA) saying that all taxes have been paid. If the seller does not provide the certificate, the buyer is entitled to hold back twenty-five percent of the entire purchase price and send it in to the CRA.

If you are not a resident of Canada but you're selling real estate here, ask your accountant what your tax liabilities will be, if any, and how much time it will take to complete your filings with the CRA.

If you are a seller and a resident of Canada, you'll be asked to provide a sworn statement to the buyer on closing stating that you are not a non-resident of Canada.

18. ADJUSTMENTS: Any rents, mortgage interest, realty taxes including local improvement rates and unmetered public or private utility charges and unmetered cost of fuel, as applicable, shall be apportioned and allowed to the day of completion, the day of completion itself to be apportioned to Buyer.

The purpose of this clause is to balance accounts between the buyer and the seller on closing. The general principle is that the seller is responsible for all costs and is entitled to all rents on the property up to the day *before* closing, and the buyer is responsible for all costs and is entitled to any rents on the property from the day of closing and in the future.

The most common adjustment is taxes. Let's say the property taxes for the year are $365 and the transaction closes on November 1. The seller has already paid all the taxes for the year but is responsible only up to October 31, the day before closing. The buyer is responsible from November 1 to December 31, sixty-one days. The buyer pays the seller $61 on closing, so the tax account is balanced. This balancing is called an "adjustment."

If the property has tenants, adjustments will be made for the rent. If closing day is the fifteenth of the month, the buyer is entitled to all rent from the fifteenth day to the end of the month. The adjustment is made on closing.

Local improvements are typically more difficult. "Local improvements" are services installed on the street at the request and expense of the homeowners, for example new street lights or sidewalks. Often homeowners agree to pay for these improvements over ten or twenty years. (This is in addition to the property tax bill.) If there are any local-improvement charges, they must be disclosed to the buyer in the agreement. We don't want unwelcome surprises later.

If the home is heated with oil, the seller usually fills the tank, and the buyer pays for the full tank on closing. For other utilities, the utility company typically sends service people to the property on the closing date to read the meters; the seller gets the final bills, and the buyer begins a new account after closing.

There is no adjustment for insurance premiums because insurance cannot be transferred. The buyer is arranging his or her own insurance, which starts on the date of closing.

Because some items can only be estimated on the closing date, buyers and sellers usually agree to co-operate after closing if there are any errors in the adjustments.

I encourage buyers to discuss all adjustments with their salesperson before they sign any agreement of purchase and sale, so they have enough money to complete the transaction on the closing date.

19. PROPERTY ASSESSMENT: The Buyer and Seller hereby acknowledge that the Province of Ontario has implemented current value assessment and properties may be re-assessed on an annual basis. The Buyer and Seller agree that no claim will be made against the Buyer or Seller, or any Brokerage or Salesperson, for any changes in property tax as a result of a re-assessment of the property.

Clause 19 reflects the current reality that provincial tax assessments of properties take a long time. The impacts of assessments may not affect your property tax bill for several years. Yet the impact can mean a dramatic increase or decrease in your property taxes. The increase or decrease is not retro-active, it is only on a going-forward basis. As a result, in this clause, the buyer and seller confirm that they will not make any claim against each other should taxes increase or decrease in the future. The situation may be different if the seller has actual knowledge that his or her taxes are going to rise dra-matically and hides this information from the buyer. When you're buying a house, ask the seller about any assessment notices that may have been sent by the local municipality.

20. TIME LIMITS: Time shall in all respects be of the essence hereof provided that the time for doing or completing of any matter provided for herein may be extended or abridged by an agreement in writing signed by Seller and Buyer or by their respective lawyers who may be specifically authorized in that regard.

In other words, every deadline in the agreement of pur-chase and sale is very important and must be adhered to. A deadline can only be changed if both buyer and seller agree in writing, or if their lawyers agree in writing.

The decision of *1473587 Ontario Inc. v. Jackson* illustrated the importance of this clause. The buyer was late paying a deposit; the judge allowed the seller to terminate the agree-ment. In the reasoning, the judge said that even if the deposit was paid ten minutes late, it was too late. Pay attention to every date in your agreement, whether it's the date conditions expire or the time deposits must be paid. If you miss a deadline, you could jeopardize your purchase or sale.

Sometimes judges look at the behaviour of a buyer or seller to determine the reason for a missed deadline. In the case of *Walker v. Jones*, decided in 2008 in Ontario, the buyer was thirty minutes late delivering the closing monies to the seller's lawyer. The seller tried to cancel the transaction. The judge reviewed the facts of the case and found out why the buyer was late in delivering the funds: the seller made it difficult for the buyer's mortgage appraiser to view the property so the mortgage could be approved. Then the seller's lawyer was late giving the buyer's lawyer closing instructions for paying the funds. The judge found that the buyer was ready to complete the transaction on closing, and ordered the seller to sell the property to the buyer on the terms indicated in the agreement.

This case tells us that when you're buying, it's a good idea to understand how your bank approves a mortgage loan. Lenders get credit approval of the buyer, but they also make sure the property is worth what you've offered to pay for it. Ask your bank to complete the appraisal as soon as possible, so you'll have your loan in time for the closing.

This case also illustrates a lesson for sellers: don't rush to litigation because a buyer is a few minutes late paying a deposit or any closing funds. You may not win in court. Buyers, be diligent about honouring your time limits.

21. TENDER: Any tender of documents or money hereunder may be made upon Seller or Buyer or their respective lawyers on the day set for completion. Money may be tendered by bank draft or cheque certified by a Chartered Bank, Trust Company, Province of Ontario Savings Office, Credit Union or Caisse Populaire.

Buyers and sellers must be able to demonstrate that they're ready, willing, and able to complete the transaction on the date set for closing. Buyer, this means you must have the money available on closing. Seller, you must have the deed signed and ready for delivery. You must be able to prove you have satisfied all the buyer's objections about title, zoning, work orders, and insurability of the property. And you must have the keys ready to hand over.

All this proof-of-readiness becomes necessary if one side cannot close a transaction, for example if the buyers can't come up with the closing funds. If the sellers want to commence legal proceedings against the buyers, the sellers have to demonstrate that on the day of closing, they were ready to close. How do you demonstrate this? The lawyer for the seller attends upon (that means the lawyer goes to the office of) the lawyer for the buyer with all the required documents, including the signed deed, to prove the sellers were ready to close the transaction.

22. FAMILY LAW ACT: Seller warrants that spousal consent is not necessary to this transaction under the provisions of the Family Law Act, R.S.O.1990 unless Seller's spouse has executed the consent hereinafter provided.

The only time you need someone other than the registered owner to sign a deed is when the owner is married and the property is used as a family residence. If that's your situation, your spouse must consent to the transaction by signing the agreement of purchase and sale and by signing the deed.

Common-law spouses are not included in this definition; they don't need to sign unless their name is on title. (There is complete information about family law in Chapter 7.)

23. UFFI: Seller represents and warrants to Buyer that during the time Seller has owned the property, Seller has not caused any building on the property to be insulated with insulation containing ureaformaldehyde, and that to the best of Seller's knowledge no building on the property contains or has ever contained insulation that contains ureaformaldehyde. This warranty shall survive and not merge on the completion of this transaction, and if the building is part of a multiple unit building, this warranty shall only apply to that part of the building which is the subject of this transaction.

Ureaformaldehyde — UFFI — is a foam insulation that was used in new homes across Canada in the 1970s. In the 1990s, there were fears that the insulation could cause a health danger to people living in UFFI-insulated homes. There was an extensive campaign to remove the insulation from these homes. Even after the insulation was removed, the home carried a stigma that reduced its market value. More recent studies have indicated that the danger to humans may have been overstated. Home inspectors still search for ureaformaldehyde.

In the clause, the sellers indicate that when they owned the house, they did not insulate it with ureaformaldehyde. They also indicate that, to the best of their knowledge and belief, the house was not insulated with ureaformaldehyde when they bought it.

Sellers, if you know ureaformaldehyde is present in the property, you must inform the buyer. (There are examples of UFFI disclosure clauses in Appendix 1.11)

24. CONSUMER REPORTS: The Buyer is hereby notified that a consumer report containing credit and/or personal information may be referred to in connection with this transaction.

The first thing people notice about this section is that it is in bold type. The clause tells buyers that a seller can get their credit checked. In Ontario, sellers have this right through the *Consumer Reporting Act*, which governs how credit bureaus are permitted to use information they collect on consumers in the province of Ontario.

The act says that consumers must consent to having their credit checked. The consent must be requested in writing, in bold type, to make sure the consumers pay attention. In other words, before a seller can conduct a credit check, the buyer has to consent.

Sellers often get a credit check if the agreement says the sellers have agreed to take back a mortgage as part of the purchase price. Buyers with poor credit histories may not make the mortgage payments. (To collect from a buyer who can't make the mortgage payments, the seller has to sell the property under the power of sale provisions contained in the mortgage.)

If the seller sees the credit report and then refuses to complete the transaction with the buyer, the seller must tell the buyer. If the buyer asks where the seller got the credit information, the seller must tell.

Similar legislation applies in the other provinces and in the territories. Sellers, ask for legal advice whenever your transaction involves a credit check on a buyer.

25. AGREEMENT IN WRITING: If there is conflict or discrepancy between any provision added to this Agreement (including any Schedule attached hereto) and any provision in the standard pre-set portion hereof, the added provision shall supersede the standard pre-set provision to the extent of such conflict or discrepancy. This Agreement including any Schedule attached hereto, shall constitute the entire Agreement between Buyer and Seller. There is no representation, warranty, collateral agreement or condition, which affects this Agreement other than as expressed herein. For the purposes of this Agreement, Seller means vendor and Buyer means purchaser. This Agreement shall be read with all changes of gender or number required by the context.

This clause has five parts.

In the first part, buyer and seller acknowledge that if there is anything written in any schedule that conflicts with the printed form, the written-in part takes precedence. For example, if the buyer adds a clause saying the seller must provide an up-to-date survey, and the printed form says a seller must only provide any survey in his or her possession, the seller must provide an up-to-date survey.

The second clause says that what is written in this agreement is the entire agreement; no oral agreements apply anymore.

The third provision states that no "representation, warranty, collateral agreement or condition" can affect the agreement other than what is stated expressly in the agreement. This clause discourages people from saying later that they were promised things they didn't get. If it's not written down, you don't get it.

If there is ambiguity in the agreement, a court may hear evidence from the buyer and seller as they try to explain what they think the agreement means. Be careful to review your agreement with your real estate salesperson to make sure everything you want is in the agreement.

What if a listing advertises special features — say, granite countertops or hardwood under the carpet — but the features are not mentioned in the agreement? If the countertops are important to you, make sure they're mentioned in the agreement.

The fourth part of the clause states that "Seller" means "vendor" and "Buyer" means "purchaser." Many lawyers still use the terms "vendor" and "purchaser" to describe sellers and buyers, and this is also true across Canada. To avoid any ambiguity, we state that the terms mean the same thing.

The fifth statement is designed to fix up any gender or number errors in the document.

Weisleder's Wisdom on the entire agreement clause

1. If something is important to you as a buyer, make sure it gets included in the agreement. This includes any promises made by the seller.
2. Review the agreement to make sure your salesperson has accurately addressed all your concerns.

---

26. TIME AND DATE: Any reference to a time and date in this Agreement shall mean the time and date where the property is located.

This clause acknowledges that buyers and sellers may be in different time zones while they're negotiating. If the agreement says the seller has until 11:00 p.m. to accept the offer, there may be confusion if the seller happens to live in B.C. — 11:00 p.m. in B.C. is 2:00 a.m. the next morning in Ontario. This clause was inserted so that any time periods relate to the time period where the property is located, not where the seller or buyer happen to be.

27. SUCCESSORS AND ASSIGNS: The heirs, executors, administrators, successors and assigns of the undersigned are bound by the terms herein.

If anyone who signed the agreement dies, the agreement is still binding on his or her estate. If anyone assigns any rights under the agreement to anyone else, the person who receives the rights is also bound by the terms of the agreement. (For information about the consequences of assignments and property flips, see Chapter 5.)

SIGNED, SEALED   IN WITNESS
AND DELIVERED   whereof I have
in the presence of: hereunto set my hand and seal:

_____   _____   ✳ DATE _____

_____   _____   ✳ DATE _____

(Witness)   (Buyer)   (Seal)

Signature and Seal

I, the Undersigned Seller, agree to the above Offer. I hereby irrevocably instruct my lawyer to pay directly to the Listing Brokerage the unpaid balance of the commission together with applicable Goods and Services Tax (and any other taxes as may hereafter be applicable), from the proceeds of the sale prior to any payment to the undersigned on completion, as advised by the Listing Brokerage to my lawyer.

SIGNED, SEALED   IN WITNESS
AND DELIVERED   whereof I have
in the presence of: hereunto set my hand and seal:

_____   _____   ✳ DATE _____

_____   _____   ✳ DATE _____

(Witness)   (Buyer)   (Seal)

Signature and Seal

The agreement must be signed by both buyer and seller to be enforceable. Sometimes a buyer or seller is not present, and the signing is done and communicated through the fax machine. This is contemplated in clause 3 of the agreement, which gives buyers and sellers the right to deliver the accepted contract through a fax machine.

Signatures are witnessed as proof that someone saw a buyer and a seller actually sign the agreement, so no one can deny signing. Your witness needs to be in the room with you when you sign; if you're faxing your agreement, you can't ask the person on the receiving end of your fax to witness your signature. Try and find someone who is physically with you to act as the witness to your signature, if possible.

As indicated in the discussion of clause 2, irrevocability, when you sign the agreement under seal, you cannot change your mind until the time limit passes. Make sure you are serious and have received expert advice before you sign any agreement to buy or sell a property.

If the buyer's deposit isn't enough to pay all the commission and GST, the seller asks his or her lawyer to pay them once the deal is completed.

SPOUSAL CONSENT: The Undersigned Spouse of the Seller hereby consents to the disposition evidenced herein pursuant to the provisions of the Family Law Act, R.S.O.1990, and hereby agrees with the Buyer that he/she will execute all necessary or incidental documents to give full force and effect to the sale evidenced herein.

_____   _____   ✳ DATE _____

If the property is a matrimonial home (see Chapter 7) and is registered in the name of only one of the married spouses, the other spouse must sign the agreement here, to indicate his or her consent to the sale. The clause is included because both spouses have matrimonial rights to the property.

CONFIRMATION OF ACCEPTANCE: Notwithstanding anything contained herein to the contrary, I confirm this Agreement with all changes both typed and written was finally accepted by all parties at _____ a.m./p.m. this _____ day of _____, 20_____ _____

(Signature of Seller or Buyer)

The last person to accept the agreement indicates the date and time, so everyone will know exactly what time the deposit is due. The buyer has twenty-four hours after acceptance to deliver the deposit cheque to the listing broker, when it states in the agreement that the deposit is payable "Upon Acceptance."

INFORMATION ON BROKERAGE(S)

Listing Brokerage _____ Tel. No. (_____)_____

_____

Co-op/Buyer Brokerage _____ Tel. No. (_____)_____

_____

You name your brokerage company here so both buyer and seller confirm that they know about the agent relationship and where to send any notices or waivers.

ACKNOWLEDGEMENT

I acknowledge receipt of my signed copy of this accepted Agreement of Purchase and Sale and I authorize the Agent to forward a copy to my lawyer.

_____ DATE _____

(Seller)

_____ DATE _____

(Seller)

Address for Service: _____

_____ Tel. No. (_____)_____

Seller's Lawyer _____

Address _____

(_____)_____   (_____)_____

Tel. No.   FAX No.

I acknowledge receipt of my signed copy of this accepted
Agreement of Purchase and Sale and I authorize the Agent to forward a copy to my lawyer.

_____ DATE _____

(Buyer)

_____ DATE _____

(Buyer)

Address for Service: _____

_____ Tel. No. (_____)_____

Buyer's Lawyer _____

Address _____

(_____)_____   (_____)_____

Tel. No.   FAX No.

Both buyer and seller must receive a copy of the final
acceptance of the agreement. Both buyer and seller sign the
acknowledgement section to confirm that the final notice has
been communicated before the deadline. It's best to hand-
deliver the copies to the address for service shown in this
section. Later in this chapter I'll give you an example of a
buyer who failed to provide personal delivery of a waiver; the
seller was able to cancel the agreement.

COMMISSION TRUST AGREEMENT

To: Co-operating Brokerage shown on the foregoing Agreement of
Purchase and Sale:

In consideration for the Co-operating Brokerage procuring the
foregoing Agreement of Purchase and Sale, I hereby declare that
all moneys received or receivable by me in connection with the
Transaction as contemplated in the MLS® Rules and Regulations

of my Real Estate Board shall be receivable and held in trust. This agreement shall constitute a Commission Trust Agreement as defined in the MLS® Rules and shall be subject to and governed by the MLS® Rules pertaining to Commission Trust.

DATED as of the date and time of the acceptance of the foregoing Agreement of Purchase and Sale. Acknowledged by:

_____
(Authorized to bind the Listing Brokerage)

_____
(Authorized to bind the Co-operating Brokerage)

The commission trust agreement protects real estate salespeople when a listing brokerage goes bankrupt before a transaction closes and the deposit is still in the broker's trust account. The money goes to the salespeople, and not to other creditors of the business. Every listing brokerage carries deposit protection insurance, so buyers and sellers are insured if anything happens to the deposit monies before the closing.

Brokerage companies have gone bankrupt recently in Toronto; the Real Estate Council of Ontario stepped in and froze their trust accounts. The deposits of consumers are always insured and protected.

CHANGES TO THE STANDARD FORM

Sellers, remember to ask questions about any change made by a buyer to the standard terms in the agreement of purchase and sale. The agreement has undergone many revisions over the years, and many of the phrases included now are the result of litigation. The agreement is worded so buyers and sellers can't avoid closing or evade their legal liability. Sometimes buyers change or add to the printed form when they fear that the market may drop. The buyers want the right to withdraw from the agreement without penalty.

If you are a seller, ask why any change is being made to the standard resale agreement form.

CONDITIONS

Many buyers believe that if they make a real estate transaction conditional on anything, they can get out of the deal easily if they change their mind. This is a dangerous assumption. Interpreting conditions and demonstrating good faith in exercising conditions have been and continue to be the subjects of many legal proceedings.

The conditions most often included in an agreement on behalf of a buyer are:

a. being able to obtain satisfactory financing to complete the purchase; and
b. conducting and being satisfied with a physical inspection of the property by a qualified home inspector.

Examples of these two conditions are in Appendix 1.3.a and 1.6. Usually these conditions are valid only for a short time, anywhere from three to seven days. Having a property "off the market" for a week probably won't materially affect the value of the property. Conditions are beneficial because they allow a buyer to make inquiries about a property before deciding to proceed. The waiving of a condition indicates the buyer is committed to completing the transaction.

When a buyer is not satisfied with the results of a home inspection and wants to terminate a transaction, my advice to sellers is to let it go. If you fight it, you'll be dealing with an unwilling buyer. It is better to find a buyer who really wants your property.

Many sellers are understandably upset when a buyer cancels a transaction because of a home inspection. Some sellers want to see a copy of the inspection report; others want to see proof that the buyer is acting in good faith. These are the signs of approaching litigation.

The case of *Marshall v. Bernard Place Corporation* is an excellent example of how to draft a condition; the case also explains how the language of conditions may be interpreted in court. It unfortunately illustrates that no legal position is guaranteed, and that most legal cases result in victories mainly for lawyers, not their clients.

This particular case involved the purchase of a renovated midtown Toronto home. Asking price: $1,510,000. Deposit: substantial — $150,000. The agreement of purchase and sale contained a home-inspection condition:

> This Agreement is conditional upon the inspection of the Property by a home inspector of the Buyer's choice and at the Buyer's sole expense, and receipt of a report satisfactory to him, in his sole and absolute discretion. Unless the Buyer/Cooperating Broker gives notice in writing, delivered to the Seller/Listing Broker on or before Wednesday August 19, 1998, that this condition is fulfilled, this Agreement shall be null and void and the deposit shall be returned to the Buyer without interest or deduction. The Seller agrees to cooperate in providing access to the property for the purpose of this inspection at reasonable times upon reasonable notice given by the Buyer. This condition is included for the sole benefit of the Buyer and may be waived at his sole option by notice in writing to the Seller/Listing Broker within the time period stated herein.

The inspection was conducted, and the buyers were not satisfied with the report. They advised the seller on August 17,

1998, in a timely manner, that they would not remove their condition, and they asked for the return of their deposit. The property was off the market for about seven days, at most, while the inspection was being conducted.

The inspection report showed only minor deficiencies; they could have been repaired for about $1,000. The seller argued that the buyers were not acting in good faith in conducting the home inspection and were thus in breach of the agreement. The seller told his salesperson not to the return the deposit, and the matter proceeded to litigation.

Many lawyers were very interested in this case. Most home inspections recommend repairs that will cost between $500 and $1,000, all for minor deficiencies. Most lawyers would probably tell you the seller had a very good legal position. But this is not what the judge determined, and his judgment was confirmed by the Ontario Court of Appeal.

The court based its decision on the wording of the clause. The wording gave the buyers the "sole and absolute discretion" to make a decision based on the inspection report. If the buyers had not conducted a home inspection at all but had merely stated that they were not satisfied with the condition of the home, the court may have said they were acting in bad faith. The sellers seemed to have an excellent legal position. The case went on for four years of legal proceedings — pleadings, motions, examinations, production of documents, trial, and appeal — and cost more than $100,000 in legal fees. It probably also stressed out both buyers and seller for the entire four-year period. All of this, when the property was "off the market" for only seven days. Or was it a case of "it's the principle of the matter, not the money"?

If you're a seller, and the buyers are attempting to cancel a transaction because they're not satisfied with a condition, my advice is to let it go. Get another offer from a buyer who is willing to conclude the transaction. And don't get too fussed up about the wording of a condition. Some sellers try to remove the words "sole discretion" because of the Marshall decision. Others demand a copy of the inspection report. In my view, it's not necessary to spend time on this kind of negotiation. You need to find buyers who want to complete the transaction. A willing buyer will give you peace of mind from the time you sign the agreement right through to the closing of the transaction. Why waste time on buyers who are looking for a way out of the deal? If they can't find an excuse in the wording of the condition, they'll look for another excuse. You don't need the aggravation.

What if your property is "sold subject to an inspection condition" and then the condition is not waived? Will there be negative remarks from other salespeople? Will they think there must be "something wrong with the property" and thus make it more difficult to sell? Believe me, it's easier to overcome skepticism from potential buyers than it is to deal with a legal proceeding.

If you're a buyer, be very careful when you review conditions, and when you try to satisfy them. Don't assume your sellers will be accommodating. Act in good faith, and always use professional home inspectors. Do not call your uncle to take a quick look at the property. If you follow these two principles, sellers will have a very hard time trying to keep your deposit if the house doesn't pass an inspection.

Sellers, if you want to see a copy of any inspection report the buyers receive, say so in the home-inspection condition in the agreement. You're not automatically entitled to see reports prepared and paid for by the buyers.

QUESTIONING CONDITIONS

A well-worded condition will always be at the sole discretion of the buyer, and should include the right to waive it. A good condition should answer the questions: Who? What? How? Where? When?

> What is the subject of the condition?
> How will the condition be satisfied?
> Where is the condition taking place?
> When do you have to notify the seller that you have satisfied the condition?
> Who will give the notice?
> And the sixth question: Can the condition be waived?

In the Marshall case, all these questions were answered in the condition as follows:
What is the subject of the condition?

> This Agreement is conditional upon the inspection of the Property by a home inspector of the Buyer's choice and at the Buyer's sole expense.

How is the condition to be satisfied?

> . . . and receipt of a report satisfactory to him [the Buyer], in his sole and absolute discretion.

Where is the condition taking place? Can it be waived?

> The Seller agrees to cooperate in providing access to the property for the purpose of this inspection at reasonable times upon reasonable notice given by the Buyer. This condition is included for the sole benefit of the Buyer and may be waived at his sole option

by notice in writing to the Seller/Listing Broker within the time period stated herein.

As we learned from the Marshall decision, the language of the condition must make it clear that the condition is for the sole and absolute benefit of the buyer. And buyers must try to satisfy the condition. If the subject of a condition is a satisfactory home-inspection report, buyers should hire a qualified home inspector. If the buyers use a qualified inspector but the house gets a bad report, this clause should allow them to get out of the transaction without incident.

The waiver must be for "the sole benefit and option of the buyer" because the buyer may want to buy the house even though the condition is not satisfied. If the waiver is *not* at the sole option of the buyer, the seller may take the position that this is a "condition precedent," and thus cannot be waived by anyone. A condition precedent means that if the condition does not happen, the deal terminates, and no party can waive it. It is normally used when you make a transaction conditional on obtaining a severance, or dividing your property, with the approval of the local municipality. If you don't get the approval, the deal cannot happen, and thus no one can waive the condition. A seller might want to take this position because the property suddenly went up in value after the original agreement was signed.

An example occurred where a buyer made a transaction conditional on a water purification system being installed on the property before closing, or else the transaction would end. It did not include any waiver rights. The seller tried but could not install the system. The buyer then tried to accept the property anyway, even without the new system. The seller refused, and since the condition was found to be a condition precedent, no one could waive it, and the deal ended.

Make sure the waiver is always for the sole benefit of and may be exercised at the sole option of the buyer.

The other popular condition used in most transactions is about financing. How do buyers satisfy the upon-obtaining-financing condition? So long as buyers make a legitimate attempt to obtain financing (that is, they go to a bank to get a mortgage), they have satisfied the condition. If the bank won't give them a loan, they can terminate the agreement. The clause should still always contain the words "sole and absolute discretion." Can a seller offer to satisfy the condition by taking back a mortgage from the buyer on the same terms as set out in the agreement? The case law is plain: the seller must make the offer to take back a mortgage in the wording of the condition. Sellers can't wait till a bank says no, then offer financing.

Pay attention during the offer negotiation: does the wording of the condition change? In a recent case, the words "subject to satisfaction with the entire property" were replaced with the words "subject to the satisfaction with the structure on the property." This subtle change had a significant change in the meaning of the condition. The buyer was concerned with the condition of the septic system on the property; the revised condition clause permitted the buyer to cancel the transaction only if there was something wrong with the house — "the structure on the property." The buyer didn't close because there was something wrong with the septic system; the seller called a lawyer, and the buyer had to pay damages, since he could only cancel if there was something wrong with the structure of the house itself. Be very careful when you review the language of the condition, and scrutinize any changes made on any sign back.

Who gives the notice? When do you have to notify the other side?

Unless the Buyer/Cooperating Broker gives notice in writing, delivered to the Seller/Listing Broker on or before Wednesday August 19, 1998, that this condition is fulfilled, this Agreement shall be null and void and the deposit shall be returned to the Buyer without interest or deduction.

The "cooperating broker" is the agent who is representing the buyer. This clause could be written in another way: It could say that if the condition is *not* waived by August 19, the agreement shall be firm and binding on both parties. Either method is satisfactory. Some drafters like to use the phrase "within five business days of acceptance" as the time allowed to satisfy the condition. I think these words invite confusion. It may not be clear when, exactly, a contract is "accepted," especially when there are many sign backs. And what is a "business day"? Is Saturday a business day if your bank happens to be open? When you choose a definite date and provide its name and number, there can be no confusion.

WAIVING CONDITIONS

Once you're satisfied with the results of a condition, immediately sign a waiver, or "notice of fulfillment of condition," and have it delivered to the seller or the seller's salesperson. If you're waiting for approval for bank financing, get written approval. Do not rely on a phone call.

In a seller's market, many buyers decide not to include a home inspection condition, so they can provide a "clean offer" to the seller. A clean offer is an offer with no conditions in favour of the buyer. This usually happens when there are multiple offers on a home. But there are other ways to protect buyers. For example, you can arrange for a home inspection *before* you submit your offer. Most sellers will be agreeable to this arrangement, because your inspection doesn't put their house "off the market." You are only asking for trouble if you don't conduct a home inspection before you decide to purchase a property.

Waivers must be delivered on time and in the exact manner indicated in the condition. In the Ontario case of *Mckee v. Montemarano*, decided in 2008, the offer contained the following condition:

> This offer is conditional upon the Buyer performing due diligence on the Subject Property. Unless the Buyer gives notice in writing delivered to the Seller not later than 5:59 pm on the first day of February, 2006, that this condition is fulfilled, this Offer shall be null and void and the deposit shall be returned to the Buyer in full with interest and without deduction and the Seller and Buyer shall both be released from any further obligations under this Agreement.

The buyers satisfied the condition on the last day, and the waiver was apparently placed by the buyer in the front-door latch of the seller's home. The seller didn't find the document until February 2. The buyer made no effort to knock on the door. (The seller was home.) The judge held that the waiver should have been hand-delivered to the seller directly, and since the seller was home and no effort was made to find out if he was home, the seller was able to cancel the agreement and sign a new agreement with a second buyer. Carefully review every word contained in a condition, and make sure you understand the condition, before you sign. Then carry out your obligations in a timely manner.

1. When drafting a condition, make sure you can answer the questions: Who? What? How? Where? When?
2. To protect a buyer, make sure both the condition and the waiver are "both in and for the sole and absolute benefit of the buyer."
3. Sellers, don't get too hung up on a condition; if a buyer wants to cancel for any reason, let it go.
4. Make sure you understand all changes made to the wording of the conditions in any sign back.
5. Buyers, always try to satisfy any condition; act in good faith.
6. Always keep a record of the times and dates by which conditions must be met.
7. Make sure you have written confirmation from your bank before you waive any financing condition.
8. Follow the exact wording of the condition when you're completing and delivering waivers.

REPRESENTATIONS

A representation is a statement of fact. It is not an opinion. You can't get in trouble for saying your property is beautiful. That's your opinion. However, the minute you make a factual statement about your property that's not correct, it's called a misrepresentation. If a buyer chooses your house because of your incorrect statement, he or she may be able to cancel the agreement or sue for damages. The moral of the story is, if you're asked to make statements of fact in your agreement, be sure everything you say has been carefully checked and is factual and correct.

If you decide to sign a form called a sellers' property information statement (also known as a property condition statement, see Chapter 2), be careful and accurate when you complete the document. The form contains many factual statements about the property. If you make a false statement — for example, if you say there has never been water in the basement even though you've seen water down there — and then the basement floods after closing, the buyer can claim damages. And, if the buyer finds evidence that you knew about the flooding problem, you'll probably have to pay those damages. If you state in the agreement that there are granite countertops in the kitchen and it turns out the countertops are ceramic, you'll have to pay whatever it would cost the buyer to replace the ceramic with granite.

What kind of misrepresentation might let a buyer cancel the whole transaction? Let's say you tell your buyers the empty lot across the street is going to become a new elementary school, so they won't have to drive their children ten miles to the existing school. Your buyers sign the agreement based on your representation, and it turns out to be a misrepresentation. If the buyers can prove they bought the house because there would be a school across the street, they will likely be able to cancel the transaction. Especially if they have young children.

If you're not sure about something, it's best not to include it in any agreement. If the topic is important to the buyers, make the transaction conditional on their being satisfied with an inquiry. For example, the buyers may want to be sure the basement apartment is legal. You may not know. Make the transaction conditional on the buyers being satisfied that the basement apartment is legal. The buyers can hire a registered planner to find out if the apartment is legal; then everyone is protected.

In rural communities, there is a great deal of litigation about the condition of the well and septic system on the property. These two issues are so complex that you may want to hire two inspectors, one to check the condition of the well and one to examine the septic system, before you decide to buy the property. The inspectors can educate you about examining wells and septic systems; you can ask them about the cost to repair and replace these systems if something goes wrong.

For wells, there are two main issues. Most important, the water must be safe for human consumption. The second issue is pressure, which must be sufficient to satisfy your normal household use — showers in the morning, running the dishwasher — without the taps running dry. In one unfortunate community in California, there was so little water pressure almost every property was unsaleable. In Ontario, we all still remember the Walkerton tragedy, where in the year 2000, seven people died as a result of the town's water supply being contaminated with E. coli bacteria. This had a negative effect for years on property values in Walkerton, even after the water supply was deemed safe to drink.

Safety of the water is most important. Hire an inspector, and make sure you get a certificate from the local health department. Make your agreement conditional on obtaining this certificate. Ask if the sellers can warrant that during their occupancy of the property, the pump and related equipment in the well have performed adequately. But it's always best to get an expert opinion — hire a second inspector if you're not sure.

Title insurance will probably not cover you if there are problems with the well after closing. Make your purchase conditional on an inspection by a local well expert.

It's hard to predict whether a septic system will break down after closing; when you buy property with a septic system, you may have to accept the risks of your system breaking down. Sellers may not be able to say anything more than that, during their period of ownership, the septic system was adequately maintained, there were no malfunctions or breakdowns, and there are no work orders on file with the Ministry of Environment. Before you sign on the dotted line, look for a local expert on septic systems; make your purchase conditional on receiving a satisfactory report about the system. (You can find sample conditions related to wells and septic systems in Appendix 1.8.a and 1.8.b.)

Another concern for buyers and sellers is the presence of old underground or above-ground oil tanks. Old oil tanks can leak and contaminate the soil. Several provinces have passed legislation requiring that all oil tanks be removed or upgraded by set dates. In Ontario, for example, all oil tanks must be removed or upgraded by October 1, 2009. If you're selling, tell your buyers about any oil tank on the property; buyers, consider making your purchase conditional on being satisfied that all provincial legislation concerning oil tanks has been complied with.

WARRANTIES

A warranty when you buy a house is similar to the guarantee you get when you purchase an appliance. If something goes wrong with the appliance during the warranty period, you can ask the manufacturer to fix it. It's the same with a home purchase. If a seller makes a warranty that the appliances will be in good working order for three months after closing, and the stove breaks down after two months, you can ask the seller to fix it. In most agreements, the warranties given by the seller expire on closing. For example, if your seller warrants that the stove will be in good working order on closing, then it has to be working on the date of closing. If it breaks down one week after closing, it's your responsibility.

If you and your seller agree that a warranty will have legal effect *after* closing, you say it "survives" closing for a specific time period. (An example is found in Appendix 1.12, under Representations/Warranties — Survive Closing — Specific Time Period.) Buyers, you may want a "surviving" warranty when you buy a home with a swimming pool. If you're buying in January, you won't be able to inspect the pool before closing.

In Canada we can purchase after-sale warranty protection from private companies on items such as the electrical and plumbing systems, the major appliances, the furnace, and the air-conditioning unit. The plans are relatively inexpensive; they're a good practical alternative for buyers, because most sellers won't usually provide warranties that extend past closing.

Weisleder's Wisdom on representations and warranties

1. Be very careful when you make a statement of fact, also called a "representation."
2. If a seller makes a false statement, or "misrepresentation," the buyer may have the right to cancel the transaction or sue for damages.
3. If you are not sure about something, don't make any statement.
4. Buyers, if the matter is important to you and the seller can't supply the information, then make the transaction conditional on finding and being satisfied with the information.
5. Wells and septic systems are becoming increasingly complex issues. Buyers, educate yourselves about the problems that can occur with these systems; have them

professionally inspected before you commit to buying the property.

6. Sellers, be hesitant about making any warranties that go beyond the closing date.

7. Buyers, consider purchasing after-sale warranty protection for appliances, furnace, air-conditioning unit, and electrical and plumbing systems, if available.

NEED FOR AN UP-TO-DATE SURVEY

I have mentioned on many occasions in this book the need to have an up-to-date survey for a property, to make sure all boundaries are clearly defined and any buildings on the property are in fact located within the boundary lines and are in compliance with all municipal zoning setback requirements. The best survey carries the seal of a registered land surveyor. If you're a seller, the survey will make your property more marketable — it gives any buyer peace of mind about boundaries. Buyers who want to make improvements to the property, such as an in-ground pool or an addition to the back of the house, will be especially reassured.

If you're a buyer, it's best to have a current and professional survey before you make a final decision to purchase a property. Ask the seller to supply the survey; make your offer conditional on your satisfaction with the contents of this survey.

An old survey may be adequate if it accurately indicates the current location of the boundary lines and any structures on the property. Walk the property with your salesperson and compare survey to fences before you waive any condition about the survey. (You'll find examples of clauses about surveys in Appendix 1.9.)

Weisleder's Wisdom on
the agreement of purchase and sale

1. Check your deed to make sure the correct seller is signing the agreement.
2. Check your deed, survey, and lawyer reporting letter carefully to make sure the legal description, including any title defects, is included in the agreement.
3. Avoid confusion: be clear about all chattels and fixtures. Buyers, take photographs – with the seller's permission.
4. Note all dates, especially the date and time you need to pay the deposit and waive conditions.
5. Arrange your closing date so you can move out of your current home or apartment and into your new home on different days.
6. Sellers must vacate their home on the date of closing no later than 6:00 p.m.
7. Once the agreement is signed under seal, buyers and sellers cannot change their minds.
8. Make sure your agreement contains conditions for financing and home inspections, as well as a survey clause.
9. Buyers, consider representations and warranties, especially if you're buying a property with a well or septic system.
10. Buyers and sellers should question when any change is made to the printed agreement of purchase and sale form.
11. Understanding the printed form will make the negotiation process less stressful for both buyers and sellers.

Multiple Offers

Bidding wars and multiple offers can occur in three types of market: seller's market, buyer's market, and balanced market. I encourage buyers and sellers to be prepared for this experience. Bidding wars are unusual and extremely stressful, and thus require both buyers and sellers to be extra careful and take precautions.

One of the main problems with the multiple offer process is that there are very few rules as to how this bidding will be conducted. This is not a silent auction where all bidders can see what others are bidding. The seller cannot give out the names of the bidders and has only a limited obligation to tell all bidders the total number of offers that have been received. In addition, the seller can demand that all offers be faxed to the listing salesperson, so the buyers will have no knowledge as to the order the offers are presented to the seller.

Sellers do not have to sign back any of the offers if they are not satisfied. They can ask all buyers to just submit new offers. Sellers do not have to accept the highest offer. For example, a seller may prefer a lower-priced offer with no conditions attached over a higher-priced offer that contains, for example, a home inspection condition, which might give a buyer the opportunity to cancel the transaction if he or she is not satisfied with the home inspection.

To encourage offers with no conditions, sometimes sellers indicate when the property is listed for sale that they, the sellers, will not entertain any offers for a five-day period. The reason for this is to create interest in the property and encourage potential buyers to conduct their home inspection during the five-day period and then submit an offer that will have no conditions at the end of the five-day period.

The unfortunate result for many buyers is that they pay the money to conduct a home inspection in advance, often three to five hundred dollars, submit an offer with no conditions, and then find out that the seller has accepted an offer from one of the other bidders.

For all of these reasons, I believe that the entire multiple offer process in general is not fair to buyers, and buyers must be properly educated about this in advance.

Even when sellers indicate on a listing that they will not entertain any offers for a five-day period, it is still open to a potential buyer to submit an offer earlier to the listing salesperson. Most real estate laws across Canada require that every offer be presented to the seller, and if the seller wants to deal with it, he or she is free to do so. This practice of submitting an offer early has been called a "pre-emptive offer," as the buyer is presenting an offer in advance of the five-day period to try to obtain a tactical advantage over other interested buyers. If a seller wants to entertain this early offer, the listing salesperson will typically immediately call all other buyer salespeople who have expressed an interest in the property to let them know the rules have changed and the seller will now accept offers immediately from anyone.

Buyers, be very careful before you agree to become part of a bidding war. First, remember to conduct your Internet and other research on the general area and walk the neighbourhood. Speak to some of the neighbours before you submit an offer (suggestions for research are outlined in Chapter 2). Has the seller supplied a property condition statement or a home inspection report? If not, be wary: there may be physical defects in the home. A home inspection is a must. Make sure your buyer salesperson asks the listing salesperson if there are any latent defects in the home, such as basement or roof leaks, and whether there are any neighbourhood conditions you should know about. (See the discussion of psychological defects in Chapter 2.)

When there are many offers on the same property, buyers must be very careful to stick to what they can afford. Too many buyers get caught up in the auction-type process and make an offer they can barely afford. Set out a realistic budget limit before you consider entering into a bidding war, and remember that you need enough funds to comfortably carry the mortgage, property taxes, maintenance and repairs, family activities and trips, and all the rest of life's expenses. Do you want to sacrifice vacations and family outings for a property you can't realistically afford? Listen to your professional buyer salesperson, who understands the bidding process and can give you objective advice and remind you about your budgetary limits.

Sellers, remember that the more you disclose, the more offers you'll probably receive. As an example, if you hire a reputable home inspection company and make the home inspection report available to potential buyers in advance, you'll probably generate more bids from more buyers. This is because buyers are more likely to present a clean offer (one with no conditions) when they've seen an inspection report. The full disclosure will also distinguish your home from others on the market.

Believe it or not, some sellers lie about how many offers they've received to encourage higher bids for their property.

For sellers, one way to satisfy buyers that you are telling the truth about the number of bids received is to tell every buyer that after the bidding process ends, you will provide the names of every buyer salesperson involved in the bidding. Smart sellers realize that acting in good faith and with integrity will probably generate even more offers.

What to do if you're unsure that another offer is coming

What do you do if your buyer salesperson is presenting your offer at 7:00 p.m. and the seller tells you they're expecting another offer later that evening? Maybe the other buyer changes their mind and decides not to present an offer. How can you protect yourself in this situation?

One solution is to instruct your salesperson not to present your offer until the seller has in fact received the other offer.

Another practice is developing: buyers insert a special clause into the purchase agreement that says the offer is being made with the understanding that it is part of a multiple offer process and that if the situation changes after the buyer submits the offer and no other offer is received by the seller, the seller agrees to inform the buyer so that the buyer will then have the right to revise or withdraw the offer. If the buyer is successful with the offer, the seller will provide the name of the other brokerage office that presented the second offer in the process.

Here's a provision for buyers and their real estate salespeople or lawyers to consider when sellers says they are expecting another offer but it has not yet been received:

This offer is being submitted on the basis that it is part of multiple offers. If the seller receives no other offers by 10 p.m., the seller will notify the buyer and the buyer shall have 1 hour to revoke or revise their offer. If the seller accepts the buyer offer, the seller shall provide the name, address and phone number of the brokerage company that submitted the competing offer.

Sharp bids

A "sharp bid" is an offer to pay $5,000 more than any other bid submitted to the seller. A sharp bid contemplates advising a buyer about a competitor's offer, which is a violation of most provincial regulatory codes of conduct. I advise sellers not to consider such a bid, and I advise sharp bidders to amend their offers by removing the clause.

Weisleder's Wisdom on multiple offers

1. Buyers and sellers, be prepared for potential bidding wars, and for the stress these bidding wars often bring. Try to keep calm during what can be an intense process.
2. Buyers should always get a home inspection before they make an offer, especially if the seller supplies no property disclosure statement.
3. Buyers should consider adding a clause allowing them to withdraw or revise their offer if the seller receives no competing offers.
4. Buyers should refrain from using sharp bids, and sellers should not accept such bids.
5. Sellers should conduct a pre-offer inspection with a reputable home inspection company and make the results available to potential buyers, to increase the marketability of the property and encourage more buyers to compete.
6. Sellers should indicate in advance that at the end of the bidding process, they will disclose the names of every brokerage office that submitted an offer on the property, to demonstrate more integrity in the process and encourage more offers from interested buyers.

CHAPTER 5

The Internet and
Scams to Watch Out For

The Internet is an evolving miracle of information accessibility, and every day it is changing the way business operates. Businesses that accept and embrace what the Internet has to offer invariably succeed in making their businesses even more profitable; those that ignore the Internet usually pay the price by going out of business very quickly.

Buyers are doing more and more research on the Internet before they make a decision about buying a home. At the same time, there is too much information on the Internet. People who are able to sift through all the information and find what they need have a distinct advantage. There's so much information that some buyers don't know where to start. But without complete information, buyers won't receive the best value for their money.

It's a good idea to check the websites of real estate salespeople before you interview any of them. Do their websites make it easier for you to learn more about the area you're interested in?

THE INTERNET BROKER

Is the Internet a threat to our current real estate salesperson commission model? We are witnessing more and more websites, each offering a different kind of selling or buying experience for a fraction of what you'd pay a traditional REALTOR®. There are some questions that we need to answer.

Is this any different from the "for sale by owner" (FSBO) methodology that has been around for years? (For a full discussion of the FSBO, see Chapter 1.)

Real estate salespeople have long been the target of uneducated buyers and sellers who fail to see the value of the services they provide. Thus the FSBO, and consumers enthralled by the "promise" that they can sell their properties easily and save the average REALTOR® commission.

Almost everyone who has tried the FSBO experience has learned a hard lesson. Sellers can't attract as many potential buyers; they don't have complete, accurate information about what their property is worth, they are not prepared for disturbing phone calls, unqualified buyers, and stressful negotiations, and they are not aware of all the potential legal and other issues that can affect the closing of their property.

I have heard people compare selling a home to being a pilot. We could all be pilots if all there was to it was flipping a switch to "automatic pilot" and then letting the plane's computers do the rest. However, it takes years to learn how to take off and land a plane, and to know what to do during an emergency. It's the same in the real estate experience. You need someone with training and experience to assist and protect you when you buy or sell a house.

Today there are many websites that offer a variety of services so people can sell real estate — kind of an Internet FSBO model. The services can range from online advertising, time on a television cable channel, sign kits to display on the property, brochures and guides on how to sell your home, and referrals to related services such as home stagers, lawyers, appraisers, and mortgage brokers. The fees can range from $250 to $1,000, depending on which services you choose. Most of the same brochures and pamphlets are available from real estate board offices and REALTORS®.

These website services have enjoyed some success in certain markets, but the main item working against the success of these models is that they don't have access to the largest group of potential salespeople and buyers, those who are looking at and comparing the properties on the local MLS® board listings.

Another problem is that any buyer who approaches a for-sale-by-owner property automatically expects to save their "share" of the REALTOR® commission. If the buyer is represented by a salesperson, the FSBO seller will usually agree to pay the buyer salesperson commission anyway, especially if they've had little or no activity on their property even though other similar properties in the neighbourhood are generating interest. Yet the buyer salesperson is acting in the best interests of their buyer client only, and doesn't provide any advice to the FSBO seller.

As I say many times in this book, sellers should disclose all the problems with the house and land, especially latent physical defects, which often don't show. If you sell your house without someone to advise you about disclosure, you may be destined for unnecessary litigation with unsuspecting buyers. And lawsuits drag on for years. If you get good advice about disclosure, your deal should close quickly and cleanly, without any aggravation afterwards.

It's easy to see how these websites make money. They don't offer much in the way of added value, save for some signs, brochures, and online advertising that few people see anyway.

Several Internet REALTOR® models have arisen in the U.S. and have had affects on the real estate industry.

The original creators of Expedia.com, the travel booking website, were Richard Barton and Lloyd Fink. After selling Expedia, they decided to create Zillow.com, a website that touches the real estate community. Their goal was similar to that for Expedia — to offer more information to the average consumer looking to buy or sell a home by providing a valuation for almost every home in the United States. To date, they claim to have a valuation for more than a hundred million homes, and the database is constantly updated using information from local property assessment rolls, recent sales, and other governmental valuations. The Zillow website also provides information on properties available for sale all over the U.S., as well as information on comparably priced properties available in those areas.

Zillow claims that it's not trying to replace REALTORS®; it's providing information to educate consumers. The consumer still requires the services of a salesperson to negotiate the agreement of purchase and sale and to market and set up inspections and all the other efforts typically associated with buying or selling a home. Zillow says it will make its money on advertisements; on the site there are ads for REALTORS®, lawyers, mortgage brokers, and other people in the real estate industry. These advertisers see the possibility of many potential leads coming from the website.

Another Internet company, Redfin.com, is taking the web one step further. Redfin is an online REALTOR® serving west coast U.S. cities such as Seattle, San Diego, and Los Angeles. They have recently expanded to some cities in New York State as well. Redfin claims to provide online search capabilities equal to what you could find on your local MLS® service. If you locate a property that interests you, then you can fill out an offer online and contact a local Redfin salesperson, who will take care of the negotiations, in person if necessary. The company primarily works for buyers. The business model is based on Redfin obtaining the average two-to-three-percent buyer portion of the sales commission directly from the seller, then refunding usually two thirds of the commission to the buyer. The Redfin salesperson gets a salary based on how satisfied the buyer is with the services. Redfin claims its salespeople will work harder for their buyer clients because, if they don't, they won't get paid. The third of the commission that Redfin keeps is refundable to the buyer if the buyer is not completely satisfied with the service. In theory, this concept does appear to overcome many of the difficulties inherent in the old FSBO websites, in that the buyers have access to all the available listings on the local MLS® service and can still use a local REALTOR® to negotiate for them — plus get part of the commission refunded.

Redfin also claims that, based on its statistics, its buyers pay on average the same price as those who buy from traditional REALTORS® in the U.S cities on Redfin.com, so Redfin's buyers end up with more money in their pockets. It's much too early to determine whether this model will hold up over the long term, or if the company has made a profit yet. It will need extraordinary sales and advertising spots on its site to survive. It's also unclear just how many services are free, and when a consumer has to start paying extra. For example, the local Redfin salesperson may provide free services to show only one or two properties, but if buyers want more showings, do they have to pay extra?

Redfin salespersons rely mostly on online information, and may not have the most up-to-date understanding of local conditions that affect properties. Most real estate salespeople are expert in a particular area, and know, for example, where the best grocery store is, where to do your dry cleaning, where to get your nails done, which schools have waiting lists. They know every business that's thinking about relocating into the area. This is just part of the "information" package they bring to the table. Much of this information will never be available on the Internet when you need it. Yet so much of it will be vital to a family thinking about moving.

Successful REALTORS® are already using the Internet to effectively market their seller's properties. Some will immediately register a new domain name for every property they list and then show the domain name right on the for-sale sign on the lawn. This makes it easy for a potential buyer to remember the site name, for example "100frederictonstreet.com." The buyer can go to the site, then take a virtual tour of the property that may answer many of their questions before they walk into the house.

In my view, real estate buyers are for the most part practical, and they understand that, as is the case with most businesses, you get what you pay for. There is no substitute for the hands-on advice of a real estate professional who is familiar with the local conditions and has the expertise to negotiate on your behalf. The general public will make the final decision about the success of these alternative brokerage models.

Weisleder's Wisdom on the Internet broker

1. The Internet is a great resource for buyers who want to research an area they're interested in moving to.
2. Check REALTOR® websites; many of them will make this research easier for you.
3. Most Internet brokerage models have the same shortcomings as the For Sale By Owner (FSBO) systems, as they don't provide the same exposure to potential buyers as the traditional MLS® systems.
4. There is no substitute for a professional real estate salesperson who understands your local market and can negotiate solely on your behalf.

IDENTITY THEFT

Identity theft is a growing nightmare for Canadians, with more than ten thousand cases reported in 2007 and 2008. To steal your identity, a fraud artist needs a copy of one or all of these:

driver's license
credit card number
social insurance number
bank account PIN

They can use this information to steal from you directly, to apply for credit cards in your name, or to otherwise damage your reputation.

We live in an age when so much of our critical personal information can be stored in the black stripe on the back of a debit or credit card. A thief can put a credit card through an illegal "reader" that accesses your password, then steals your bank or credit card funds. Never let your credit card out of sight when you're using it. You won't know the thief has used your card PIN until you look at your next credit card statement. How many of us carefully review every item on the statement every month?

Thieves go through recycling boxes outside people's homes looking for discarded credit cards or bank statements; they steal mail from mailboxes. Before doing something as simple as taking out the blue box, consider buying a shredder to destroy any personal information that, if stolen, could compromise your finances.

Never give out your social insurance number unless you absolutely must. In a real estate transaction, if a buyer earns more than $50 in interest on a deposit, the listing brokerage is required to issue a T5 form for the buyer, so the buyer is required to provide a social insurance number to the brokerage. If I asked any of you reading this book the last time anyone asked you for your social insurance number or birth certificate, most of you will probably say it has been years. Well, consider this: if you lose your wallet and someone acquires your social insurance number, he or she can immediately apply for dozens of credit cards in your name. Do yourself a favour and keep these cards in a safe place in your home. Don't carry them around.

Another technique thieves use is called "phishing." In this scam, you receive an e-mail from a website that looks exactly like it's from one of the chartered banks. The e-mail explains that there has been a security breach and that you need to change your password or update your account information to make sure you are protected. Invariably, you're asked to provide your old and new passwords, "as a security measure." The thieves use the information you provide to take the money from your account.

You may also receive a phone call or e-mail solicitation claiming that you have either won a lottery or that your account security has been compromised, and you need to provide your password. Even replying to these e-mails could provide unauthorized access to the hard drive on your computer.

You can report this type of economic crime at www.recol.ca, a website developed by the RCMP and other international security firms. Do not hesitate to use this service; don't try to deal directly with the con artists.

Many people link all their home computers using a network, so every computer has access to the same information. But this network may not be as private as you think: it could be accessed by a neighbour or a thief with a laptop in a car parked outside your home. Be sure to have a firewall installed in your network to prevent access to anyone outside your home. The computer technician who set up your network should be able to help you.

It's a good idea to make copies of your credit card, driver's license, and health card numbers and keep them in a safe place, so if you ever do lose your wallet, you can quickly cancel all of your credit cards and alert the police and your provincial health provider. You may also want to go directly to www.equifax.ca and www.transunion.ca, Canada's main consumer credit agencies, to report the theft and to find out if anyone has tried to obtain credit cards in your name.

Weisleder's Wisdom on identity theft

1. Never share personal information, whether on the phone or through e-mail or the Internet, unless you have initiated the contact.
2. Ignore e-mails that seem to be from your financial institution asking for user names, passwords, or account numbers.
3. Use a firewall to protect your home computer network from hackers.
4. Try never to let your credit card out of sight when paying for any item.
5. Shred all documentation before you toss it in the trash.
6. Make copies of your credit card numbers, driver's license number, and health card number, in the event you lose your wallet. Do not carry your social insurance number with you.
7. Always have adequate password protection on your computers.
8. Have your mail delivered through a mail slot instead of a mailbox outside your home, if possible.
9. Don't reply to any phone or Internet solicitation asking for personal or bank account information.

10. Don't carry sensitive information like your social insurance number with you in your wallet.
11. When you shop at a store, provide only the minimum personal information required to process your transaction.
12. Regularly check your bank and credit card statements.

NO-MONEY-DOWN REAL ESTATE SEMINARS

How many times have you seen late-night infomercials or advertisements in your local newspapers inviting you to a seminar on how you can become a millionaire in real estate by buying property with no money down, even if you have a poor credit history?

The live infomercials attempt, typically in a two-hour presentation, to convince you to attend a three-day workshop in which you'll learn the "secrets" to become an instant real estate entrepreneur. You are then invited to pay three or four thousand dollars to attend the three-day seminar, with a promise that you'll make tens of thousands of dollars within thirty to sixty days of completing the course.

As I say many times in this book, if something seems too good to be true, it probably is. There are no shortcuts to making money in real estate. It takes a lot of experience, research, hard work, and in most cases financial risk. It is not for the faint of heart. Buying a home should be more about your family future than about making short-term profits. It's easy to make money in real estate when markets are rising. It is a different story if you're overextended when the market drops.

Here are some of the methods used and the "secrets" given out at these presentations.

1. The instructor will spend half an hour telling you about all the vacations he is taking now that he is financially secure, and that he has personally purchased several hundred properties in your area using his system.
2. The main principle is that the seminar will help you find properties in distress and the owners who owe more on the mortgage than they can afford.
3. One of the main "secrets" you'll learn is how to place advertising in key real estate magazines to help you find these owners who are in distress.
4. Your ad could be as simple as "if you need help with your mortgage, or if you are in foreclosure, call me."
5. You will then apparently receive at least 50-100 calls from sellers in trouble, either through job loss, marriage breakdown or a death in the family.
6. Apparently distressed homeowners will be happy to give you their property if you take over their mortgage payments, so they can avoid having their credit score ruined for the next ten years.
7. According to the seminars, even if you have bad credit, you will still be able to take over an owner's mortgage without getting approval from the owner's bank.
8. The people who sponsor the seminars will provide you with the names of lenders who will lend you money at high interest rates for a short period of time – usually thirty to sixty days – because in two months you can resell your property and make your first profit.
9. The seminar presenters also claim to have a database of properties in your area that are in a category called "pre-foreclosure," and you'll find out about them before anyone else.

Notice the phrase "pre-foreclosure." That's a term rarely used in Canada, but it's common in the U.S. Many other principles in the seminars are taken from similar U.S. seminars. In Canada, most banks use the power of sale remedy in the mortgage if it goes into default; they typically do not use the foreclosure remedy because it takes too long. And we are not experiencing the real estate meltdowns people are facing in the U.S., because most lenders in Canada have been more responsible than lenders in the U.S.

More than fifteen years ago, some trust-company mortgages allowed buyers to take over a mortgage without bank approval, but it's very unlikely you'll find one of those mortgages today. (You can learn more about buying property from a bank under power of sale in Chapter 9.)

In Canada, no lender will give you money, even at high interest rates, unless you can demonstrate that you'll still have at least twenty to twenty-five percent equity in the property. So why would owners in this situation not sell their properties themselves to pay off their mortgages?

As in most schemes, remember, if it seems too good to be true, it is.

Weisleder's Wisdom on
no-money-down real estate seminars

1. There are numerous seminars claiming to teach you how to buy real estate with no money down and no credit.
2. Most of these seminars are based on principles adapted from the U.S. experience, and are based on principles that have little or no application in Canada.
3. If it seems too good to be true, it is.

REAL ESTATE FRAUD

There are two kinds of real estate fraud buyers and sellers need to be aware of. The first is fraud by forgery, and the second is fraud by identity theft and impersonation.

In a forgery situation, a fraud artist will generally look for a property where the owner may not be personally living in the home. The owner could be out of the country for the winter, or the home might be rented to tenants. The fraud artist will then prepare a phony deed that transfers the title to the property into his name, and sign the real owners' name on the deed, without their knowledge. The fraud artist may also obtain unauthorized computer access to a provincial title registry and effect the same forged electronic transfer of the owner's title to the property into his name. Once the name of the fraud artist appears on the actual title to the property, using these forgeries, the thief pretends to be the legitimate seller of the property when he approaches a real estate salesperson to sell the property or goes to a bank to apply for a new mortgage on the property.

Fraudsters will probably have valid ID to prove they are the person or persons now named on title. Once they've sold the property or receive the funds from the new mortgage, they disappear. The original homeowner, or the person who buys the house from the forgers, the financial institution that approved the new mortgage, and the bank that had their title and mortgage transferred or discharged — all have been duped.

In an identity-theft situation, the fraudster uses forged or false ID to impersonate the homeowner, arranges either a sale or a mortgage of the property, then runs away with the money. These fraudsters also usually choose a house the owner doesn't live in.

In the Ontario case of *Reviczky v. Meleknia*, decided in 2007, the tenants living in the house forged a power of attorney from the absent owner and used it to list and sell the house to an unsuspecting buyer. The tenants managed to fool the listing salesperson, the lawyer who acted for them, and the buyer's lawyer. In an interim decision, the judge had to deal with the competing claims of three innocent parties: the original owner, who had his property stolen; the new buyer, who paid fair value for the property; and the bank that gave the buyer a mortgage on the property. The listing salesperson's For Sale sign didn't cause any suspicion only because the original owner was in a retirement home. The court ruled in favour of the original owner, stating that since the buyer and the bank had the opportunity to suspect something might be wrong with the power of attorney, they should suffer the loss.

A separate legal action is still continuing against the listing salespeople, the seller lawyer, and the buyer lawyer, on the basis that they should have suspected something was wrong with the power of attorney because it was a continuing power of attorney granted by a man who was 88 years and 11 months old; it was valid until his death; it had no limitation of any kind; it could be revoked at any time; and only one person witnessed the signature. (Ontario's *Substitute Decisions Act* requires two signatures for a continuing power of attorney.) It may still be several years before the action comes to trial to determine what duties may have been expected from the salesperson and the lawyers involved. I won't offer any opinion as to how the case may be decided, but I can say it is clear that if the listing salesperson or the lawyers had asked questions about the power of attorney, the fraud would probably have been uncovered right away.

As a result of this case, the government made changes to the way title transfers are registered in Ontario and the rest of Canada, and there are more stringent requirements before making a title transfer based on a power of attorney.

I advise buyers and sellers to always obtain title insurance. Title insurance can help you correct encroachment or other survey issues, zoning setback violations, tax arrears, or errors made by the municipality in answering inquiries. The most important benefit is protecting a buyer's or seller's title from any theft, whether through forgery or impersonation. Once a fraud has occurred, the average cost to repair a title, including all legal and other expenses, is more than $30,000. If you don't have a title insurance policy, you can't get this money back.

To obtain a title insurance policy, contact your lawyer. The process is quick and the cost is reasonable. If you don't have title insurance, obtain a policy today and have peace of mind always.

FINTRAC

The Financial Transactions and Reports Analysis Centre of Canada, or "FINTRAC," collects, analyzes, and discloses financial information and intelligence about suspected money laundering and terrorist financing, both domestic and international. When businesses and industries report to FINTRAC, they must keep records of personal information of the clients they deal with, especially when clients deliver large sums of money.

In every real estate transaction, buyers and sellers deal with large sums of money. Accordingly, real estate brokerages must comply with the provisions of FINTRAC, and keep a record of the identity of everyone who provides funds for the purchase of any property. Buyers and sellers are routinely asked by real estate salespeople to provide personal ID, such as a driver's license or passport, to demonstrate that they are who they claim to be. Don't carry or provide your social insurance number unless absolutely necessary.

This FINTRAC process provides many advantages to the real estate industry. The ID check should prevent real estate frauds.

Under Canada's privacy rules (see Chapter 10), the real estate brokerage must always protect the personal information of buyers and sellers in their files. The FINTRAC process should also provide sellers with the comfort that a buyer's identity and the source of his or her deposit funds have been verified by the buyer salesperson involved in the transaction.

> ### *Weisleder's Wisdom on real estate fraud*
>
> 1. Every homeowner should have title insurance on their property.
> 2. Fraud artists try to impersonate an owner who doesn't live on the property, in order to steal the owner's title.
> 3. FINTRAC was designed to ensure that businesses, including real estate brokerage companies, know where their client's funds are coming from.

BUYER TRICKS TO WATCH OUT FOR IN THE AGREEMENT OF PURCHASE AND SALE

In difficult economic times, when real estate markets are volatile, many buyers attempt to insert various legal "tricks" in offers — usually offers prepared by lawyers or buyer salespeople. The buyer's goal is to legally walk away from the deal without penalty if he or she decides not to close the transaction for any reason.

Be aware of these tricks when you're presented with any offer from a buyer. If you use a REALTOR® you'll have professional help negotiating the agreement of purchase and sale and dealing with any unusual change or addition to the agreement before you accept it.

The deletion in clause 10

A common trick of a trickster buyer is to delete subclauses 10(a), (b), (c), and (d) in the fine print of the agreement. Clause 10 (discussed in detail in Chapter 3) is where buyers acknowledge that on closing they will accept minor utility easements on the property, as well as any restrictive covenant or city agreement registered against title to the property. With this deletion, if the buyers' lawyer finds even a minor Bell easement on the property during the title search, the buyers will have the right, but not the obligation, to cancel the transaction with no penalty.

It's not a good idea to permit any buyer to change the printed form, unless you question the reason for the change, then obtain legal advice, before you sign the agreement.

Addition of "discharge" clause

Some trickster buyers try to insert the following discharge clause to the agreement:

The seller agrees to discharge from the property all mortgages, liens or encumbrances, at their expense, on or before closing.

As indicated in Chapter 3 under clause 25, when you add anything into the agreement that somehow conflicts with the standard form, then the added provision takes precedence. The addition of the above discharge clause means that the seller will have to remove any minor easement, covenant, or bank mortgage that the buyer agreed to accept under clauses 10 and 12 of the agreement. (This is discussed more fully in Chapter 3.) Again, with this clause, the buyer will have the right, but not the obligation, to cancel the agreement without penalty. I advise sellers to reject this clause. If your buyer insists on this discharge clause, add the phrase "subject to the provisions of clause 10 and 12 contained herein" at the end of the clause, to protect yourself.

Extra copies of the agreement and the "missing" schedule B
Be extra careful to review all copies of the agreement of purchase and sale before you sign them, to ensure that they are all exactly the same (for more detail see the discussion of purchase price in Chapter 3). Unscrupulous buyers try to change the price on one of the offers and then take the amended offer to their bank, so they can get a higher mortgage loan. Their goal is to complete the transaction without making any down payment.

This is a fraudulent action by the buyer against the bank. The bank may suspect that you, the seller, were part of this fraud, and you may be dragged into legal proceedings when the buyer disappears. Even if you're innocent of any wrongdoing, you'll incur legal fees, because you'll need to defend yourself.

Another trick buyers try is to tell you they'll agree to your asking price of $400,000 if the purchase price shown on page one is $440,000. They then add a schedule that says the buyer will receive a special "rebate" of $40,000 on closing. The buyers don't show the schedule to the bank, so they obtain a loan for the property based on the $440,000 price. The buyers hope to buy the property with no money down, and to take the extra money they borrow and disappear. The bank may suspect that the seller was involved, meaning costly legal proceedings for the seller.

PROPERTY FLIPS AND THE ASSIGNMENT CLAUSE

Buyer have the right to sell their interest in the agreement of purchase and sale even before the transaction closes, because there is nothing in the agreement that prevents the buyer from doing this. (Clause 27 is explained in detail in Chapter 3.) To protect themselves, home builders and condominium developers typically insert a clause indicating that buyers are prohibiting from assigning or transferring their interest in the agreement to buy a new home or new condominium before the closing. Builders and developers sell homes or units before they're built; they don't want buyers competing with them. Buyers who try to transfer their interest in the unit risk forfeiting all their deposits, at the discretion of the builder or developer.

However, there is nothing preventing a buyer from signing a resale agreement on Monday night and transferring their interest in the agreement to a new buyer on Tuesday morning — except when the original agreement called for the first buyer to give back a mortgage to the seller. If the closing proceeds are by bank draft, then no permission is required. In a seller's market, when prices were rising, these resales were common, even though sellers didn't like the idea of buyers making a quick profit on their property.

There's only one way to ensure this does not take place: insert a clause into your agreement prohibiting the buyer from assigning or transferring any interest in the property prior to closing.

Some buyers still include the following assignment clause into agreements:

The buyer may assign this agreement at any time before closing, and upon such assignment, the buyer shall have no further liability under this agreement.

On the surface, this does not seem to be a difficult clause, but in practice, it has serious implications. The important words are: "the buyer shall have no further liability under this agreement."

Let's say the buyers sign an agreement for $300,000, with a $5,000 deposit, and they've inserted this clause. Before the closing, the market drops significantly, and the buyers do not want to close the transaction. They tell the seller that in accordance with the assignment clause, they have transferred the agreement to a company called Helium Investments Limited. This company has no assets of any kind. Helium Investments Limited then refuses to close the deal.

The seller then sells property to a second buyer for $250,000, suffering a $50,000 loss.

As a result of the assignment clause, the seller cannot sue the buyers, he or she can only sue Helium Investments Limited, and as that company has no assets, a lawsuit is pointless. If there was no assignment clause, the seller could have sued the original buyers for the entire $50,000. By using this clause, the buyers effectively limited their total loss on the transaction to $5,000, being the deposit, instead of $50,000.

WHO IS YOUR BUYER?

If an offer is prepared in the name of a numbered company, be wary. The company may have no assets. The only way to protect yourself against the numbered-company buyer or the assignment clause is to obtain a significant deposit, at least ten percent of the purchase price, to make it difficult and expensive for your buyers if they try to cancel the transaction.

Weisleder's Wisdom on
Internet brokers and other scams to watch out for

1. There are different Internet brokerage models who claim to provide REALTOR® services at a reduced cost.

2. Most Internet models don't provide maximum exposure or the negotiation skills of a professional REALTOR®.

3. Identity theft is an ever increasing problem; be very diligent in safeguarding your personal information.

4. No-money-down real estate seminars in general offer outdated information that's not worth your time and money. Remember, "if it sounds too good to be true, it usually is."

5. Always have title insurance on your property, so you'll be protected if someone tries to fraudulently transfer your title.

6. Sellers, be wary of any changes made by the buyer to the printed provisions of the agreement of purchase and sale; also watch out for any unusual additional clauses.

7. Sellers, carefully check all copies of the agreement, especially any schedules designed to let the buyer escape their obligations without penalty, or defraud a bank.

CHAPTER 6

Landlord and Tenant Rights

Most of us have been landlords or tenants at some point in our lives. When you're buying or selling a home, the rules regarding landlord and tenant rights and obligations will have a major impact, so you need to understand your basic rights and obligations as landlords or tenants before you buy or sell a home that has apartments or is being rented by a tenant.

FIRST-TIME BUYERS CURRENTLY RENTING AN APARTMENT OR HOUSE

If you're renting an apartment and thinking of buying a home, find out when your lease expires, because you're responsible for all rental payments until the end of your lease. If you have a lease that expires on November 30, you're responsible for all rental payments until November 30 — even if you buy a house and move into it in May or June or July. You may be able to sublease your apartment, or obtain the landlord's permission to leave earlier without penalty. Most landlords will want the rent unless they have a waiting list of new tenants ready to take over your apartment.

If your lease has already expired and you're on a monthly lease, in most provinces you still need to give the landlord sixty days' notice before you move. If you move out without giving notice, the landlord has the right to claim the two months' rent from you.

BE CAREFUL BEFORE SIGNING ANY RESIDENTIAL LEASE RENEWAL

To rent an apartment in a building that has more than four units, you usually have to sign a one-year lease. When the lease expires, many landlords ask you to sign a one-year renewal of the lease. If you sign the renewal, you're responsible for all the rent until the end of the renewed lease. In most provinces, as long as you pay the rent on time and don't bother the other tenants, the landlord can't evict you. Don't sign the renewal. Your tenancy will switch to a monthly lease and you'll be able to terminate your lease at any time with only sixty days' notice.

If you are renting a home, a condominium, or a unit in a building with four or fewer units, you may want the security of a one-year renewal term, because your landlord can terminate a monthly lease at any time by providing sixty days' notice, if he or she wants the property for family use or, if the building is for sale, for a buyer who requires vacant possession.

SELLING A HOME OCCUPIED BY TENANTS

If you have a tenant and you decide to sell your home, you may need to sell your home with vacant possession, as most buyers will want to move in after closing. In my experience, unless you have a very good relationship with your tenant, you are much better off ending your relationship with your tenant before you put the property up for sale. Tenants generally don't maintain a home the way an owner would; your home may not show as well to buyers if a tenant is living there.

The 24-hour notice

Under the *Residential Tenancies Act* of Ontario, and in most other similar provincial statutes, landlords must provide twenty-four hours' notice to the tenant every time they want to show a property to a potential buyer. These showings must be between 8:00 a.m. and 8:00 p.m. Many buyers would prefer to see a property immediately. An unco-operative tenant can refuse entry by leaving the chain lock in place. Some landlords have had to obtain a court order to get the tenant to co-operate. Court orders sometimes take several months.

The termination process for landlords

A landlord must have a legitimate reason to terminate a residential lease. Even with a legitimate reason, it can be time-consuming and costly to obtain vacant possession of a property. As an example, if you're a landlord in Ontario, you can terminate a lease at any time for non-payment of rent by providing fourteen days' notice to the tenant. If the tenant does not make the payment by the end of the fourteen days, you can ask for a hearing date at the Landlord and Tenant Tribunal Board; it usually takes three to four weeks to get a hearing. If you're successful at the hearing, you wait an additional week to obtain a signed court order for possession. If the tenant doesn't leave, you can take the court order to the county sheriff, pay the fee — four to five hundred dollars — and the sheriff will remove the tenant from the property.

In my experience, removing a tenant typically takes two months, and that's when there are no significant delays. Unfortunately, professional tenants who know how to work the legal system can delay proceedings by up to six months. Such tenants can cause severe financial hardship for landlords. How can you avoid these tenant-warriors? You can carefully qualify your tenants, doing credit checks, obtaining references from previous landlords, and making sure the tenants have regular employment. Ask to see a copy of their last pay stub from their current employer.

When a tenant interferes if you want to show the property by, for example, keeping the chain on the front door to deny you access, that is a breach of conduct. In Ontario, you can terminate a tenancy for breach of conduct by providing the tenant with twenty days' notice. If the tenant won't move out, you'll have to go through the same two-month court process to obtain vacant possession of the property.

If you want to sell a property with vacant possession, consider the termination date in the tenant's lease; you can't obtain vacant possession before the lease expires. The only way to sell the home in this situation is to find a buyer who agrees to accept the tenant. Most buyers are unwilling to do this, unless they require the income from a basement apartment in the home.

If you have a tenant who is on a monthly lease, you'll still have to provide sixty days' notice to terminate the tenancy. However, you may provide this notice only *after* you have signed an agreement of purchase and sale with a buyer. So be very careful when you select your closing date. You may still face the risk of your tenant refusing to leave, so you may be faced with the two-month court process to obtain vacant possession. The buyer may not be able to wait, and the transaction may fail as a result of the delay.

If your buyer is planning to rent the home after closing, you can't terminate your existing tenant's lease, and the buyer must assume your existing tenant. There was a case where a landlord gave a notice to terminate a tenant's lease based on a new buyer taking over possession of the property. But after closing, the buyer immediately rented the property to a new tenant. The original tenant was successful in a court action against the first seller landlord; the landlord had to pay all the tenant's moving costs because the notice to terminate was not valid, as the buyer did not move into the property.

There is a clause you can use when you have an existing tenant and the buyer requires vacant possession on closing; be careful as there is no way that a seller can ever guarantee that the tenant will leave prior to closing. (See Appendix 1.13, Vacant Possession Notice.)

Sellers can expect to get a higher purchase price from a buyer if they properly stage a home before putting it on the market. However, tenants are usually very unco-operative about changes to their rental accommodations. For example, one of the first lessons of staging is that the home should be free of clutter. A landlord does not have a right to tell a tenant to de-clutter their home to make it more attractive to buyers.

MAKE A DEAL

All these potential problems can be avoided, in my view, by making a deal with the tenants so they'll leave the premises before you put your home up for sale. You may, for example, offer the tenant one month's free rent, or offer to pay their moving costs — much better than having to call the sheriff! If you arrange in advance for vacant possession you can stage the home and get your best selling price. You won't have to worry about providing twenty-four hours' notice before any showing of the property. And you'll be able to deliver vacant possession to your buyer on the date scheduled for closing.

Weisleder's Wisdom on landlord and tenant rights

1. If you're living in an apartment and you want to buy a house, look at your lease and find the termination date. Synchronize the end of the lease with the purchase of your new home, so you won't have to pay rent for an apartment you're not living in.
2. If you're renting in a building that has more than four units, don't sign any lease renewal agreements, especially if you're considering buying a home within the next twelve months.
3. If you're selling your home, you may have difficulty terminating the leases of unco-operative tenants.
4. Consider paying your tenants an incentive to leave so you'll have vacant possession before you put your home on the market and you can get the maximum selling price with no aggravation.

Family Law Rights

Both buyers and sellers should understand their rights under the *Family Law Act* legislation in their provinces, so they can make informed decisions about ownership, buying a home, and who needs to sign documents when properties are bought or sold.

MARRIED SPOUSES

The *Family Law Act* in Ontario recognizes two different kinds of spousal relationships. The first is a married spouse: two people who have entered into a marriage in Ontario that is recognized as a legal marriage under the province of Ontario. Some marriages performed outside of Ontario are also recognized as legal marriages by the province of Ontario.

COMMON-LAW SPOUSES

People in the second relationship are generally referred to as "common-law spouses." The phrase refers to two people who are not married but have been living together for more than three years or have been living together less than three years but are also the natural or adoptive parents of at least one child. If you have no children and you have not been living together for at least three years, you would not be considered to be a common-law spouse.

SUPPORT OBLIGATIONS

Under the laws of Ontario and in most jurisdictions in Canada, there is no difference to support awards for depen-dants whether a couple is married or living in a common-law relationship.

In Ontario, support is the only area of family law that treats a common-law couple the same as a married couple. The very important laws regarding property rights and the matrimo-nial home apply only to married couples and not to common-law couples. Common-law spouses have charged that this law is unconstitutional under the *Canadian Charter of Rights and Freedoms*, but the provisions have been upheld by the Supreme Court of Canada.

PROPERTY RIGHTS FOR MARRIED SPOUSES

The rest of the information about property rights in this chapter applies only to married spouses. The main principle under the legislation is that marriage is a partnership, and it does not matter who is making all the money or who is look-ing after the children; the two contributions are equally important. Furthermore, there is no penalty against a spouse when a marriage breaks down. What happens is that all the property assets the spouses have accumulated during their married lives are added together. "All the property assets" includes real estate, businesses, stocks, jewelry, and bank accounts. Together, all these assets form a married couple's "net family property." This net family property is divided equally between the two married spouses. It makes no difference if a property is registered in the name of only one spouse. All property acquired during the marriage is added to net family property and divided equally.

There is one main exception: property that was owned by one spouse before the marriage is treated differently. Typically, the value of the property on the day of marriage is excluded from the calculation of net family property. For example, if on the date of the marriage one spouse owned a plaza that was worth $200,000. On the date of separation, the plaza was worth $500,000. Only the gain in value during the marriage — $300,000 — is included in the calculation of net family property.

However, if one spouse owned a house before the marriage, and both spouses moved into the house, the house becomes the matrimonial home. The spouse who moved in after the marriage would now be entitled to fifty percent of the value of the entire home on the date the spouses separate. A matrimonial home is defined as "a property which is owned by at least one of the spouses and is ordinarily occupied by the spouses as their family residence." Married spouses can have more than one matrimonial home. For example, if a couple uses both a home in the city and a cottage in the country during the year, then both properties will be treated as matrimonial homes and divided equally if the couple separates. Using the above example, let's say someone owned a home before they were married that was worth $200,000 on the date they got married, and their spouse moved into the home, making it a matrimonial home. On the date they split up, the home is now worth $500,000. In this example, each of the married spouses will be entitled to $250,000, being one half the value of the entire home.

Marriage contracts

A married couple is permitted to change the rule of fifty-fifty division of assets if they sign a marriage contract before they get married. In a marriage contract a couple can state that one spouse will receive more than fifty percent if they ever separate. There are cases where a spouse agreed to receive nothing if the marriage broke down, and the judge upheld the agreement. The point is that if you don't like the terms of the marriage contract, don't get married.

Despite what may be written in a marriage contract, married spouses always are given the right of possession to any matrimonial home. To sell any matrimonial home, even if it's registered in only one married spouse's name, and even if there is a signed marriage contract limiting the other spouse's right to the value of the home, both married spouses must consent to the sale of the matrimonial property. This is true even if the couple has separated and only one spouse is living in the home. If the couple has not yet divorced and the home was used as a matrimonial home at the time of separation, both married spouses must consent to the sale of the home.

If you are married and buying a matrimonial home, based on the above information, it is not necessary to take title in both spouses' names. Yet for practical purposes, especially if the couple will be applying for a mortgage loan to help finance the purchase, it may make more sense for both spouses to have their names on title.

If you're living common law and your home is registered in only one spouse's name, the other spouse has no rights to the home, and his or her signature is not required to sell the home. When you're living common law with someone, the only way you can claim an interest in the real estate is if you can prove you either a) paid part of the down payment when the home was purchased or b) you contributed significantly to the ongoing maintenance of the home. Married people don't have to prove anything as they are automatically entitled to a fifty-percent interest.

For common-law couples considering buying a home together, the moral of the story is that to protect your rights, you must make sure your name is on title to the property. When your name is on the title, your legal interest will always be protected, and your common-law spouse will need your agreement to sell or mortgage the home.

In some communities, there have arisen some disturbing examples where one of the married spouses is working overseas for an extended period of time and the other spouse tries to sell the home and scoop the money, without telling their spouse. You must be careful as a buyer not to buy from this type of fraudulent seller, as a claim may be made against you by the overseas spouse when they return only to find that their property has been sold. This is another reason buyers should walk the neighbourhood of any home they may be interested in buying, and talk to the neighbours to make sure there is nothing untoward taking place in the home they are interested in buying.

In other Canadian provinces, such as Manitoba, common-law couples have property rights that are not available in Ontario. No matter where you reside, ask a lawyer what property rights you may have when you are in a common-law relationship.

Weisleder's Wisdom on family law rights

1. In Ontario, common-law spouses do not have the same rights to matrimonial property as married spouses.

2. If you're married and want to sell a matrimonial home, you need a signature from your spouse on the agreement of purchase and sale, even if the home is registered in your name only.

3. If you're living common law and your name is not on title to the home, you have no entitlement to the property; the home can be sold without your agreement.

4. If you're a common-law spouse, make sure your name is placed on the title when you and your common-law spouse buy any property together.

Resale Condominiums and Other Co-Ownerships

Condominium ownership is one of the more popular forms of home ownership, especially for first-time buyers, as it offers many of the advantages of home ownership at a much lower cost. Yet when you own a unit in a condominium corporation, you are part of a democracy, and you can no longer make all the decisions about your home, as you can when you own a private house.

CREATING A CONDOMINIUM

To explain your rights as a condominium owner, I'll take you through the steps a condominium developer typically goes through when creating a new condominium.

Initially, the developer will be involved in four separate processes at the same time to get a condominium project ready for construction.

First, the total land of the condominium, including its units and common elements, whether it is a high-rise building or townhouses, must be registered in the land titles system. It takes about a year to convert land in the registry system to the land titles system. (The two systems are described in detail in Chapter 2.)

For step two, the developer approaches the local city government to obtain any zoning changes required to construct a high-rise building (if that's what's being built), as well as any agreements with the city for utility and other services that must be provided to the development. This step can take two to three years to complete.

In step three, the developer prepares the two main condominium documents, the "declaration" and the "description," then sends them to the province for approval. (These documents are explained more fully in the next few paragraphs.) This process can take one to two years.

Fourth, the developer usually builds a presentation centre that includes a sample finished unit and a model of the finished building. The developer then starts pre-selling units.

DECLARATION

The declaration is commonly explained as the bill of rights in a condominium. It contains all your rights of ownership in the building, as well as any important restrictions of ownership. A controversial restriction in many condominium declarations is a prohibition against pet ownership, which means you can't bring a pet into your unit. If pets are prohibited, the condominium corporation has the power to go to court to have your pet evicted.

The declaration also divides the condominium building into units and common elements. As an owner, you buy your unit plus a percentage interest in the common elements. The unit typically includes everything inside your four walls, but may also include your balcony or a patio if you're in a townhouse building. Unit owners are generally responsible for repairing and maintaining anything in their unit; the condominium corporation is responsible for repair and maintainance of the common elements. The definition of "unit" is in the declaration of every condominium corporation. Sometimes there is confusion over the HVAC system in your unit. Be careful to check the declaration to find out who is responsible for maintaining the heat and air conditioning. If it's the unit owner's responsibility, make your purchase conditional on a condominium home inspection (discussed later in this chapter). Unit owners have the right to paint and decorate their unit, but if you want to make major changes to the interior walls, you'll need approval from the condominium corporation. Every unit owner is entitled to share in the use and enjoyment of the common elements, which can include party rooms, swimming pools, tennis courts, lobby, and elevators.

To determine how owners pay their fair share of expenses in the condominium building, the corporation makes the calculation based on the percentage interest that you own in the common elements. The principle is that 100% of the owners pay 100% of the condominium expenses according to their individual percentage-share ownership. Let's say there are 100 unit owners in a building, with 20 one-bedroom units, 60 two-bedroom units, and 20 three-bedroom units. To keep things simple, let's say the percentages in the declaration are:

20 one bedrooms, 0.5% each = 10% total
60 two bedrooms, 1% each = 60% total
20 three bedrooms, 1.5% each = 30% total

100 units = 100% total

Let's say the total sum needed to run the condominium corporation in a given year is $500,000. Each one-bedroom unit will contribute $500,000 x 0.5%, or $2,500 a year, with monthly payments of approximately $208.33. Each two-bedroom unit will pay $500,000 x 1%, or $5,000 a year, with monthly payments of $416.66. Each three-bedroom unit will pay $500,000 x 1.5%, or $7,500 per year, about $624.99 per month.

This is how all amounts payable to a condominium corporation are collected from the unit owners, and the percentages are always listed in the declaration itself.

DESCRIPTION

The description tells you what the condominium will look like and contains detailed plans, including the survey of the entire property, the location and layouts of each of the units, and the common elements. For example, you may be able to see by looking at the plans exactly where your proposed parking space will be in relation to the elevator.

MAKING CHANGES TO THE DECLARATION AND DESCRIPTION

Once the declaration and description have been finalized and reviewed by the unit owners, there can be no changes made to these important documents unless at least 80% or 90% of the owners agree; exact agreement depends on the change being requested. In our example, to change the percentage ownership from 0.5%, 1%, and 1.5% to something different, at least 90 out of the 100 unit owners must agree to the change.

PRE-SALE OF UNITS

There is no requirement in the *Condominium Act* that a developer pre-sell a certain number of units before starting construction, but from a practical standpoint, most developers will not undertake construction and most banks won't lend money unless a specific percentage of the units, usually seventy percent, are already sold. Whenever a buyer enters into an agreement with a developer to buy a unit in a condominium that has not yet started to be constructed, the developer is obliged to provide the buyer with a "statement of disclosure." This package includes the main condominium documents, the declaration, the description, all the bylaws, and the proposed first-year budget for the condominium. The buyer has ten days — called the cooling-off period — to read all the documents; if the buyer is not happy with anything contained in the statement of disclosure, he or she can cancel the agreement, and the deposit will be returned. (There is no cooling-off period when a buyer purchases a resale condominium.) If developers make material changes to the declaration or the description before closing, they must again provide the buyer with the ten-day cooling-off period. The buyer can cancel the transaction if he or she does not agree with the proposed changes.

Once these steps are completed, the developer begins construction. When the building is completed, the developer must obtain a certificate from an architect, an engineer, and a registered land surveyor confirming that the building has in fact been constructed and completed in accordance with the plans that were approved by the government. These certificates are then attached to, and form part of, the description.

Next, the developer registers the declaration and the description (including all certificates) on title to the property. This registration creates a condominium corporation, and the property is governed by the terms and provisions of the *Condominium Act*. The land titles office assigns the next available corporation number to the new corporation. As an example, if you own a unit in Metropolitan Toronto Condominium Corporation No. 824, you own part of the 824th condominium building registered in the City of Toronto.

THE CONDOMINIUM CORPORATION

There are differences between a condominium corporation and a regular business corporation. If you want to buy an interest in a regular business corporation, you purchase something called a "share." There are no shares in a condominium corporation. When you buy an interest in a condominium corporation, you buy a unit, to which you have exclusive use, and a percentage interest in the common elements, to which you share use with the other owners in your condominium. Another major difference between the two kinds of corporations is the concept of "limited liability." If a business corporation incurs any debts or other liabilities, the creditors cannot sue the shareholders; they can seek to recover damages only from the business corporation. This is why people incorporate businesses: to limit their liability if something goes wrong later. There is no limited liability in a condominium corporation. If someone slips and falls outside a condominium building and sues the condominium corporation, damages are paid out of the condominium's assets. If there are not enough assets, the owners are responsible for the debt, in accordance with their percentage ownership as stated in the declaration. In the above example, if there was $100,000 still owing on a lawsuit, the one-bedroom units would each have to pay $500 toward the settlement, the two-bedroom units would each pay $1,000, and the three-bedroom units would each pay $1,500.

Bylaws

Once the condominium corporation is formed, the next step is to register the bylaws of the corporation. Bylaws govern how the first board of directors of the corporation will be elected; the number of directors on the board; the term of office a director will serve; and the process all meetings will follow in the future. In Ontario, the *Condominium Act* states that all boards shall consist of at least three directors, and the term of office shall be three years, but unit owners may change both the number of directors and the term of office. The bylaws also state that if the situation warrants, fifteen percent of the unit owners may call a meeting to replace the directors. Any changes to the bylaws require the approval of a majority of the unit owners. In our example, at least fifty-one unit owners need to approve a change to the bylaws.

Duties of the board of directors

Directors have two main functions: to propose rules and to prepare budgets. Condominium corporations have rules so unit owners can enjoy the use of the common elements. For example, a board of directors could propose a rule that prohibits unit owners from parking in the parking spots allocated for visitors, or to permit swimming or tennis only between the hours of 9:00 a.m. and 10:00 p.m. Proposed rules are approved by the owners at a meeting with at least twenty-five percent of all owners and with a majority of the owners present at the meeting itself. If twenty-five out of a hundred owners attend a meeting, and thirteen vote in favour of the rule, it passes. To be part of the decision-making process, unit owners have to attend meetings.

The board of directors also prepares a yearly budget for approval by the owners. The budget contains all amounts the directors expect will be required to effectively maintain the condominium corporation for the coming year. Budgets include ordinary repairs and maintenance for all systems in the building, security, insurance, cleaning, landscaping, and snow removal. There is also a reserve fund — ten percent of the budget — for major repairs and replacements of the common elements or other assets of the condominium corporation. The board also orders a reserve fund study, usually performed by engineers and verified by auditors, that states how much money will be required to maintain the common elements going forward, and whether there are sufficient funds in the reserve fund to pay for the maintenance. The reserve fund study must be updated every three years.

If you're buying a resale condominium, review the reserve fund study and find out what's in the reserve fund. This will assist you in not only finding out the condition of major items like the building roof and parking garage, but, more important, will let you know whether there is enough money set aside in the reserve fund to make the repairs, when necessary, in the coming years. (Every owner can get a copy, as well.)

If the board wishes to make major alterations to the common elements, such as installing an additional tennis court, the directors must obtain the approval of two-thirds of all the owners. If there are a hundred owners, the board needs approval from sixty-seven of them.

The budget must be approved by the owners at a meeting. Once the budget is approved, owners pay their percentages. This collection of money is called the "common expense fees" and is payable monthly.

Sometimes a condominium corporation incurs a sudden, unanticipated expense, such as a major leak in the roof. If there are insufficient funds in the budget or the reserve fund to pay for a repair, the board of directors may issue a special assessment to every unit owner, again based on each owner's percentage of ownership.

PAYMENT OF THE COMMON EXPENSE FEE

If a unit owner doesn't pay the common expense fee or a special assessment approved by the unit owners, the condominium corporation has the right to register a lien on title to the property against the owner's unit. The lien is for the amount owed, and the cost to remove a lien is usually $350. Most mortgages include a provision that registration of a lien against your unit constitutes a default under your mortgage. If the lien is not paid immediately, your bank could commence power of sale proceedings. (For information about power of sale, see Chapter 9.) Or the condominium corporation can sell your unit to collect what you owe. And your neighbours will be upset that you're not contributing your share of expenses. If you buy a condominium unit, keep your common expense payments up to date! Most condominium corporations don't have a line of credit at a bank; they need the money from the common expense payments so they can pay the bills. There are no excuses for not paying your share on time.

CAN YOU DECORATE YOUR UNIT?

Most condominium corporations allow owners to decorate the interior of their unit; however, owners are not permitted to remove walls or change plumbing fixtures without the permission of the board of directors. Restrictions on decorating are printed in the condominium declaration. Most condominium declarations prohibit satellite dishes on balconies.

THE STATUS CERTIFICATE

Some important issues if you're buying a resale condominium:

How is the common expense payment calculated?
What is the common expense payment for the unit I want to buy?
What are the restrictions against pets and decorating?
Are there any lawsuits against the corporation?
Is the corporation contemplating any major additions to the building?
Are there any special assessments coming due?
When was the last reserve fund study completed?
How much money is in the reserve fund?

You can find answers to all these questions in the condominium corporation's status certificate. This document is prepared by the corporation management office, so people can find out the status of affairs in the condominium building. The status certificate includes a copy of the condominium declaration, description, bylaws, and rules, as well as a copy of the reserve fund study and information about any lawsuits or special assessments. If you're thinking about buying a resale condominium, make your purchase conditional on reviewing the status certificate with your lawyer. The cost to a buyer of obtaining a status certificate is usually $100. You can see an example of the condition in Appendix 1.2.

When you buy a new condominium, there are, in effect, two closings. The first is an occupancy closing, when you move into the unit. The second is title closing, when you receive the deed, registered on title, for your unit. Once the building is ready for occupancy, the province requires certificates from the architects, engineers, and surveyors; it may take several months to satisfy the provincial requirements before the condominium registration is finalized. During this period, you pay a "rental fee" to the developer; the rental fee is your portion of the common expenses, real estate taxes, and mortgage interest that you would have paid if you had paid for the unit in full.

For example, if you paid $200,000 as the full price for your new one-bedroom unit, your monthly expenses after closing might be $208.33 as your common expenses, $200 for property taxes, and if you had taken out a mortgage for $150,000, a monthly interest payment of $800. So your total monthly payment would be $1,208.33. This is how your rental fee would be calculated and what you would pay each month until you receive title to your unit. At that time, you make the payments directly to your own bank.

Buyers of new condominiums receive another protection: if the first year's budget exceeds the number given to you by the developer in the disclosure statement when you signed your agreement of purchase and sale, the developer must make up the difference, but only during the first year of the condominium's operation.

BUYING A RESALE CONDOMINIUM UNIT

For a resale condominium buyer, the "neighbourhood" is often the condominium building. Try to speak to people who already live in the building. Are they happy with the way the building is maintained? Do they seem to be comfortable living in the building? Are the units occupied by owners or tenants?

Often, tenants may not take good care of the units and common elements.

Is there good sound control between the units, or will you hear every chair scrape from the unit above or beside you? What about the piano in the unit below you?

Find out who manages the building. Is it a professional manager with lots of experience, a management company, or a group of owners who want to keep the expenses low? If it's owners on a budget, be wary about committing to the purchase.

Will you require a traditional home inspection when you purchase a resale condominium? Opinions vary. I advise an inspection, especially if the declaration indicates you'll be responsible for the maintenance and replacement of certain building elements, such as your portion of the HVAC system. Have an inspector check these elements before you commit to buying the unit. (An example of a condominium inspection is included in Appendix 1.3.b.)

An inspection may also reveal problems with the maintenance and repair of the building. The reserve fund study can tell you whether there are sufficient funds for anticipated repairs; an inspection may tell you if the building is run down. A building that's slightly worn will probably have some "special assessments" coming up in the near future.

If the unit inspection reveals problems within the unit, you can discuss this with the seller and perhaps negotiate a compromise. You can't negotiate anything after the deal closes.

Weisleder's Wisdom on condominium ownership

1. Condominium ownership provides many of the benefits of home ownership without many of the accompanying maintenance obligations.

2. In a condominium you are part of a democracy. Attend meetings: because you'll be affected by the outcome, so you may as well participate in making the decisions.

3. The main condominium documents are the declaration and the description. These two documents tell you your rights, restrictions, and obligations as a condominium owner.

4. If you fail to pay common expenses, the condominium corporation can sell your unit.

5. Condominium owners are personally responsible for any lawsuits successfully brought against the condominium corporation.

6. Buyers, make any resale condominium purchase conditional on a review of the status certificate, the reserve fund study, and all condominium documents, bylaws, and rules.

7. If you buy a resale condominium, make the purchase conditional on a home inspection of the unit and the building.

THE CONDOMINIUM RESALE AGREEMENT

When you buy a resale condominium unit, you'll be asked to sign a form of the resale agreement of purchase and sale. The agreement has been revised over time to effectively deal with many issues specific to condominium ownership. I'll explain each clause in the agreement. In some cases, I repeat information from Chapter 3, where clauses are similar, for easy reference.

Agreement of Purchase and Sale
Condominium Resale

for use in the Province of Ontario

This Agreement of Purchase and Sale dated this _____ day of

_____ 20_____

BUYER, _____, agrees to purchase from

　　　　(Full legal names of all Buyers)

SELLER, _____, the following

　　　　(Full legal names of all Sellers)

When you buy a condominium, use your full legal name. In some cases, only one buyer signs the offer but title will be placed in the name of two or more owners. And sometimes the buyer who signs the offer does not take title to the property. Every person who signs the offer as a buyer will have a legal obligation to perform everything in the offer, unless there is a clause that limits his or her liability. (The concept of liability is discussed in detail in Chapter 5.) What this means is that once you put your name on the agreement as a buyer, you obligate yourself to be legally responsible to complete any promise you make in the offer, which means paying a certain amount of money to buy a property. If your agreement is accepted and you don't complete the agreement for any reason, you may forfeit your deposit and also may be liable for any other losses the seller suffers because the house didn't sell for the stated price.

If you're not married but are living with a partner and you both put an offer on a condominium, I recommend that you both sign the agreement of purchase and sale, and that you both take title to the property together, to ensure that your ownership interests are protected if you later break up. Unmarried couples are not generally afforded the same kind of protections as married spouses when it comes to real property in Canada; make sure your name always goes on title to any property you purchase with your partner.

Often a seller who gets an offer from a married couple will usually insist that both husband's and wife's names are shown as the buyers for the property. The reason is that sometimes a couple decides to make the offer in the name of the spouse who has no assets, so if anything goes wrong, the couple can limit their liability — the seller may not bother to get damages from someone who has few assets. Or a couple may decide to insert the name of a corporation as the buyer. The reason is that the corporation also has no assets other than the deposit that is being submitted. If the corporation doesn't complete the deal, again there is no further liability on the couple. Sellers who see these maneuvers on an agreement usually insist on a substantial deposit, so that the buyers don't walk away from their commitment.

The agreement should only be signed and submitted when you are seriously interested in purchasing a property. This is also one of the advantages of using a qualified REALTOR®. A buyer salesperson usually qualifies the buyer clients before they make an offer; this invariably gives confidence to the sellers and the sellers' salesperson that the buyers are serious.

When you're the seller, check your title deed, which you received when you purchased your condominium, and use the exact names and spellings registered on title when you fill in the agreement to sell. If the property is registered in the names of husband and wife, then both must sign the agreement as the sellers. If the seller is a corporation, make sure the person signing for the corporation has the authority to bind the corporation to the agreement. If one of the sellers named on the deed has passed away, the will of the deceased owner must first be probated by the estate trustees (formerly referred to as the executors) named in the will. If no dispute arises during the probate, the estate trustees will sign the agreement on behalf of the selling estate. There is an old expression, "Where there's a will . . . there's a relative." Don't assume any probate will proceed smoothly. A disgruntled relative may object to the provisions of a will, and it may take years to resolve the objection. If you are acting as the trustee for an estate, don't enter into agreements for the estate to sell any real estate until you're sure the probate has been completed and you have the authority to deal with the property.

What happens if the property is registered in only one married spouse's name, but it's a matrimonial home — a home that is ordinarily occupied by the spouses and their children as a family residence? In this situation, both spouses have an interest in the home, so the registered owner signs the agreement on the "seller" line and the partner signs in the "spousal consent" section, which is shown on page 296. If a couple has separated but has not signed a separation agreement, and only one spouse is on title and is living in the condominium, both spouses will still have to sign the agreement of purchase and sale, again on the seller line and the spousal consent section. Did you know that couples can have more than one matrimonial home? They can, so the same rules apply for the family cottage or ski chalet that's ordinarily used by the family. If you are buying from a couple going through a divorce, make sure both spouses have accepted the agreement. You don't want to deal with either spouse trying to cancel the agreement later.

Weisleder's Wisdom on buyers and sellers

1. Buyers, submit your offers in your full legal names, especially when two or more people are involved.
2. Sellers, demand a higher deposit if an offer is signed by only one of two spouses, or if an offer is submitted in the

name of a corporation that may have no assets except the deposit.

3. Look at your original deed and make sure the person listed on title to the property signs in the seller line.

4. If the property is owned by a corporation, make sure the person signing for the corporation has the authority to sign for the corporation.

5. When you're acting as a trustee for an estate, be sure that the probate application has been completed before you sign any agreement to sell the property.

6. If a matrimonial home is involved, a non-registered spouse signs the agreement in the spousal consent section.

7. If you are not married and buying a condominium with your partner, make sure your name is registered on title, to adequately protect your interests.

PROPERTY:

a unit in the condominium property located at _____

in the _____ being

Unit No. _____ Level No. _____

Condominium Plan No. _____

Building No. _____ known as _____ No. _____

(Apartment/Townhouse/Suite/Unit)

together with ownership or exclusive use of Parking Space(s)

_____, together with

(Number(s), Level(s))

ownership or exclusive use of Locker(s) _____,

(Number(s), Level(s))

together with Seller's proportionate undivided tenancy-in-common interest in the common elements appurtenant to the Unit as described in the Declaration and Description including the exclusive right to use such other parts of the common elements appurtenant to the Unit as may be specified in the Declaration and Description: the Unit, the proportionate interest in the common elements appurtenant thereto, and the exclusive use portions of the common elements, being herein called the "Property".

Before it is registered, the entire condominium property must be put into the land titles system so there will be no boundary-line issues. Be accurate about the unit number, the level number of your unit, which parking spaces you can use, and your locker. In some condominiums, the parking spaces are recorded as separate units, which may make them easier to buy and sell among unit owners. (If the parking units were created by deed, you can transfer your interest in a parking spot by deed. If the parking space is part of the common elements, and the seller has exclusive use of the space, you'll need approval from the condominium corporation to transfer the exclusive right — that is, the parking space — to another unit owner).

If you're buying apartment 712 in a condominium build-ing, the unit is legally described as Unit 12, Level 7. The condominium corporation number is assigned at the registry office and included in your deed. Make sure the parking-space and locker-unit description in the agreement exactly matches the description given in the status certificate; you may also want to take the status certificate down to the parking lot and make sure you are shown the correct parking space.

The language in the agreement of purchase and sale indi-cates that you're buying the seller's interest in the common elements of the condominium corporation. Your ownership percentage is used to determine how much you pay for the monthly common expenses.

Weisleder's Wisdom on property

1. Make sure that you visit the condominium building and make a note of the actual unit apartment number, parking space, and storage locker.

2. Review the condominium declaration and description to confirm that the parking space and storage locker that you visited is actually the parking space and storage locker described in the Agreement.

3. It will be easier to sell your parking space if it is described as a separate unit in the condominium building, as opposed to your having the exclusive use of this common element.

PURCHASE PRICE: Dollars (CDN$) _____

"Purchase Price" means the total money the seller will receive in exchange for transferring the condominium property to the buyer. Use both words and numbers, the same as when you write a cheque, to avoid any confusion. Often salespeople prepare four copies of the agreement for signature by the buyers and sellers, one each for buyer, seller, buyer's lawyer, and seller's lawyer. Make sure all copies are identical; double check the total purchase price. There was a case where the purchase price was changed from $419,000 to $499,000 on the fourth copy of the offer by an unscrupulous buyer, who never intended to pay $499,000. The buyer used the phony copy to obtain a high-ratio mortgage for $450,000. The buyer used the mortgage proceeds to pay the seller $419,000, then disappeared. The sellers and salespeople were accused of fraud and had to answer questions when the mortgage company investigated. Be careful: even though you're innocent, you may be investigated by police and read about yourself in the local paper. Review every copy of the agreement before you sign.

DEPOSIT: Buyer submits _____
_____Dollars (CDN$)
(Herewith/Upon Acceptance/as otherwise described in this Agreement)

by negotiable cheque payable to _____ "Deposit Holder" to be held in trust pending completion or other termination of this Agreement and to be credited toward the Purchase Price on completion.

For the purposes of this Agreement, "Upon Acceptance" shall mean that the buyer is required to deliver the deposit to the Deposit Holder within 24 hours of the acceptance of this Agreement. The parties to this Agreement hereby acknowledge that, unless otherwise provided for in this Agreement, the Deposit Holder shall place the deposit in trust in the Deposit Holder's non-interest bearing Real Estate Trust Account and no interest shall be earned, received or paid on the deposit.

Buyer agrees to pay the balance as more particularly set out in Schedule A attached.

SCHEDULE(S) A _____ **attached hereto form(s) part of this Agreement.**

For clarity, the deposit should also be listed in both words and numbers, the same as when you're writing a cheque. And you will be writing a cheque: the cheque for the deposit is usually made payable to the listing brokerage and used to pay the commission to the listing brokerage after the transaction is completed. If there is any money left after the commission and the GST are paid, the balance is forwarded to the seller. If the commission plus GST was $12,600 and there was only $10,000 paid as a deposit, then after closing, the lawyer for the seller will pay the balance of $2,600 to the listing broker out of the closing funds received from the buyer.

In most provinces, the deposit monies are paid to the seller "herewith," which means the seller gets the cheque and the signed offer from the buyer at the same time. Or the deposit can be paid "upon acceptance," which means within twenty-four hours of the seller accepting the offer.

In Ontario, though, most salespeople use the words "upon acceptance." Under the *Real Estate and Business Brokers' Act* in Ontario, all listing brokerages must place any deposits they receive into their trust accounts within five days of receipt. If a buyer hands over an offer with a cheque attached, the cheque usually goes immediately into the listing broker's trust account even if the seller hasn't yet accepted the offer. The difficulty occurs if the seller does not accept the offer and the deposit now has to be paid back to the buyer. In order to remove the funds from the listing broker's trust account, both the buyer and seller must agree by signing a mutual release, to confirm that both parties are in agreement to return the deposit. This process can take several days and the buyers will be prevented from using these deposit monies to make an offer on a different property. Since most buyers cannot afford to wait to get their deposit money back, they use the words "upon acceptance" so that they do not have to hand over the deposit unless and until the seller actually accepts their offer.

When the offer is made "upon acceptance," it states further that buyers have twenty-four hours from acceptance to actually pay the deposit. The twenty-four-hour requirement was recently added to the standard form in Ontario to resolve confusion about the meaning of the words "upon acceptance." On the last page of the agreement, in the "Confirmation of Acceptance" section, there is a place to note the date and time the acceptance is completed, so that we can figure out when the twenty-four-hour time period starts. The logical question is then: "What happens if you are late in paying the deposit?" Can the seller sue the buyer? Can either of them get out of the deal?

In the decision of *1473587 Ontario Inc. v. Jackson*, decided in 2005, an offer was prepared by Loblaws to purchase property. The agreement provided that the deposit was due and payable within five days of acceptance. It turned out that, because of an administrative error, the deposit was not delivered until seven days after the date stipulated in the agreement. The seller refused to accept the deposit and took the position that the agreement was over; the seller then sold the property to a different buyer. Loblaws sued and lost. The judge focused on the standard form clause 19 (clause 23, "Time Limits," in the condominium agreement). Clause 19 stated, "Time shall be of the essence of this Agreement," meaning time limits are significant and must be followed. The judge ruled that the delay by Loblaws constituted a fundamental breach of the contract, so the seller could take the position that the agreement was at an end.

As a postscript, the second buyer eventually also failed to close the deal, and Loblaws acquired the property after all. Unfortunately, they incurred thousands of dollars in legal fees before it was all over.

How will this decision affect a buyer who takes more than twenty-four hours to pay a deposit? Could a seller take the position that the deal is over? In a seller's market, where prices are rising, many sellers may say a transaction is over if they know there is another buyer willing to pay more for the property. I don't like litigation. If I was the seller and I tried to cancel a deal, I would be running the risk of the buyer starting a lawsuit and tying up the property in court for several years. If your buyer doesn't get the deposit delivered in time, immediately contact your lawyer for advice. The best solution may be to obtain the deposit from your buyer and close the transaction quickly.

When you're a buyer, you can't predict how your seller is going to react. If you know you'll need two or three days to get the deposit together, then say so in the agreement, so that there is no confusion. Change the twenty-four hours to forty-eight or seventy-two hours, especially if you need to get a bank draft or certified funds, or arrange to courier the deposit to a location in another city. In other provinces, the agreement states that the deposit must be paid "on a certain date." Make sure you write that date in your diary, so the deposit is always paid on time. It's always a good idea to avoid litigation.

What if the deposit cheque bounces? Will the deal be cancelled? Based on the Loblaws decision, a bounced cheque could very well be grounds to cancel an agreement. However, I caution sellers from taking this position. Sometimes cheques bounce for reasons that are beyond the control of the buyer. What I would do is contact my lawyer for instructions. As a seller, for example, you may decide to continue with the deal, provided the buyer increases the amount of the deposit, to give you more assurance that the transaction will indeed close on time.

Sellers, be vigilant about who is writing the cheque for the deposit. A new fraudulent practice has emerged: unscrupulous buyers steal a company cheque from an organization that writes many cheques, then change the "payee" name to the seller's brokerage company. They submit the "deposit" with an agreement and a short home inspection conditional period. Then they cancel the deal, claiming they're not satisfied with the results of the condominium home inspection, and they ask for their money back. The innocent brokerage company writes them a cheque; the buyers take the money and run. You never want to be connected in any way to a fraudulent transaction. When you're accepting an offer, ask where your deposit cheque will be coming from.

More and more sellers and brokerage companies are insisting on certified cheques or bank drafts for all deposits to eliminate bounced or forged cheques. This is perfectly legal; if you're a buyer, agree if you think it's appropriate.

Some buyers think they may sign an agreement, have it accepted by the seller, and then simply get out of the deal by not paying the deposit. Those buyers are wrong. The moment a buyer signs an agreement that is accepted by a seller, the buyer is bound to all the legal promises and obligations described in the offer to purchase, including the obligations to pay the deposit and also the balance due on closing. Suppose, as an example, you sign an agreement as a buyer and agree to pay $400,000 for a condominium property, with a $20,000 deposit, and your offer is accepted by the seller. You then change your mind, decide to keep the $20,000 deposit, and cancel the transaction. If the seller sells the condominium to someone else for $375,000, you may have to make up for the seller's lost $25,000.

Buyers and sellers should know the legal significance of the deposit and a listing brokerage's trust account. A deposit cannot be disbursed from a brokerage's trust account until the transaction closes, or unless there is a mutual release signed by the buyer and seller, or there is a court order. If there is a dispute and the matter goes to court, the deposit is paid to the court or stays in the trust account until the legal matter is decided. If a buyer defaults on an agreement, the court usually determines that the deposit will be forfeited to the seller, even if the seller sells the property for more money later. By paying the deposit, a buyer is paying part of the total purchase price and is also showing good faith; in other words, they are indicating they intend to complete the transaction. A buyer who doesn't close violates this good faith obligation and thus forfeits the deposit.

If a deal falls apart and the seller is awarded the deposit, the listing brokerage can't keep any part of the deposit for themselves unless the seller promised to share it with the listing broker in the listing agreement under these circumstances. Sellers sometimes agree to such a provision in commercial listing agreements, but it's rare in residential listing agreements.

Weisleder's Wisdom on deposits

1. Buyers, all deposits must be paid when stated in the agreement; if you need more time, change the wording on the offer.
2. Sellers, if a deposit is not being paid directly by the buyer, ask where the money is coming from.
3. Consider asking for certified cheques for large deposits.
4. Get a lawyer's advice if a deposit cheque bounces, but avoid litigation, if possible.

The schedules attached to an agreement typically include provisions regarding payment of the balance due on closing, as well as clauses about conditions, representations, warranties and any other matter important to buyers and sellers. These provisions and clauses are discussed in detail in Chapter 3.

1. IRREVOCABILITY: This Offer shall be irrevocable by _____ until _____ a.m./p.m. on the _____ day of
(Seller/Buyer)
_____ 20 _____, after which time, if not accepted, this Offer shall be null and void and the deposit shall be returned to the buyer in full without interest.

Typically, the agreement process starts with a buyer making an offer to a seller. In some provinces, the section where you do this appears at the end of the agreement, just before the buyer signs. No matter where the section is located, the buyer agrees to leave the offer "open" for a specific time, so the seller may consider the offer and then either accept it, reject it, or sign it back with a counter-offer. If the seller signs a counter-offer, then the word "buyer," written in the first blank, is crossed out and replaced with the word "seller," because now it's the seller making an offer to the buyer. In some provinces, there is a separate section for a counter-offer, for greater clarity.

Let's try to understand this process a little more. Although the buyer has agreed to leave the offer "open" for acceptance for perhaps several hours, he or she has not received any money or other consideration for doing this. Therefore, you would think that the buyer could just change their mind and cancel their offer up to the time that the seller actually accepts it.

However, if you look at the back of the offer, beside the area where the buyer and seller sign, are the words, "I have hereunto set my hand and seal." The legal significance of the seal is that it means that the person signing cannot change their mind about anything contained in the offer until the irrevocable date expires. It means that they were so serious about making this offer that it must have been important enough to them that they did not need extra money to leave the offer open for a specific time period. But if an offer is not signed under seal, then a buyer has the right to change their mind and cancel the offer at any time before the seller actually accepts it. Once the seller accepts any offer, whether under seal or not, it is too late for the buyer to change their mind.

If you forget to indicate a time limit in the irrevocable clause, no one will think your offer is open "forever." The law says an untimed offer will remain open for "a reasonable time." So complete this clause very carefully: important legal obligations flow from it.

If you submit a deposit with the offer and the offer is not accepted, the deposit is returned to you. Once an offer is accepted, a deposit can be returned only when the buyer and seller agree by signing a mutual release.

Weisleder's Wisdom on irrevocability

1. When you sign "under seal," it means you can't change your mind.
2. Buyers and sellers, once you sign an agreement "under seal," legal liability ensues, even if the buyer never remits a deposit.
3. If the offer is left open indefinitely, through carelessness, the courts will infer that it is to be left open for only a reasonable period.

---

2. COMPLETION DATE: This Agreement shall be completed by no later than 6:00 p.m. on the _____ day of _____, 20 _____. Upon completion, vacant possession of the Property shall be given to the Buyer unless otherwise provided for in this Agreement.

Think carefully about your completion or closing date. Make sure the date you choose is a regular business day, from Monday to Friday, as title cannot be transferred on a weekend or statutory holiday.

Many buyers automatically choose the last day of a month because they have given notice that they'll be vacating their apartment, or are planning to close the sale of their house on the last day of the month. You may be adding an enormous amount of stress by choosing the same day.

It is always preferable to close the purchase of your condominium a few days before you have to leave your current location, if at all possible, so the entire move-out move-in process is not rushed. If you're living in an apartment, you have to be careful to provide the correct written notice before you leave. There's a thorough discussion of leaving your apartment and the required notices to be given in Chapter 6.

If you are moving out at the end of a month, try to schedule your purchase closing date at least a week before that. This will give you the time to inspect your new condominium, and you can paint, clean, or make minor repairs to get it ready for you to move into. If you don't rush the process, there is also less likelihood of things breaking or being damaged during the move.

If you're selling one condominium and buying another, you can still sell a few days after you purchase. Ask your bank and obtain interim financing, called a "bridge loan," so you can pay for your new condominium before you get the proceeds from selling your old condominium. You have to pay interest on the bridge loan, but the cost of the interest for a few days will be well worth it, and you'll be moving in a much more relaxed atmosphere.

If you're selling a condominium that's rented to tenants, and your buyer has asked for "vacant possession on closing," the tenants must be off the premises. (We discuss this in Chapter 6.) Suffice to say that it may be easier to just pay your tenants an incentive to leave your condominium even before you put it up for sale, to avoid any potential problems on closing.

In Ontario, the clause indicates that the condominium unit must be vacant no later than 6:00 p.m. on the day of closing. In today's environment, lawyers can electronically transfer title from a seller to a buyer from the computers in their offices, and the transaction may be completed as early as 10:00 a.m. on the day of closing. Legally, once the title has been transferred and keys are exchanged, the buyer should have vacant possession. A time of 6:00 p.m. was specified in the agreement because the Ontario government registry offices close at 5:00 p.m., so it's possible to transfer title up to 5:00 p.m.; the extra hour is so the lawyers can still make arrangements if anything goes wrong at the last moment. It happens:

the buyer's funds may not reach the seller's lawyer by five because the courier got stuck in traffic.

If the seller is late in leaving the condominium and granting the buyer vacant possession, and the buyer incurs extra moving expenses as a result, the seller is responsible for the costs. In one case, the seller was not out of the home until after 9:00 p.m. The movers would not wait, and the buyers had to pay to put their goods in storage until they could arrange a new moving time. The seller had to pay these costs. If you're a seller and you believe you'll need more time to move, protect yourself. Insert a clause into the agreement stating that vacant possession will not be granted until, for example, 9:00 p.m. on the date of completion. If you're a buyer, insist on an early time for vacant possession, so you don't incur extra moving expenses.

In other provinces, the agreement indicates the closing date, without reference to a specific time. In my view, the legal principle is still the same: vacant possession must be provided once title has been transferred, which typically occurs during the afternoon. Sellers, if you will require extra time to get everything out of the condominium, add that amount of time to the agreement. No confusion, and no unnecessary moving expenses.

What does the phrase "vacant possession" mean? Can sellers leave unwanted items in the condominium unit? Can they leave you with a very messy condominium? In general, buyers expect an empty home, in a broom-swept condition. In most offers, buyers request this in a specific clause. (The clause is in the Appendix) Sellers, arrange to have all unwanted items, especially large items, such as old furniture or metal bed frames, removed before the closing. These days there are many companies that, for a reasonable fee, will attend at the seller's condominium and remove all unwanted items. If a seller does leave large items and other junk in the condominium or a townhouse garage after closing, a buyer can hire such a company and charge the costs to the seller.

If you're a buyer, don't wait for closing to be "surprised" by a seller's junk. Stay involved. Ask your salesperson to find out if the junk is being removed. Check the condominium during your pre-closing visit to see if the seller is cleaning up. If it's not being done, ask your salesperson to be a pest and offer to arrange a bin for the seller. If you are a seller, leave the condominium the way you want your new home to be left for you.

Weisleder's Wisdom on completion or closing date

1. Make sure the closing date is a regular weekday, not a Saturday or Sunday and not a holiday.
2. Schedule the closing of your condominium purchase to happen before your sale closes or your lease ends.
3. Provide adequate notice to your landlord.
4. Make a deal with your tenants so they'll leave before you put your condominium up for sale.
5. In the agreement, set a specific time vacant possession is to be granted to avoid unnecessary moving costs.
6. Hire a bin company to remove all junk before closing.

---

3. NOTICES: seller hereby appoints the Listing Brokerage as Agent for the purpose of giving and receiving notices pursuant to this Agreement. **Only if the Co-operating Brokerage represents the interests of the buyer in this transaction**, the Buyer hereby appoints the Co-operating Brokerage as Agent for the purpose of giving and receiving notices pursuant to this Agreement. Any notice relating hereto or provided for herein shall be in writing. This offer, any counter offer, notice of acceptance thereof, or any notice shall be deemed given and received, when hand delivered to the address for service provided in the Acknowledgement

below, or where a facsimile number is provided herein, when transmitted electronically to that facsimile number.

FAX No. _____ (For delivery of notices to Seller)

FAX No. _____ (For delivery of notices to Buyer)

The agreement of purchase and sale includes many important provisions, conditions, and obligations. To avoid vagueness, uncertainty, or misunderstanding, almost all notices under the agreement must be given in writing and should be signed by the sellers or the buyers. If buyers want to waive a condition, for example the home inspection condition, they have to sign a waiver, or a "notice of fulfillment of the condition," then hand it to the buyer representative. Clause 6 permits the buyer representative to deliver the notice directly to the listing sales-person or brokerage so the sellers know the condition has been waived. For matters that are fundamental to the validity of the agreement — for example whether the offer has been accepted — the signed agreement is sent directly to the seller or the buyer, as the case may be. There are also guidelines for delivering a notice: by hand to the buyer or seller's address, as shown on the back of the agreement in the acknowledgement section, or by fax to the fax number written into the acknowl-edgement section on the back of the agreement.

We sign the acknowledgement section on the back of the offer to provide confirmation from both seller and buyer that the final acceptance of the agreement has been communicated to both seller and buyer in a timely manner and there are instructions to deliver a copy to the buyer and seller lawyers.

Don't ask your salesperson to sign any notice on your behalf, or initial any changes to the agreement on your behalf. This is how lawsuits get started. Sometimes it's inconvenient to wait up late at night to make sure all signatures and changes are finalized by both parties, but this contract is too important to leave anything to chance.

Buyers and sellers ask whether real estate agreements can be accepted through other electronic means, such as e-mail. If any method of acceptance is not printed on the agreement form, you can't use it. No agreement of purchase and sale form in Canada allows notice to be given via e-mail, but the question is being reviewed, given the realities of the amount of business done over the Internet. Until changes are made in the forms, e-mail is not permitted.

Make sure you initial all changes and finalize everything before the irrevocable date and time noted in clause 1. Until you do, the agreement has not yet been accepted; buyers and sellers could take the position that there is no binding agreement. Be especially careful when there are multiple offers on a property. Work closely with your buyer or seller salespeople to make sure your agreement is signed, accepted, and delivered in a timely manner, and deal with all notices as soon as possible.

Weisleder's Wisdom on notices

1. Buyers and sellers, always personally sign any notice under the agreement.
2. Make sure all notices are signed and delivered to the address noted in the acknowledgement on the back of the offer.
3. Never ask your salesperson to initial any document on your behalf.
4. Electronic methods of giving notice are not yet available in the agreement of purchase and sale forms across Canada.

4. CHATTELS INCLUDED: _____

_____

_____

_____

5. FIXTURES INCLUDED: _____

_____

_____

_____

6. RENTAL ITEMS: The following equipment is rented and not included in the Purchase Price. The Buyer agrees to assume the rental contract(s), if assumable:

_____

_____

_____

One of the more problematic areas between buyers and sellers is the rights and obligations regarding chattels included with the purchase price and fixtures that will be removed or replaced before closing. First, what's a "chattel"? What's a "fixture"? Here's a simple principle to remember: "If it takes a tool, that's the rule."

In other words, if you require a tool to remove something from the condominium, it is most probably a fixture. If you can pull it out easily, like a plug from a wall, it's a chattel. But even with simple principles, it can be very confusing. A front door key is a fixture because it is a part of the front door lock. What about mirrors or sliding doors you can remove by lifting them out of their slots? What about carpets that are not tacked down, or a dishwasher that's connected by a simple valve you can remove with your hand? To avoid confusion later, educate yourself before you list your condominium for sale or put in an offer.

If you're a seller, it's a good idea to remove or replace any fixtures you intend on taking with you when you move. If you want to keep the dining room chandelier, the gold-plated faucets in your bathroom, your drapes, the broadloom, a built-in oven or stove, or any other items you may have an emotional attachment to, take them out of your condominium before you list it. Replace the chandelier with a cheaper version, or make it very clear in the agreement that you're taking the chandelier with you.

When you're a buyer, there is no such thing as too much detail regarding the chattels you expect to receive on closing. My best advice is to list the make and model (and serial numbers, if available) of all appliances that are being included, and also note the colour and location of all drapes, carpeting, and anything else you expect to be in the condominium when you move in. Salespeople may have lengthy lists of chattels and fixtures to help buyers and sellers keep track of what's included and what's not. Leave nothing to chance. During any home inspection, take photographs of all of the chattels and fixtures so you'll know if they've been replaced before the closing. Arrange for a pre-closing visit so you can satisfy yourself that all the chattels and fixtures that are supposed to remain on the property are still there. (There's a clause for the pre-closing visit; see Appendix 1.3.c.) Some chattels and fixtures may contain a seller's personal information, such as family photographs on magnets placed on a fridge; get permission from the seller before you take photographs. Sellers, I encourage you to be cooperative in this regard. Most home inspectors take these pictures anyway, as part of their inspection duties.

Chattels and fixtures are important to sellers and buyers alike. For sellers, remember to leave the home you're selling just the way you want to receive the home you are buying.

What about rental contracts? Some contracts are not transferable. So do your homework: ask about the satellite receivers and any air conditioning unit. The seller may have to incur a penalty for cancelling the contract before it expires. Look at all contracts carefully; ask any rental suppliers if their contracts can be assumed and what costs may be involved. Again, the trick is to have no surprises.

What about the condition of the chattels and fixtures? In most agreements, the buyers typically request that the chattels and fixtures, including all heating, air conditioning, and plumbing, will be "in good working order," or "in working order," on closing (see Appendix 1.1.a and 1.1.b). There is no difference between "working order" and "good working order." Both phrases mean that all chattels and systems will be working when the buyer takes possession of the property. They do not mean the seller warrants that everything will be working one month after closing. Sometimes buyers can't check all the chattels and fixtures on the date of closing; a clause deals with this:

> The seller represents and warrants that all chattels, the furnace and the heating, plumbing and air conditioning systems will be in good working order on closing. This warranty shall survive closing but only to the extent that the said chattels, fixtures and systems are in good working order on closing.

What this clause means is that if there is not enough time on the day you move in to check all the appliances and systems in your condominium, and you find out when you try them a few days later that they are not working, then you can still ask the seller to repair them, as they were likely also not working on the day of closing either.

When we say that a warranty survives closing for a month, it is like a warranty that you receive when you buy an electronic item, like an iPod. It means that if something breaks down during this one-month period, the seller is responsible to repair it. Sellers do not like to give these kinds of warranties on anything in the condominium after they move out because there is always the problem of deciding whose fault it was that the item broke down. That is why, for the most part, sellers only give a warranty that everything will be working on the day you move in and no longer.

If you know that some of your appliances are not working when a buyer submits an offer to buy the condominium, disclose the condition of the appliances immediately. If an appliance breaks down after the agreement has been signed but before closing, the seller has to conduct the repairs.

In a court decision in Ontario, a seller was caught switching appliances after the agreement was signed and before closing. The buyer had video evidence, taken during the home inspection, that clearly showed the appliances — but not the appliances in the house on closing. The sauna wasn't working; some other systems were also not working. The court ordered the seller to pay for replacing the appliances and to repair the sauna and the disabled systems. The seller also had to pay "punitive damages" — an extra $10,000 — for attempting to deceive the buyers. This case serves as a lesson to sellers that this type of behaviour will not be tolerated. It's also a lesson to buyers: make and keep a detailed list or photographs of any chattels or fixtures you expect to receive on closing, and conduct a pre-closing visit to make sure everything you expect to get is still on the property.

**Weisleder's Wisdom on
chattels, fixtures, and rental items**

1. If it takes a tool, that's the rule.
2. Sellers, before you show your condominium to any potential buyers, remove or replace any fixtures or chattels you want to retain after closing.
3. Describe all chattels and fixtures clearly, with make, model, and serial numbers, and photograph where possible.
4. Buyers, always include a pre-closing-visit clause in the agreement, so you can check that all chattels and fixtures are being left behind.

5. Buyers, quickly check all chattels, fixtures, and systems as soon as possible after you take possession, and bring up any problems or questions with the sellers or the seller's salespeople as soon as possible after closing.

6. Contact all rental-contract suppliers to determine what contracts, if any, can be transferred to a buyer; clearly identify the transferrable contracts in the agreement.

7. Sellers, if you know a chattel, fixture, or system is not working on the day an offer is submitted by a buyer, and if you have no intention of repairing the item, provide full disclosure to the buyer before you accept any offer, to avoid any confusion on closing.

8. Sellers, don't switch any chattels or fixtures once the agreement is signed, or you may face legal liability and punitive damages.

7. COMMON EXPENSES: Seller warrants to Buyer that the common expenses presently payable to the Condominium Corporation in respect of the Property are approximately $_____ per month, which amount includes the following: _____

_____

_____

_____

8. PARKING AND LOCKERS: Parking and Lockers are as described above or assigned as follows: _____ at an additional cost of _____

For condominium buyers, the amount of the common expenses payable each month makes up a significant portion of your costs to maintain your unit going forward and you must be careful to insert the exact amount. In addition, you need to make clear whether this also includes the cost to maintain your parking space and storage locker. If there is an extra charge for the parking space and storage locker, then this needs to be detailed in paragraph 8 as well. As noted above, a failure to pay common expenses when due can result in liens being placed on your unit by the condominium corporation as well as a possible sale of your unit by the condominium corporation if the default is not remedied.

> **9. GST:** If this transaction is subject to Goods and Services Tax (GST), then such tax shall be _____ the
> (included in/in addition to)
> Purchase Price. If this transaction is not subject to GST, Seller agrees to certify on or before closing, that the transaction is not subject to GST.

Virtually all residential resale transactions, whether single-family dwellings or condominiums, are not normally subject to GST, so usually buyers will always insert the words "included in" for this clause, so they won't be subject to any additional payment of GST. For example, if your purchase price is $105,000 with GST included, and it later turns out that GST should have been collected on the transaction, the purchase price will be changed to $100,000, plus $5,000 GST. The seller remits the $5,000 to Revenue Canada, and the buyer's purchase price remains unchanged. This process can be very costly to sellers, who may not know whether GST is in fact payable. If you have run a business out of your condominium or are writing off any expenses related to your home against your business, you may have to charge GST on part or all of the purchase price, in which case you'll insert the words "in addition to" in this clause.

If you do run a home business, consult your accountant and find out your tax status before you place your condominium on the market. If you find out you have to charge GST, immediately advise your listing broker.

In Nova Scotia, New Brunswick, and Newfoundland and Labrador, there is already a harmonized sales tax (HST), which includes provincial sales tax on the sale of certain real estate. An example of an HST clause is:

All conveyances of real property are subject to the Harmonized Sales Tax ("HST"), unless the conveyance is specifically exempt pursuant to the Excise Tax Act. The facts required to determine exemption from HST are entirely dependent upon the use of the property by the seller and are therefore accordingly within the knowledge of the seller only. The conveyance contemplated by this Agreement shall be:

Exempt from HST

Not exempt from HST; included in the purchase price

Not exempt from HST; over and above the purchase price

The printed agreements in the HST provinces ask the seller to state if the property is exempt from HST; if the buyer will have to pay HST on closing; or if the HST is included in the purchase price. The HST can increase the cost of the home significantly. In its 2009 budget, the Ontario government announced a similar HST, scheduled to apply to new-home and new-condominium purchases with a value of more than $400,000, commencing July 1, 2010. Exemptions may be considered and passed by the Ontario government before July 1, 2010.

10. TITLE SEARCH: Buyer shall be allowed until 6:00 p.m. on the _____ day of _____, 20_____, (Requisition Date) to examine the title to the Property at Buyer's own expense and until the earlier of: (i) thirty days from the later of the Requisition Date or the date on which the conditions in this Agreement are fulfilled or otherwise waived or; (ii) five days prior to completion, to satisfy Buyer that there are no outstanding work orders or deficiency notices affecting the Property, and that its present use (_____

_____) may be lawfully continued. If within that time any valid objection to title or to any outstanding work order or deficiency notice, or to the fact the said present use may not lawfully be continued, is made in writing to Seller and which Seller is unable or unwilling to remove, remedy or satisfy or obtain insurance in favour of the Buyer and any mortgagee, (with all related costs at the expense of the Seller), and which Buyer will not waive, this Agreement notwithstanding any intermediate acts or negotiations in respect of such objections, shall be at an end and all monies paid shall be returned without interest or deduction and Seller, Listing Brokerage and Co-operating Brokerage shall not be liable for any costs or damages. Save as to any valid objection so made by such day and except for any objection going to the root of the title, buyer shall be conclusively deemed to have accepted Seller's title to the Property. Seller hereby consents to the municipality or other governmental agencies releasing to buyer details of all outstanding work orders and deficiency notices affecting the Property, and Seller agrees to execute and deliver such further authorizations in this regard as Buyer may reasonably require.

11. TITLE: Buyer agrees to accept title to the Property subject to all rights and easements registered against title for the supply and installation of telephone services, electricity, gas, sewers, water, television cable facilities and other related services; provided that title to the Property is otherwise good and free from all encumbrances except: (a) as herein expressly provided; (b) any registered restrictions, conditions or covenants that run with the land provided such have been complied with; (c) the provisions of the Condominium Act and its Regulations and the terms, conditions and provisions of the Declaration, Description and By-laws, Occupancy Standards By-laws, including the Common Element Rules and other Rules and Regulations; and (d) any existing municipal agreements, zoning by-laws and/or regulations and utilities or service contracts.

Due to the fact that all condominiums are registered in the land titles system, it is unlikely that a buyer's lawyer will find any title defects that may permit a buyer to refuse to complete a transaction. The main difference between these clauses and the similar clauses in the Residential Agreement found as Paragraphs 8 and 10 in Chapter 3 is that the buyer is also accepting the terms of all the condominium documents that are registered against the title to the condominium.

12. CLOSING ARRANGEMENTS: Where each of the Seller and Buyer retain a lawyer to complete the Agreement of Purchase and Sale of the Property, and where the transaction will be completed by electronic registration pursuant to Part III of the Land Registration Reform Act, R.S.O. 1990, Chapter L4 and the Electronic Registration Act, S.O. 1991, Chapter 44, and any amendments thereto, the Seller and Buyer acknowledge and agree that the exchange of closing funds, nonregistrable documents and other items (the "Requisite Deliveries") and the release thereof to the Seller and Buyer will (a) not occur at the same time as the registration of the transfer/deed (and any other documents intended to be registered in connection with the completion of this transaction) and (b) be subject to conditions whereby the lawyer(s) receiving any of the Requisite Deliveries will be required to hold same in trust and not release same except in accordance with the terms of a document registration agreement between the said lawyers. The Seller and Buyer irrevocably instruct the said lawyers to be bound by the document registration agreement which is recommended from time to time by the Law Society of Upper Canada. Unless otherwise agreed to by the lawyers, such exchange of the Requisite Deliveries will occur in the applicable Land Titles Office or such other location agreeable to both lawyers.

There has been an increase in fraudulent activity relating to real estate in the past several years. Phony buyers forge certified cheques or bank drafts to buy a property, wait until the funds are paid out by lawyers or brokerage companies, then disappear. In this clause, sellers and buyers give their respective lawyers authority to complete the registration and closing of a real estate transaction via electronic means. Registration of the deed on the title register can be done electronically, and so can the wiring of funds directly from the buyer lawyer's bank account to the seller lawyer's bank account. Law firms and brokerage companies may require that all funds from a buyer are deposited by wire directly from the buyer bank to the brokerage or law firm trust account. This system will provide a clear electronic verification that funds are, in fact, on deposit and available for transfer on closing, and will protect against fraud.

13. STATUS CERTIFICATE AND MANAGEMENT OF CONDOMINIUM: Seller represents and warrants to Buyer that there are no special assessments contemplated by the Condominium Corporation, and there are no legal actions pending by or against or contemplated by the Condominium Corporation. The Seller consents to a request by the Buyer or the Buyer's authorized representative for a Status Certificate from the Condominium Corporation. Buyer acknowledges that the Condominium Corporation may have entered into a Management Agreement for the management of the condominium property.

In this clause, sellers are saying that, as far as they know, the condominium corporation is not planning any "special assessments" — extra fees for unit owners. They're also saying they haven't heard that the corporation is having any legal troubles, but that you may ask to see the corporation's status certificate. Buyers, if there is a special assessment coming, you will have to pay for it. And if the corporation is in legal trouble, so are you. You should definitely request a status certificate.

14. DOCUMENTS AND DISCHARGE: Buyer shall not call for the production of any title deed, abstract, survey or other evidence of title to the Property except such as are in the possession or control of Seller. Seller agrees to deliver to Buyer, if it is possible without incurring any costs in so doing, copies of all current condominium documentation of the Condominium Corporation, including the Declaration, Description, By-laws, Common Element Rules and Regulations and the most recent financial statements of the Condominium Corporation. If a discharge of any Charge/ Mortgage held by a corporation incorporated pursuant to the Trust And Loan Companies Act (Canada), Chartered Bank, Trust Company, Credit Union, Caisse Populaire or Insurance Company and which is not to be assumed by Buyer on completion, is not available in registrable form on completion, Buyer agrees to accept Seller's lawyer's personal undertaking to obtain, out of the closing funds, a discharge in registrable form and to register same, or cause same to be registered, on title within a reasonable period of time after completion, provided that on or before completion Seller shall provide to Buyer a mortgage statement prepared by the mortgagee setting out the balance required to obtain the discharge, and, where a real-time electronic cleared funds transfer system is not being used, a direction executed by Seller directing payment to the mortgagee of the amount required to obtain the discharge out of the balance due on completion.

This paragraph contains two separate topics. The first sentence discusses the seller's obligation regarding the survey and any other title document in his or her possession. The rest of the paragraph describes how a bank mortgage or a mortgage from another lending institution is discharged from title.

The survey clause

The first sentence says sellers must provide buyers with any survey or other title document, for example a sketch, that they have in their possession. Since every condominium is registered in the land titles system, there will always be an up-to-date survey of the land that is included as part of the condominium description, and the outside boundary lines of the entire condominium building are guaranteed to be correct by the province. When you are buying a townhouse, with a private backyard, you may want to check the survey a little more carefully.

The mortgage discharge

Most sellers will have a mortgage on their condominium, and most of these mortgages will need to be discharged when the sale closes. Yet the practical reality is that it usually takes three to four weeks for a bank to process the discharge document that will be registered on title. When the buyer acquires title to the condominium from the seller, the seller's mortgage will still stay on title for a few weeks after closing, so the bank can process the discharge. This section of the agreement provides a mechanism so the lawyers can deal with the slowness of the banks. The seller's lawyer provides a discharge statement from the bank showing exactly how much money is required to discharge the mortgage on closing. The buyer writes a cheque for this amount as part of the closing proceeds. The seller's lawyer delivers the cheque directly to the bank that holds the mortgage. The seller's lawyer then agrees to register the discharge as soon as he or she receives it from the bank, and to notify the buyer's lawyer of the details. However, this process applies only for mortgages from banks, trust companies, credit unions, and insurance companies. If you have a private mortgage on your property, for example if a relative lent you money, you have to discharge your debt on or before closing, and get a written discharge. You will have to make arrangements with your relative to come in and sign the discharge paper at the lawyer's office before your deal closes, so that upon closing, your lawyer registers the discharge.

15. MEETINGS: Seller represents and warrants to Buyer that at the time of the acceptance of this Offer the Seller has not received a notice convening a special or general meeting of the Condominium Corporation respecting (a) the termination of the government of the condominium property; (b) any substantial alteration in or substantial addition to the common elements or the renovation thereof; OR (c) any substantial change in the assets or liabilities of the Condominium Corporation; and Seller covenants that if Seller receives any such notice prior to the date of completion Seller shall forthwith notify Buyer in writing and Buyer may thereupon at Buyer's option declare this Agreement to be null and void and all monies paid by Buyer shall be refunded without interest or deduction.

In this clause, sellers list three meetings they have *not* received notices about. The first is a meeting to change the corporation's government — the people who run the building. Second is a meeting about alterations to the common elements in the building. Third is a meeting about changes to the condominium's assets or liabilities. If the condominium corporation *does* set up a meeting about any of these topics, buyers need to know, because any of these three changes would probably make a very large change in the cost of living in the building. This clause is part of the concept of full disclosure we discussed in Chapter 2, the section about preparing to sell property.

16. INSPECTION: Buyer acknowledges having had the opportunity to inspect the Property and understands that upon acceptance of this offer there shall be a binding agreement of purchase and sale between Buyer and Seller. **The Buyer acknowledges**

having the opportunity to include a requirement for a property inspection report in this Agreement and agrees that except as may be specifically provided for in this Agreement, the Buyer will not be obtaining a property inspection or property inspection report regarding the property.

The first thing you notice about this paragraph is the bold print. Then you may notice that the first sentence appears to be unnecessary. Isn't it obvious that when the offer is accepted there will be a binding agreement between the seller and the buyer? But in fact, the first sentence says much more: it states that the buyer has had the opportunity to inspect the property. *Then* it states that the buyer's acceptance of the offer means there's no going back on the deal. In between the inspection and the acceptance, there are all those obvious defects in the property the buyer should have noticed and now has accepted. A "defect" would include cracked tiles on the floor that you can easily see. If you don't say in the agreement that the seller will repair the cracks in the tiles, the legal doctrine of *caveat emptor* — buyer beware — applies. Unless you specify them and state that the seller will repair them, you must accept every patent defect that was in the condominium the day you signed the agreement. If, on the other hand, the tiles cracked after you signed the agreement and before closing, the seller is responsible for making the repair. Insist on a pre-closing visit, to make sure the condominium is exactly as it was on the date you signed the agreement of purchase and sale.

"Latent," or hidden, defects are not easily observable during a routine inspection. These can include leaks from the roof or basement, cracks in the foundation, or the presence of asbestos or other potentially dangerous insulation, all of which should be disclosed in any status certificate.

Sellers, be up front about all defects you're aware of. You don't want legal proceedings after closing.

As discussed at the beginning of this chapter, it is always advisable to make any resale condominium agreement conditional on the buyer being satisfied with the results of a home inspection report.

17. APPROVAL OF THE AGREEMENT: In the event that consent to this sale is required to be given by the Condominium Corporation or the Board of Directors, the Seller will apply forthwith for the requisite consent, and if such consent is refused, then this Agreement shall be null and void and the deposit monies paid hereunder shall be refunded without interest or other penalty to the Buyer.

In most condominium declarations, unit sales don't have to be approved by the condominium corporation or the board of directors. Check your declaration carefully: if it asks for approval, you have to comply. If you don't get approval, your sale will be cancelled. Co-operatives almost always require approval, because the owners are much more reliant on each other; if you sell to someone who doesn't pay on time, every owner in the co-op feels the effect.

18. INSURANCE: The Unit and all other things being purchased shall be and remain at the risk of the Seller until completion. In the event of substantial damage to the Property Buyer may at Buyer's option either permit the proceeds of insurance to be used for repair of such damage in accordance with the provisions of the Insurance Trust Agreement, or terminate this Agreement and all deposit monies paid by Buyer hereunder shall be refunded without interest or deduction. If Seller is taking back a Charge/Mortgage, or Buyer is assuming a Charge/Mortgage, Buyer shall supply

Seller with reasonable evidence of adequate insurance to protect
Seller's or other mortgagee's interest on completion.

The insurance clause

This clause says it's the responsibility of the seller to maintain
the property until closing. Say you're buying: there is a fire in
the condominium unit or the building and the unit is substantially damaged. You have two choices: take the insurance
proceeds and complete the transaction, or refuse to close. You
have to decide by the closing date, even though you probably
won't know by the closing date, if the insurance company will
pay the claim, or how much they'll pay. If the insurer suspects
the fire was deliberately set, or that the condominium owner
or condominium corporation violated a provision of the
policy, they may refuse coverage entirely. Most buyers who are
put into this position refuse to complete the transaction.

If you're buying, always include a pre-closing site visit to
the property to make sure there has been no damage since you
signed the agreement. And ask your buyer salesperson to confirm that the seller has removed any junk that has
accumulated in or on the property. It's much easier to conduct
the final site inspection if you don't have to move any junk to
get a good look at the place. And make sure the seller hasn't
replaced any appliances with cheaper models.

No insurance is transferred on closing. Sellers cancel their
policies on the day of closing; buyers obtain insurance that
will become effective on the day of closing. In condominiums,
the condominium corporation takes out an insurance policy
to cover the building itself, and the owners pay their share of
the cost of the policy as part of their common expenses. But
the unit owners also need to take out their own individual
insurance for all of their contents and any improvements that
they make to their unit.

19. DOCUMENT PREPARATION: The Transfer/Deed shall, save for the Land Transfer Tax Affidavit, be prepared in registrable form at the expense of Seller, and any Charge/Mortgage to be given back by the Buyer to Seller at the expense of the Buyer.

It is the seller's responsibility to prepare the deed that will be delivered to the buyer on closing. It is the buyer's responsibility to prepare the land transfer tax affidavit and any mortgage documentation needed for the transaction. In Ontario, because most lawyers now use the electronic method of registration, the buyer's and seller's lawyers have the authority to complete this information on behalf of their clients.

20. RESIDENCY: Buyer shall be credited toward the Purchase Price with the amount, if any, necessary for Buyer to pay to the Minister of National Revenue to satisfy Buyer's liability in respect of tax payable by Seller under the non-residency provisions of the Income Tax Act by reason of this sale. Buyer shall not claim such credit if Seller delivers on completion the prescribed certificate or a statutory declaration that Seller is not then a non-resident of Canada.

What if a person selling a condominium is not a resident of Canada? In this clause, sellers provide proof that they are residents of Canada, typically by a sworn statement. Sellers who are not residents of Canada must pay any income taxes owing on the property before closing, and they must obtain a certificate from the Canada Revenue Agency (CRA) saying that all taxes have been paid. If the seller does not provide the certificate, the buyer is entitled to hold back twenty-five percent of the entire purchase price and send it in to the CRA.

If you are not a resident of Canada but you're selling a condominium here, ask your accountant what your tax liabilities will be, if any, and how much time it will take to complete your filings with the CRA.

If you are a seller and a resident of Canada, you'll be asked to provide a sworn statement to the buyer on closing stating that you are not a non-resident of Canada.

21. ADJUSTMENTS: Common Expenses; realty taxes, including local improvement rates; mortgage interest; rentals; unmetered public or private utilities and fuel where billed to the Unit and not the Condominium Corporation; are to be apportioned and allowed to the day of completion, the day of completion itself to be apportioned to the Buyer. There shall be no adjustment for the Seller's share of any assets or liabilities of the Condominium Corporation including any reserve or contingency fund to which Seller may have contributed prior to the date of completion.

The purpose of this clause is to balance accounts between the buyer and the seller on closing. The general principle is that the seller is responsible for all costs and is entitled to all rents on the property up to the day *before* closing, and the buyer is responsible for all costs and is entitled to any rents on the property from the day of closing and in the future.

The most common adjustments are the monthly common expense payments and the property taxes. Let's say the property taxes for the year are $365 and the transaction closes on November 1. The seller has already paid all the taxes for the year but is responsible only up to October 31, the day before closing. The buyer is responsible from November 1 to December 31, sixty-one days. The buyer pays the seller $61 on closing, so the tax account is balanced. This balancing is called an "adjustment."

If the property has tenants, adjustments will be made for the rent. If closing day is the fifteenth of the month, the buyer is entitled to all rent from the fifteenth day to the end of the month. The adjustment is made on closing.

There is also no adjustment for anything in the reserve fund. These monies are for the benefit of all the owners, and are used to make timely repairs and replacements in the condominium as they are required.

Because some items can only be estimated on the closing date, buyers and sellers usually agree to co-operate after closing if there are any errors in the adjustments.

I encourage buyers to discuss all adjustments with their salesperson before they sign any agreement of purchase and sale, so they have enough money to complete the transaction on the closing date.

22. PROPERTY ASSESSMENT: The Buyer and Seller hereby acknowledge that the Province of Ontario has implemented current value assessment and properties may be re-assessed on an annual basis. The Buyer and Seller agree that no claim will be made against the Buyer or Seller, or any Brokerage or Salesperson, for any changes in property tax as a result of a re-assessment of the Property.

Clause 22 reflects the current reality that provincial tax assessments of properties take a long time. The impacts of assessments may not affect your property tax bill for several years. Yet the impact can mean a dramatic increase or decrease in your property taxes. The increase or decrease is not retroactive, it is only on a going-forward basis. As a result, in this clause, the buyer and seller confirm that they will not make any claim against each other should taxes increase or decrease in the future. The situation may be different if the seller has actual knowledge that his or her taxes are going to rise dramatically and hides this information from the buyer. When you're buying a condominium, ask the seller about any assessment notices that may have been sent by the local municipality.

23. TIME LIMITS: Time shall in all respects be of the essence hereof provided that the time for doing or completing of any matter provided for herein may be extended or abridged by an agreement in writing signed by Seller and Buyer or by their respective lawyers who may be specifically authorized in that regard.

In other words, every deadline in the agreement of purchase and sale is very important and must be adhered to. A deadline can only be changed if both buyer and seller agree in writing, or if their lawyers agree in writing.

The decision of *1473587 Ontario Inc. v. Jackson* illustrated the importance of this clause. The buyer was late paying a deposit; the judge allowed the seller to terminate the agreement. In the reasoning, the judge said that even if the deposit was paid ten minutes late, it was too late. Pay attention to every date in your agreement, whether it's the date conditions expire or the time deposits must be paid. If you miss a deadline, you could jeopardize your purchase or sale.

Sometimes judges look at the behaviour of a buyer or seller to determine the reason for a missed deadline. In the case of *Walker v. Jones*, decided in 2008 in Ontario, the buyer was thirty minutes late delivering the closing monies to the seller's lawyer. The seller tried to cancel the transaction. The judge reviewed the facts of the case and found out why the buyer was late in delivering the funds: the seller made it difficult for the buyer's mortgage appraiser to view the property so the mortgage could be approved. Then the seller's lawyer was late giving the buyer's lawyer closing instructions for paying the funds. The judge found that the buyer was ready to complete the transaction on closing, and ordered the seller to sell the property to the buyer on the terms indicated in the agreement.

This case tells us that when you're buying, it's a good idea to understand how your bank approves a mortgage loan. Lenders get credit approval of the buyer, but they also make sure the property is worth what you've offered to pay for it. Ask your bank to complete the appraisal as soon as possible, so you'll have your loan in time for the closing.

This case also illustrates a lesson for sellers: don't rush to litigation because a buyer is a few minutes late paying a deposit or any closing funds. You may not win in court. Buyers, be diligent about honouring your time limits.

> **24. TENDER:** Any tender of documents or money hereunder may be made upon Seller or Buyer or their respective lawyers on the day set for completion. Money may be tendered by bank draft or cheque certified by a Chartered Bank, Trust Company, Province of Ontario Savings Office, Credit Union or Caisse Populaire.

Buyers and sellers must be able to demonstrate that they're ready, willing, and able to complete the transaction on the date set for closing. Buyers, this means you must have the money available on closing. Sellers, you must have the deed signed and ready for delivery. You must be able to prove you have satisfied all the buyer's objections about title, zoning and work orders on the property. And you must have the keys ready to hand over.

All this proof-of-readiness becomes necessary if one side cannot close a transaction, for example if the buyers can't come up with the closing funds. If the sellers want to commence legal proceedings against the buyers, the sellers have to demonstrate that on the day of closing, they were ready to close. How do you demonstrate this? The lawyer for the seller attends upon (that means the lawyer goes to the office of) the lawyer for the buyer with all the required documents, including the signed deed, to prove the sellers are ready to close the transaction.

> **25. FAMILY LAW ACT:** seller warrants that spousal consent is not necessary to this transaction under the provisions of the Family

Law Act, R.S.O. 1990 unless seller's spouse has executed the consent hereinafter provided.

The only time you need someone other than the registered owner to sign a deed is when the owner is married and the property is used as a family residence. If that's your situation, your spouse must consent to the transaction by signing the agreement of purchase and sale and by signing the deed.

Common-law spouses are not included in this definition; they don't need to sign unless their name is on title. (There is complete information about family law in Chapter 7.)

26. UFFI: Seller represents and warrants to Buyer that during the time Seller has owned the Property, Seller has not caused any building on the Property to be insulated with insulation containing ureaformaldehyde, and that to the best of Seller's knowledge no building on the Property contains or has ever contained insulation that contains ureaformaldehyde. This warranty shall survive and not merge on the completion of this transaction, and if the building is part of a multiple unit building, this warranty shall only apply to that part of the building which is the subject of this transaction.

Ureaformaldehyde — UFFI — is a foam insulation that was used in new homes across Canada in the 1970s. In the 1990s, there were fears that the insulation could cause a health danger to people living in UFFI-insulated homes. There was an extensive campaign to remove the insulation from these homes. Even after the insulation was removed, the home carried a stigma that reduced its market value. More recent studies have indicated that the danger to humans may have been overstated. Home inspectors still search for ureaformaldehyde.

In the clause, the sellers indicate that when they owned the condominium, they did not insulate it with ureaformaldehyde. They also indicate that, to the best of their knowledge and belief, the condominium building is not insulated with ureaformaldehyde.

27. CONSUMER REPORTS: The Buyer is hereby notified that a consumer report containing credit and/or personal information may be referred to in connection with this transaction.

The first thing people notice about this section is that it is in bold type. The clause tells buyers that a seller can get their credit checked. In Ontario, sellers have this right through the *Consumer Reporting Act*, which governs how credit bureaus are permitted to use information they collect on consumers in the province of Ontario.

The act says that consumers must consent to having their credit checked. The consent must be requested in writing, in bold type, to make sure the consumers pay attention. In other words, before a seller can conduct a credit check, the buyer has to consent.

Sellers often get a credit check if the agreement says the sellers have agreed to take back a mortgage as part of the purchase price. Buyers with poor credit histories may not make the mortgage payments. (To collect from a buyer who can't make the mortgage payments, the seller has to sell the property under the power of sale provisions contained in the mortgage.)

If the seller sees the credit report and then refuses to complete the transaction with the buyer, the seller must tell the buyer. If the buyer asks where the seller got the credit information, the seller must tell.

Similar legislation applies in the other provinces and in the territories. Sellers, ask for legal advice whenever your transaction involves a credit check on a buyer.

28. AGREEMENT IN WRITING: If there is conflict or discrepancy between any provision added to this Agreement (including any Schedule attached hereto) and any provision in the standard pre-set portion hereof, the added provision shall supersede the standard pre-set provision to the extent of such conflict or discrepancy. This Agreement including any Schedule attached hereto, shall constitute the entire Agreement between Buyer and Seller. There is no representation, warranty, collateral agreement or condition, which affects this Agreement other than as expressed herein. For the purposes of this Agreement, Seller means vendor and Buyer means purchaser. This Agreement shall be read with all changes of gender or number required by the context.

This clause has five parts.

In the first part, buyer and seller acknowledge that if there is anything written in any schedule that conflicts with the printed form, the written-in part takes precedence. For example, if the buyer adds a clause saying the seller must provide an up-to-date survey for the townhouse, and the printed form says a seller must only provide any survey in his or her possession, the seller must provide an up-to-date survey.

The second clause says that what is written in this agreement is the entire agreement; no oral agreements apply anymore.

The third provision states that no "representation, warranty, collateral agreement or condition" can affect the agreement other than what is stated expressly in the agreement. This clause discourages people from saying later that they were promised things they didn't get. If it's not written down, you don't get it.

If there is ambiguity in the agreement, a court may hear evidence from the buyer and seller as they try to explain what they think the agreement means. Be careful to review your agreement with your real estate salesperson to make sure everything you want is in the agreement.

What if a listing advertises special features — say, granite countertops or hardwood under the carpet — but the features are not mentioned in the agreement? If the countertops are important to you, make sure they're mentioned in the agreement.

The fourth part of the clause states that "Seller" means "vendor" and "Buyer" means "purchaser." Many lawyers still use the terms "vendor" and "purchaser" to describe sellers and buyers, and this is also true across Canada. To avoid any ambiguity, we state that the terms mean the same thing.

The fifth statement is designed to fix up any gender or number errors in the document.

Weisleder's Wisdom on the entire agreement clause

1. If something is important to you as a buyer, make sure it gets included in the agreement. This includes any promises made by the seller.
2. Review the agreement to make sure your salesperson has accurately addressed all your concerns.

29. TIME AND DATE: Any reference to a time and date in this Agreement shall mean the time and date where the Property is located.

This clause acknowledges that buyers and sellers may be in different time zones while they're negotiating. If the agreement says the seller has until 11:00 p.m. to accept the offer, there may be confusion if the seller happens to live in B.C. — 11:00 p.m. in B.C. is 2:00 a.m. the next morning in Ontario. This clause was inserted so that any time periods relate to the time period where the property is located, not where the seller or buyer happen to be.

30. SUCCESSORS AND ASSIGNS: The heirs, executors, administrators, successors and assigns of the undersigned are bound by the terms herein.

If anyone who signed the agreement dies, the agreement is still binding on his or her estate. If anyone assigns any rights under the agreement to anyone else, the person who receives the rights is also bound by the terms of the agreement. (For information about the consequences of assignments and property flips, see Chapter 5.)

SIGNED, SEALED   IN WITNESS
AND DELIVERED   whereof I have
in the presence of: hereunto set my hand and seal:

_____   _____   ✳ DATE _____
_____   _____   ✳ DATE _____
(Witness)   (Buyer)   (Seal)

I, the Undersigned Seller, agree to the above Offer. I hereby irrevocably instruct my lawyer to pay directly to the Listing Brokerage the unpaid balance of the commission together with applicable Goods and Services Tax (and any other taxes as may hereafter be applicable), from the proceeds of the sale prior to any payment to the undersigned on completion, as advised by the Listing Brokerage to my lawyer.

SIGNED, SEALED   IN WITNESS
AND DELIVERED   whereof I have
in the presence of: hereunto set my hand and seal:

_____   _____   ✳ DATE _____
_____   _____   ✳ DATE _____
(Witness)   (Buyer)   (Seal)

The agreement must be signed by both buyer and seller to be enforceable. Sometimes a buyer or seller is not present, and the signing is done and communicated through the fax machine. This is contemplated in clause 3 of the agreement, which gives buyers and sellers the right to deliver the accepted contract through a fax machine.

Signatures are witnessed as proof that someone saw a buyer and a seller actually sign the agreement, so no one can deny signing. Your witness needs to be in the room with you when you sign; if you're faxing your agreement, you can't ask the person on the receiving end of your fax to witness your signature. Try and find someone who is physically with you to act as the witness to your signature, if possible.

As indicated in the discussion of clause 1, irrevocability, when you sign the agreement under seal, you cannot change your mind until the time limit passes. Make sure you are serious and have received expert advice before you sign any agreement to buy or sell a condominium property.

If the buyer's deposit isn't enough to pay all the commission and GST, the seller asks his or her lawyer to pay them once the deal is completed.

SPOUSAL CONSENT: The Undersigned Spouse of the Seller hereby consents to the disposition evidenced herein pursuant to the provisions of the Family Law Act, R.S.O.1990, and hereby agrees with the Buyer that he/she will execute all necessary or incidental documents to give full force and effect to the sale evidenced herein.

_____   _____

(Witness)   (Spouse)

✳ DATE _____

(Seal)

If the condominium is a matrimonial home (see Chapter 7) and is registered in the name of only one of the married spouses, the other spouse must sign the agreement here, to indicate his or her consent to the sale. The clause is included because both spouses have matrimonial rights to the property.

CONFIRMATION OF ACCEPTANCE: Notwithstanding anything contained herein to the contrary, I confirm this Agreement with all changes both typed and written was finally accepted by all parties at _____ a.m./p.m. this _____ day of _____, 20_____   _____
                         (Signature of Seller or Buyer)

The last person to accept the agreement indicates the date and time, so everyone will know exactly what time the deposit is due. The buyer has twenty-four hours after acceptance to deliver the deposit cheque to the listing broker, when it states in the agreement that the deposit is payable "Upon Acceptance."

INFORMATION ON BROKERAGE(S)
Listing Brokerage _____ Tel. No. (_____)_____
_____
Co-op/Buyer Brokerage _____ Tel. No. (_____)_____
_____

You name your brokerage company here so both buyer and seller confirm that they know about the agent relationship and where to send any notices or waivers.

ACKNOWLEDGEMENT

I acknowledge receipt of my signed copy of this accepted Agreement of Purchase and Sale and I authorize the Agent to forward a copy to my lawyer.

_____ DATE _____

(Seller)

_____ DATE _____

(Seller)

Address for Service: _____

_____ Tel. No. (_____)_____

Seller's Lawyer _____

Address _____

(_____)_____   (_____)_____

Tel. No.   FAX No.

I acknowledge receipt of my signed copy of this accepted Agreement of Purchase and Sale and I authorize the Agent to forward a copy to my lawyer.

_____ DATE _____

(Buyer)

_____ DATE _____

(Buyer)

Address for Service: _____

_____ Tel. No. (_____)_____

Buyer's Lawyer _____

Address _____

(_____)_____   (_____)_____

Tel. No.   FAX No.

Both buyer and seller must receive a copy of the final acceptance of the agreement. Both buyer and seller sign the acknowledgement section to confirm that the final notice has been communicated before the deadline. It's best to hand-deliver the copies to the address for service shown in this section.

FOR OFFICE USE ONLY

COMMISSION TRUST AGREEMENT

To: Co-operating Brokerage shown on the foregoing Agreement of Purchase and Sale:

In consideration for the Co-operating Brokerage procuring the foregoing Agreement of Purchase and Sale, I hereby declare that all moneys received or receivable by me in connection with the Transaction as contemplated in the MLS® Rules and Regulations of my Real Estate Board shall be receivable and held in trust. This agreement shall constitute a Commission Trust Agreement as defined in the MLS® Rules and shall be subject to and governed by the MLS® Rules pertaining to Commission Trust.

DATED as of the date and time of the acceptance of the foregoing Agreement of Purchase and Sale. Acknowledged by:

_____

(Authorized to bind the Listing Brokerage)

_____

(Authorized to bind the Co-operating Brokerage)

The commission trust agreement protects real estate sales-people when a listing brokerage goes bankrupt before a transaction closes and the deposit is still in the broker's trust account. The money goes to the salespeople, and not to other creditors of the business. Every listing brokerage carries deposit protection insurance, so buyers and sellers are insured if anything happens to the deposit monies before the closing.

Brokerage companies have gone bankrupt recently in Toronto; the Real Estate Council of Ontario stepped in and froze their trust accounts. The deposits of consumers are always insured and protected.

SPECIAL PROVISIONS: APPROVAL OF CERTIFICATE OF STATUS

In Appendix 1.2 there is a clause making the transaction conditional on buyers and their lawyers being satisfied with a review of the status certificate issued by the condominium corporation. Buyers, it's best that you understand all the costs you may be assuming when you buy a unit; you should also understand all your rights, restrictions, and obligations. You'll find these in the corporation's declaration, description, bylaws, and rules.

When you're choosing a real estate salesperson, ask them about their experience with the condominium buildings you're interested in. In many cases, real estate salespeople are familiar with the condominium documents and status certificates, and they can give you information about financial situations, reserve funds, and how the buildings have been maintained.

If you buy a unit and the condominium corporation has given you an incorrect status certificate or doesn't include, for example, a special assessment that has already been approved, you have the right not to pay the assessment.

TIMESHARE AGREEMENTS

A timeshare is a form of ownership governed by the *Condominium Act* in Ontario and in other provinces. Timeshares are popular in resort and vacation properties. Buyers use the property for only a few weeks or months of the year, so they buy a period of time instead of buying a unit. The property is owned by the condominium corporation, and the building has units and common elements. Each unit is divided into fifty-two weeks; the first week usually starts on the first Saturday or Sunday in a given year. Forty-eight weeks are sold for each unit; the other four weeks are usually held back for maintenance and upgrades. In many timeshare developments, a unit owner has the right to use other vacation properties that may be owned by the same developer.

In my experience, timeshares don't pay much as investments, certainly not as much as owning a condominium unit. Timeshare owners often say they would have been much better off with just paying for a two-week vacation.

Be careful when you check out the reputation of the timeshare developer, and review the condominium declaration carefully as it will likely contain many restrictions on the use of your unit. For example, you will probably not be permitted to do any decorating at all.

Think hard before you decide to buy a timeshare. Review the documents carefully, and also consider whether the investment makes sense for you and your family.

CO-OPERATIVE AGREEMENTS

Co-operative are typically high-rise buildings that contain many residential units. They look like regular apartment buildings. But a co-operative building is owned by a business corporation. Let's say Rosehill Investments Limited owns a 100-unit building. The name on the deed to the property is Rosehill Investments Limited. Like all business corporations, Rosehill is made up of shares. For our 100-unit building, Rosehill has issued 100 shares. To buy into the building, you buy a share of the company. When you own a share, you have the right to occupy one of the units in the building.

Once all 100 shares are sold, you will have 100 share owners — usually called shareholders — who have the right to occupy the 100 units in the building.

How is this different from a condominium? When you buy a condominium, your name is registered against title to your unit at the land titles office. When you buy a share in a co-operative, your name does not appear on title. This means you'll probably find it difficult to arrange financing for your purchase. A bank can't register a mortgage against title to a unit in a co-op. You can offer to "pledge" your share to your bank as security for your loan, but it's still not as easy as getting approved for a condominium mortgage.

Co-ops don't have the traditional condominium documents, such as declarations, descriptions, and bylaws. Instead, co-op shareholders enter into a "shareholder agreement" — a very detailed document that outlines all your rights, restrictions, and obligations as a co-operative share owner. Restrictions in a shareholder agreement may include a no-pets policy or a no-subletting rule. Review the shareholder agreement carefully with your lawyer before you commit to buying a share in any co-operative.

Co-operative buildings don't have separate property-tax assessments for each unit. Instead, one tax bill is assessed against the entire building. If the municipal tax bill for the entire building is $200,000, the shareholder agreement may provide that each of the 100 shareholders pays the same amount, which would be $2,000 each, as their share of property taxes. If one owner defaults, the rest of the owners have to make up the difference. (It takes only one delinquent owner to attract the attention of the city's tax department; cities have the right to sell a building to collect outstanding tax payments.) In a condominium, you pay only the taxes for your unit; you are never responsible for the taxes on any other unit in your building.

Because co-operative shareholders are more reliant on each other, there is almost always a provision in the shareholder agreement that any sale of a share must be approved by the board of directors of the co-operative corporation. The board usually conducts a credit and reference check on any proposed buyer, to make sure the buyer has the financial means to contribute their share of ongoing expenses.

In my opinion, co-operative buildings should be run by a professional manager; find out if the management firm prepares a document similar to the condominium's status certificate, and if there's an available reserve fund and reserve fund study. You can make your offer conditional on approving the two documents and the shareholder agreement you'll be expected to sign. Finally, make the agreement conditional on a home inspection; ask the inspector to look at the unit and the building as a whole.

In New York City, co-operatives are as popular as condominiums. Many owners prefer co-operatives because they get to approve all new potential buyers. Many co-operative buildings in New York don't approve "celebrity" buyers because the owners don't want reporters and photographers hanging around the building.

Co-operative ownership is not as popular as condominium ownership in Ontario.

Co-operative resale agreement

When you buy an interest in a co-operative, the agreement will look very similar to the condominium resale agreement — except you're not buying units and common elements, you're buying a share in a corporation and the right to occupy a unit and parking space. Most co-operative resale agreements begin with this paragraph:

REAL PROPERTY AND SHARES:

The exclusive right to occupy and use _____ (the "Unit") in the Co-operative Apartment Building located at _____ in the _____ Parking Space(s) _____ Locker _____ (the "Property") and _____ shares (the "shares") in the Capital of _____ (the "Corporation")

This first paragraph states that you're buying shares, and not a unit in the building. In most other respects, the resale co-operative agreement is the same as the resale condominium agreement.

CO-OWNERSHIP AGREEMENTS

Co-ownership is a relatively recent form of ownership. Co-ownership occurs when the owners of an apartment building begin selling percentages of their building to buyers. As an example, we'll use a building with 100 apartments. The owners sell an apartment to a buyer, who receives a deed on closing. The deed is for a one-percent interest in the property registered against title. The buyer also signs a co-ownership agreement with the original owners; the agreement conveys to the buyer the exclusive right to occupy one of the apartments and use of a parking space. However, even though you receive a deed on closing, it is still very difficult to obtain a mortgage loan from a bank on this type of investment.

If the building is rented to tenants, the owners give the tenants the first right to buy their apartment. The tenants don't have to buy their apartment; they can't be evicted from their apartment for refusing to buy. The owners can sell an occupied apartment only when the tenant vacates voluntarily.

Every buyer will have to sign the co-ownership agreement, which outlines owners' rights, restrictions, and obligations.

If you're interested in this form of ownership, find out what percentage of the units are still occupied by tenants and how many are owned by unit owners.

It's best to choose a co-ownership property run by a professional manager; make your transaction conditional on the receipt and approval of the building's co-ownership agreement, status certificate, and reserve fund study. And make your offer conditional on a home inspection of the apartment unit and the rest of the building.

Weisleder's Wisdom on
timeshares, co-operatives, and co-ownerships

---

1. Read all corporation documents; know your rights, restrictions, and obligations as an owner.
2. Condominium ownership is preferable to other forms of group ownership.
3. Always ask if the building is run by a professional management firm.
4. Make your transaction conditional on a home inspection report and a review of all corporation documents.

Special Purchases: New Homes, New Condominiums, Buying from a Bank Under Power of Sale

NEW HOMES AND CONDOMINIUMS

When it comes to buying a brand-new home or condominium in Ontario, there are three processes that buyers need to be familiar with in doing their homework. They are the following:

1. Understand your rights under your provincial new home warranty program.
2. Research the builder. This includes looking at all the company references.
3. Hire a lawyer to explain the home-builder or new-condominium standard form agreement of purchase and sale; look for hidden charges.

In Ontario, the Tarion Warranty Corporation provides protection for new-home buyers. Their warranty programs are designed to ensure that all new home and condominium builders are properly licensed, and that all new homeowners receive the home warranty coverage they are entitled to. Tarion also distributes annual awards to recognize excellence in building in Ontario. You can read about the winners for the last four years on the Tarion website (www.tarion.com). Similar public and private programs across Canada provide protection for buyers of new homes and condominiums.

Yet as a buyer, it's your responsibility to research the builders. Visit new homes and condominiums built by the same builders, and speak to the people living in them. Ask them what the builders did after the closing. Did they repair any deficiencies that were noted on the pre-delivery inspection in a timely manner? In Ontario, go to the Tarion site. Search the web for convictions or other offences noted against builders who did not comply with their obligations under the warranty program.

The first question to ask about builders is: are they registered with the provincial warranty protection program? In Ontario, you can check the Tarion website under the heading "Find a Builder." You can find out how many homes they have built in the past ten years, and whether they have had any claims made against them.

If the builder is not registered with the provincial program, there is a real risk the home won't meet the requirements of the provincial building code. The builders may have begun work without obtaining any of the required municipal permits or inspections. Make sure your builder is registered. In Ontario, this means Tarion.

THE TARION WARRANTY PROGRAM

In Ontario, every new home and condominium is covered by a warranty backed by the Tarion Warranty Corporation. The warranty protects deposits of up to $20,000 for new condominium units and $40,000 for new homes. If your agreement requires you to pay more than $40,000 in advance as deposits for a new home, make certain that these funds are paid directly to the builder lawyer in trust, or ask for proof that the builder has a separate insurance policy to protect any deposit over $40,000. There were unfortunate cases where unsuspecting buyers paid builders more than $40,000 in deposits and the builders subsequently went bankrupt. The buyers were only compensated $40,000 by Tarion, which is the limit for deposit protection.

Up to $5,000 can be claimed if your closing occurs more than 120 days late for a new home and 135 days late for a new condominium.

A one-year warranty covers all work and materials used, so you know your new home was constructed in a workmanlike manner. This warranty also protects you against any violations of the Ontario Building Code.

You get a two-year warranty against water penetration through the basement or foundation walls, and against defects in the electrical, plumbing, and heating systems; it also ensures that your home is free of any structural defects.

There is a seven-year warranty on anything — including major defects in the building structure — that significantly affects the use of the building as a home.

In other provinces there are similar warranty plans, as well as some private companies offering the same protection. Discuss warranty coverage with your lawyer before you buy any new home.

ADVANTAGES OF USING A REAL ESTATE SALESPERSON

Many buyers don't know the advantages of using a real estate salesperson to buy a newly built home. Buyers typically rely on the salespeople working for the builder. But the builder's sales-people are working primarily for the builder, and their goal is to obtain the highest price possible for their builder client.

Many buyers think it will cost them more to use their own real estate salesperson because the builder will have to pay the buyer salesperson's commission. This is not true. Most builders recognize real estate salespeople have relationships with many interested buyers; these builders are only too happy to permit salespeople to bring interested buyers into a new home or new condominium development. Buyer salespeople and developers co-operate with each other regarding the pay-ment of any commission, at no additional cost to the buyer.

Here's a list of some of the knowledge and experience real estate salespeople bring to a new home or new condominium transaction:

Layout and location of the home: Real estate salespeople can pro-vide timely advice about north and south exposures and other advantages when you're choosing a new home from the home builder's plans. In many cases, builders try to sell the less choice locations first, holding back more premium lots. An experienced salesperson will ask questions to ensure that you get a look at all options before making any purchase decisions. A salesperson can also help you visualize the completed subdivision, and tell you what view and sunlight you'll have once all the homes are completed.

Upgrades: Typically, builders make most of their profits by offering upgraded finishings at inflated prices. Real estate salespeople can tell you if the upgrades will bring you the same additional value when you're selling your home. You'll be able to focus your dollars on upgrades that give you the maximum return on your investment.

This same reasoning applies when it comes to choosing a specific unit in a new condominium building. There will be differences in layout, view, and finishings throughout the condominium building.

Resale value: Because real estate salespeople have detailed knowledge of prices in a particular area, they can also provide timely advice about which new home or new condominium development is likely to retain or increase in value. Their advice will be based on factors, both social and economic, in the development's area.

Hidden charges: Experienced salespeople should be familiar with some of the hidden charges in the agreement of purchase and sale for a newly built house or condominium building, as discussed in the next section on the fine print. They are in a better position to negotiate some of the charges before you accept the agreement of purchase and sale. Your buyer salesperson may, for example, ask to add a clause to the agreement that puts a cap on all extra charges, so you know the maximum you'll have to pay on closing, besides the actual purchase price.

THE FINE PRINT

There is no such thing as a "standard" new-home or new-condominium agreement. Builders usually hire a law firm to create the agreement; these agreements can differ significantly from builder to builder. So can costs to buyers. Every new-home or new-condominium agreement must be made conditional upon the review and approval of the buyer's lawyer. An example of this condition is found at Appendix 1.5.

Hidden in the agreement may be all kinds of additional fees payable by the buyer. These could include the buyer's share of city connection fees, a Tarion enrolment fee, and the reimbursement of other developer fees. Ask the builder's salesperson for a detailed list of every single charge expected of you on closing, and review the list with your lawyer. Make sure what is written in the standard form accurately reflects the charges on the builder's list of charges.

When you're buying a home that hasn't been built yet, measurements and floor plans are very important. Builders usually calculate their measurements to the outside wall, so the area inside your new home will be smaller than what you may be expecting. Be sure you obtain all interior measurements, so you know the real size of your rooms. Don't be afraid to measure the model suite or model home, and make sure the expected floor plan with all the expected room sizes is attached to your purchase agreement. You can add a clause to your agreement that states that if the new home is more than two percent smaller than promised, you may terminate the transaction or receive a rebate in the purchase price. A professional real estate salesperson can help you write the clause and get the best deal for your new home.

The agreement will also tell you when you may make selections for the interior and exterior finishes. If you make changes partway through the construction, you'll have to pay surcharges.

THE PRE-DELIVERY INSPECTION

This inspection gives you the opportunity to view your new home in a completed state and to note any deficiencies, damages, or items that may be missing on the pre-delivery inspection ("PDI") form. During this inspection, the builder will show you how to operate the heating, plumbing, electrical, and air conditioning systems in your new home. Take your time and test everything in the house very carefully. Turn on the heating, run water in all the sinks, flush the toilets, turn the air conditioning on, check all the lights and electrical outlets, and make sure the appliances are working. Are there any scratches or chips on the countertops, bathtubs, or toilets? Do all windows and doors open easily? Bring your list of selected finishes with you; make sure you received everything you paid for, and that there are no substitutions. If you fail to mention something on the PDI form, you may have difficulty claiming for it later. A builder could say the damage happened after you moved in and was caused by you.

Make sure you follow up regularly with your builder to ensure all deficiencies noted on your PDI form are rectified as soon as possible after your closing. You don't want to have to file a complaint with Tarion to have the work completed.

NEW CONDOMINIUMS

The Tarion warranty program also works for buyers of new condominiums. There is also a PDI form to complete when the unit is ready for occupancy; be careful to note any deficiencies, damaged, and missing or substituted items.

Developers must give you a disclosure statement when you buy a new condominium unit. The form includes copies of the declaration, the description, and the first year's proposed budget. You have a ten-day "cooling off" period, during which you can change your mind for any reason, or cancel the agreement and receive a return of your deposit.

When you check the budget, be careful to look at what the developer is including as ongoing expenses of the condominium corporation after closing. Many developers try to reduce the cost of the unit by increasing the cost of the common expenses after closing. For example, if a developer buys all the heating and air-conditioning equipment initially, there will be only a maintenance charge payable after closing. But if the developer leases the equipment, the ongoing carrying cost for the system will be much higher after closing, resulting in higher monthly common expense payments for each owner.

The ten-day cooling-off period is not available to buyers of new houses; they can protect themselves by making the transaction conditional on the review and approval of the agreement by their lawyers.

Condominium developers and home builders also typically include an "economic-viability clause" in their agreements: if they don't sell sufficient units or homes, or if unforeseen factors occur, they can cancel the project without penalty and refund only your deposit. Try to buy from a developer who has already started construction. The farther along the developer is with construction, the less likely he or she will cancel the project.

A change in your circumstances is much more problematic. For example, let's say you agree to buy a new condominium unit in a building that won't be built for three years. Say you pay twenty-five percent in deposits over the three-year period. Then you lose your job, or the stock market has a meltdown. If you can't close, the builder has the right to keep your deposit, then sue you if the unit sells for less than you promised to pay. You can add a clause to your purchase agreement to minimize your losses. For example, the clause can say that if you and your spouse are buying the unit together, and if you or your spouse dies before the closing, you have the right to cancel the transaction on payment of an agreed-upon amount, perhaps five to ten percent of the purchase price. Depending on market conditions, builders should be willing to accept such a provision.

New condominiums may also contain commercial units on the main floor. These units typically are not part of the condominium corporation, and developers have the right to rent them out to the tenants of their choice. Ask who the commercial tenants are; the commercial units may affect the continued enjoyment of your unit after closing.

In other forms of shared ownership, such as co-operatives or co-ownerships, the buildings are not covered by the Tarion warranty, even if they are brand new. Buyers, be careful to conduct home inspections and to check the references of the builder before you buy.

BUYING FROM A BANK UNDER POWER OF SALE

In most provinces in Canada, when a borrower defaults on an obligation under a mortgage the lender has a variety of remedies to consider. The two most common remedies are a power of sale and foreclosure. Under a power of sale, the lender, most often a bank, sells the property to recover the mortgage debt that is owed. The power to sell the property is contained in the mortgage. If there are insufficient funds from the sale to pay the debt, the bank can sue the borrower for any difference. If the sale yields excess funds, the bank must send the extra money to the borrower. For example, if the mortgage debt is $250,000 and the bank sells the property, then pays all expenses, and is left with $225,000, the bank can sue the borrower for $25,000. If the bank nets $300,000, the bank sends $50,000 to the borrower.

In a foreclosure action, the bank is seeking a court order to take over ownership of the property. If the bank gets the ownership, the debt is extinguished. If the bank then sells the house and gets less than the owner owed them, the bank can't sue the borrower. If the bank sells the house for more, they can keep the profit.

The main difference between a power of sale and foreclosure proceeding is time. It takes a lot longer for a lender to complete a foreclosure proceeding. If the borrower contests the foreclosure, the process can take one or two years. A power of sale can be completed within six months. Foreclosure is used as a remedy when the property has fallen greatly in value and the borrower is facing bankruptcy; the bank may decide to foreclose then wait until the market improves before selling the home. Such foreclosures occurred in the U.S. subprime mortgage mess. Properties fell more than sixty percent in value, and borrowers had no money, so the only real remedy for the banks was to take over the properties through foreclosure. In Ontario and most provinces in Canada, bank lending practices have been much more conservative in the past five years, so home equity in Canada is still strong, and lenders use the power of sale as their method of choice when a borrower defaults in the payment of their mortgage.

How does a power of sale work? In Ontario once a mortgage has been in default for a minimum of fifteen days, the lender may issue a power of sale notice. The notice gives the owner thirty-five days to put the mortgage into good standing. If the owner fails to pay the arrears, the lender has the right to list and sell the property. During the thirty-five days, the lender is not permitted to take any steps to sell the property, for example, have the house appraised, sign any listing agreement, or advertise the property for sale.

In a separate process, the lender applies to the court for an order to obtain possession of the property. Once the lender obtains possession, and the thirty-five-day time period expires, the lender will then appraise, list, and try to sell the home. Banks have a legal obligation to act reasonably in obtaining a fair price for the property. They make sure their salesperson completes a thorough appraisal and gives them an idea what the property is worth; banks try to sell a property at a value as close as possible to the appraisal. The law indicates that on the date the bank signs an unconditional agreement of purchase and sale with a buyer, the original borrower has no further legal right to pay off his mortgage. But the borrower's rights may be extended by the bank in certain circumstances. Those circumstances are described in the next paragraph.

If you buy a home under power of sale, you'll face two difficulties. First, the bank will always include a provision that the home is being sold on an "as is" basis and that the bank accepts no responsibility for any damage or missing items that may occur before closing. Second, banks may add a provision stating that if the original borrower comes up with the money to pay off the mortgage in full on or before closing, they get their house back. You'll be in a very difficult position if you've already sold your current house. The banks include the provision to protect themselves from borrowers who claim the bank sold the property too cheaply and thus caused damages to the borrower.

The "as is" clause and the right of the borrower to pay off the mortgage and thus cancel the deal can be found in Appendix 1.7.

When you buy from a bank under power of sale, it is most important to make the transaction conditional on a home inspection report and, if possible, an up-to-date survey of the property. In most power of sale deals, you'll receive no real disclosure.

Sometimes a property may be listed by both the borrower's listing salesperson and the lender's listing salesperson. In other words, two different brokerages are trying to sell the same property at the same time, one on behalf of the owner and the other on behalf of the bank. If, as a buyer, you face this choice, I recommend that you make your offer to the owner, and make it conditional on the bank providing its consent to your offer. You won't have to accept an "as is" clause, since the owner can control the property until closing, and you won't have to worry about losing the property on the last day if the owner comes up with the arrears.

> ### *Weisleder's Wisdom on*
> ### *new homes, condominiums, and buying from a bank*

1. Understand the protection offered you under the Tarion warranty plan or any other provincial plan for new homes and condominiums.
2. Research any builder you are thinking of buying a house from.
3. Include all floor plans and measurements with your agreement, so there is no misunderstanding about the square footage you expect your unit to contain; consider adding a clause giving you the right to terminate the deal if you don't receive the square footage you expected.
4. Use a professional salesperson to assist you, especially when you're looking at layout of the home, finishings, hidden charges, and potential resale value.
5. When you're looking at new-condominium agreements, consider adding a clause to limit your liability if you or your partner passes away prior to closing.
6. Review the fine print of any agreement with your lawyer; pay particular attention to any hidden charges; consider adding a clause to cap all additional expenses beyond the purchase price.
7. Be prepared for your pre-delivery inspection.

8. Conduct a detailed review of the condominium disclosure statement, especially the proposed budget for the first year.

9. Understand the process and pitfalls when buying from a bank under power of sale.

CHAPTER 10

The Federal Privacy Act and Do Not Call Legislation

As of January 1, 2004, the new federal *Privacy Act* became applicable to most commercial activities in Canada. The main purpose was to prevent businesses from disclosing consumers' personal information without their permission. The Do Not Call legislation came into effect on September 30, 2008, and took the laws of privacy one step further, making it an offence to make marketing phone calls to any consumer who has registered his or her number on the Canada Do Not Call list.

In this chapter I will explain the principles behind the legislation and tell you how the laws will affect buying and selling a home.

THE PRIVACY ACT

The privacy legislation passed by the federal government is called the *Personal Information Protection and Electronic Documents Act* and is commonly referred to as PIPEDA, or the *Privacy Act*. The act is divided into two parts. The first part deals with the protection of personal information. The second part promotes electronic commerce by providing for the use of electronic means to communicate or record information or transactions.

The main purpose of the first part of the act is stated in section 3:

> The purpose of this part is to establish, in an era in which technology increasingly facilitates the circulation and exchange of information, rules to govern the collection, use, and disclosure of personal information in a manner that recognizes the right of privacy of individuals with respect to their personal information and the need of organizations to collect, use, or disclose personal information for purposes that a reasonable person would consider appropriate in the circumstances.

The creation of the Internet was the driving force behind worldwide privacy legislation. Countries were concerned about how businesses shared consumer information with other businesses in the same country, and about the implications when businesses have the ability to transmit this information to other companies all over the world.

In Canada's constitution, matters of personal information are typically under the jurisdiction of the provincial governments. In Ontario, for example, the government has passed the *Consumer Reporting Act*, which deals with how consumer reporting agencies, commonly known as credit bureaus, handle the personal and credit information of customers. There is an express provision in PIPEDA that it will no longer be effective in a province once that province passes its own privacy legislation. Quebec, Alberta, and British Columbia have already passed privacy legislation, and Ontario was expected to pass its own privacy law at the end of 2004. The Ontario government instead took the position that it will wait to see how the federal legislation is interpreted in practice before introducing its own privacy legislation. The principles of all the privacy laws are alike.

"Personal information" is any information that can identify an individual, excluding their name, business address, and business phone number. In the real estate business, any facts about a person's home, including the property address and its sale price, are considered personal information, because those facts can be used to identify the owner of the property. It makes no difference that you can find this information in other public databases, such as the local land registry office. You can use personal information only with the consent of the individual.

Why was the *Privacy Act* introduced in the first place? One of the main objectives of privacy legislation is to protect ordinary consumers from invasions of their personal privacy, including the sharing of personal information about them without their permission.

If I asked you to indicate what you felt was the most annoying daily invasion of your privacy, you would probably answer telemarketing calls at home, closely followed by spam e-mails, unwanted fax advertisements, and the direct mail and junk mail that cascades out of your mailbox. How did these people and businesses obtain your telephone and fax numbers, your e-mail and home addresses? Initially, most telemarketers went through the phone book to obtain this information. When they were successful in selling their products or services to a list of customers, that list became very valuable information, and the telemarketers sold it to other telemarketers. The *Privacy Act* prevents the selling of lists, unless individuals have consented to have their names on the list and to have the list distributed to others.

I also receive many annoying recorded voice messages telling me to call a number to hear about a great product or marketing opportunity. I used to wonder why any telemarketer would think anyone would bother to make such calls, as I usually hang up the phone within two seconds of realizing I'm on the other end of a canned pitch. Then I learned that telemarketers are more interested in *when* we pick up the phone than in how we respond to the pitch. What *time* we pick up the phone is valuable information telemarketers can share with other telemarketers. (I have also learned that you can abort this fact-gathering by pressing the # key six times before hanging up.)

Before the Do Not Call list legislation, Canadians could go to the website of the Canadian Marketing Association (CMA), at www.the-cma.org, and register their phone number, fax number, and mailing address if they did not wish to receive invasions of their privacy. The list is updated every three months and then circulated to all the members of the CMA. About eighty percent of all telemarketers in Canada are members of the CMA and abide by the list. Telemarketers who did not honour the list could have their number disconnected by the local phone service provider.

Although the Do Not Call list has replaced the CMA registry, you can still use the website to register your home address, which should reduce the amount of direct mail advertising you receive.

The U.S. experience with their own Do Not Call list demonstrates just how annoyed the U.S. consumer is with phone invasions. When the U.S. introduced the Do Not Call list in January of 2003, they expected that 2 million consumers would sign up during the first few years. As of December 31, 2008, more than 145 million consumers in the U.S. had signed up. As a direct result of these lists, and the penalties associated with calling someone who is registered on the list, several U.S. call centres have closed, and companies are reducing their workforces in these areas.

As of the end of 2008, more than 5 million Canadians had registered their numbers on Canada's Do Not Call list.

E-MAIL SPAM

E-mail spam and e-mail scams are a worldwide problem. It's a good idea to install filters and firewall systems to prevent unwanted e-mails from entering your mailbox. How many of you have received an e-mail indicating that you just won the latest internet lottery and all you have to do to claim your multimillion-dollar prize is send a "courier" fee of $200? Or just fill out the attached application form with your personal details, including your bank account information.

The lottery scam is no different than the "Nigerian scams" of the 1980s, which offered unwary consumers millions for helping officials move money out of Nigeria. Consumers who responded were cheated out of thousands of dollars in "transfer fees" before finding out they had been the victim of fraud. Remember, if it seems too good to be true, it is.

If you provide your own personal information, fraud artists can steal your identity; they can also transfer funds directly out of your bank accounts. Be very careful about giving out your personal information.

There is now a website you can use to report any unauthorized e-mail scams. The site, www.recol.ca, is run by the Royal Canadian Mounted Police (RCMP); the "recol" in the web address stands for Reporting Economic Crime Online. The RCMP works with law enforcement agencies around the world to combat e-mail crime.

TEN PRINCIPLES OF PRIVACY

The *Privacy Act* codifies ten principles of privacy that were introduced by the Canadian Standards Association in 1996. However, if you understand three simple principles, you'll understand how the *Privacy Act* works in ordinary business dealings between a consumer and a business.

1. Every company must have a privacy policy and must make sure all its employees understand the importance of protecting your personal information.
2. Before a company asks for your personal information, or when they are asking, they must explain to you why they are collecting the information.
3. The company must obtain your consent to collect your personal information.

And now the ten principles of privacy, including examples of how these relate to the real estate industry and how they affect the rights of buyers and sellers.

Principle 1 — Accountability

An organization is responsible for personal information under its control and shall designate an individual or individuals who are accountable for the organization's compliance [with the principles of the act].

Every business must have its own privacy officer, someone responsible for all issues related to privacy in that office. Every real estate brokerage must have a privacy officer who can answer all your inquiries.

Principle 2 — Identifying Purposes

The purposes for which personal information is collected shall be identified by the organization at or before the time the information is collected.

This is the main principle of all privacy legislation. Any company, including any real estate brokerage company, must tell a consumer in advance how your personal information will be used. In the real estate experience, the salesperson collects personal information: facts about the property being sold, the listing price, and the final sale price. The use of personal information is explained in clause 11 of the listing agreement and clause 8 of the buyer representation agreement. A seller's consent gives the salesperson the right to advertise that the property is for sale, by any means necessary.

This may seem obvious when the salesperson is listing a home, but it becomes less clear in other instances. One example is the sign-in sheet buyers are asked to sign when they visit an open house. Buyers usually are told the names and addresses are collected for "security reasons," that is, the seller needs to know who was visiting the property. If salespersons at the open house want to contact someone on the sign-in sheet, they must have the person's consent to do so. If you visit an open house, let the salesperson know when you sign in that you do not wish to be contacted.

What happens if you're a seller and your listing has expired? Can other salespeople contact you to get your business? Your personal information — name and address — is available on most MLS® services. However, when you consented to list your property, you gave permission to the salesperson to do only what was necessary to sell the property "during the listing."

In a case before the Privacy Commissioner of Canada in 2006, a consumer complained after being contacted by a salesperson after her listing expired. She had given no express consent to the second salesperson. As expected, the privacy commissioner's office considered the salesperson's call a violation of the second privacy principle.

The privacy commissioner recognized that this was an industry issue and suggested that the real estate boards across the country solve the problem by obtaining consent from the consumer when the listing was originally obtained. Accordingly, there is new language in most listing agreements in Canada:

> In the event that this Agreement expires and the Property is not sold, the Seller Does _____ Does Not _____ consent to allow other real estate board members to contact the Seller after expiration of this Agreement to discuss listing or otherwise marketing the Property.

If the consumer agrees, the board may add it to the MLS® listing so every board member will know when they can contact a consumer once a listing has expired. Other provinces have made similar changes to their listing processes.

If you do not wish to be contacted by other salespeople when your listing expires, be sure to indicate this explicitly by marking the box "Does Not" when you sign your listing agreement.

After a successful sale, some real estate salespersons send out cards announcing that they have sold the property at, for example, 102% of the listing price. The amount a house sells for is personal information. In a typical listing agreement, the salesperson has not identified this marketing tool to the seller; therefore, it is not permissible under privacy law. (The salesperson *is* permitted to state that he or she has sold a home in the area, or three homes in the area, with an average price of, for example, $300,000.) If a salesperson receives permission to advertise the selling price, he or she may send out the cards immediately after the sold sign is placed on the property. The point to remember is that a seller must give permission for a real estate salesperson to send out these cards. If the real estate salesperson also wants to indicate the actual price the property sold for, he or she must obtain the consent of the buyer. You do not have to agree to the advertisement of the price your home sold for.

However, newspapers are not subject to these privacy rules. Newspapers regularly list the details of properties that have recently sold, including the property address and the price it sold for. You can't prevent the newspapers from advertising the price your home sold for.

What about taking photographs of the chattels and fixtures of a property during an inspection? Would this be permitted? Chattels and fixtures could be considered personal information as defined by the *Privacy Act*. People might wonder what harm taking pictures could do to anyone. In Ottawa recently, a cabinet minister sold his home; his salesperson told him she had permitted the buyer salesperson to take pictures of the home. The cabinet minister was extremely upset, and feared that the pictures could find their way onto the Internet or into magazines, which would embarrass him. Photographs of a house for sale could clearly be a violation of the seller's privacy.

If you want to take photos, make it clear that the sole purpose of taking them is to provide documented proof of what you expect to receive from the seller after closing, so there are no misunderstandings. Then obtain the consent of the seller to take the pictures.

Principle 3 — Obtaining Consent

The knowledge and consent of a customer are required for the collection, use, or disclosure of personal information except where inappropriate.

The third rule is the easy answer to all privacy questions. A company must obtain the permission of a consumer before using the consumer's personal information for any purpose.

In Ontario, in paragraph 11 of the listing agreement and paragraph 8 of the buyer representation agreement, sellers and buyers explicitly give limited permission to the use of their personal information to advertise (for sellers) and find (for buyers) a property. Similar language is included in the other provincial agreements.

METHODS OF OBTAINING YOUR CONSENT

As indicated in Principle 2, if a salesperson wants to use information from the sign-in sheet at an open house, he or she must obtain the consumer's informed consent on the sign-in sheet itself. Consumers must understand what they are consenting to. There has been much debate about how to obtain the consent, and two methods have been deemed acceptable by the privacy commission: opt-in consent and opt-out consent.

In opt-in consent, consumers must check off a separate box on the form, besides their signature, indicating that they agree to have their personal information disclosed for a particular purpose. For an open house sign-in sheet, example, the clause is:

The undersigned consents to X using my personal information to contact me about this property and other similar properties.

In an opt-out consent, unless the consumer checks off the box, he has agreed to accept the information. For example:

> You agree that X may use your personal information to send you information about this property or similar properties. If you do not wish to receive this information, please check the box.

Customers who have not checked the box are deemed to have consented to receiving information.

What if your name is already on a company mailing list? Companies that are already doing business with you for your home, such as your cable or phone provider, may continue to call you or send you e-mail marketing. If you do not wish to receive any calls or e-mails from these companies, you must expressly tell them to stop.

Principle 4 — Limiting Collection

Members shall limit the collection of personal information to that which is necessary for the purposes identified.

There is no reason for a real estate brokerage company to collect personal information beyond what is required to carry out its responsibilities. For example, there is only one reason to give your social insurance number to any real estate brokerage: the interest earned on a deposit will exceed $50, and the brokerage has to issue a T5 slip for income tax purposes. There is no other reason to give any company your social insurance number. A social insurance number is one of the best tools for stealing a person's identity. (There's more information about identity theft in Chapter 5.)

Principle 5 — Limiting Use, Disclosure, and Retention
Members shall use or disclose personal information only for the reason it was collected, except with the consent of the consumer or as required by law.

On the surface, this appears to be an easy concept to understand. Unless the information is required by law, a real estate salesperson cannot disclose personal information without permission from the client. We tend to associate "required by law" to mean "if required pursuant to a legal warrant" or a subpoena or a similar demand. But what if a seller says the following to his or her listing salesperson:

> This used to be a grow house operation, but I have cleaned it up so no one has to know about it. It's personal information.

> The previous owner committed suicide in the house, but that's a private family matter. It's no one else's business.

Under privacy law, all these facts fall under the definition of "personal information." However, think about this for a minute. Is what the seller said material information you would want to know if you were buying the property? If the answer is yes, then you know you should be disclosing such information to any buyer. In Chapter 2 I discuss the concept of full disclosure by a seller; no privacy rule can change a seller's obligation to disclose what should be disclosed.

Principle 6 — Accuracy
Members shall keep personal information as accurate, complete, current, and relevant as necessary of its identified purpose.

When a company is relying on information to make a decision about a consumer, it makes sure the information is as accurate and current as possible. For example, any time you apply for a new apartment, mortgage loan, or credit card, you must pass a credit check. The laws and regulations surrounding the credit reporting agencies, also called credit bureaus, are governed by provincial legislation, but the principles are very closely related to privacy legislation. The credit reporting agencies are constantly updating their files because they understand that companies are relying upon credit information to make decisions about granting credit to consumers.

Principle 7 — Protecting Information
Members shall protect personal information with safeguards appropriate to the sensitivity of the information.

It is common sense that if we entrust our personal information to a company, the company should do its best to protect our information. This is especially true given identity theft and fraudulent use of social insurance numbers, credit cards, and automatic banking cards. We read about hackers who get inside an organization's computer to obtain sensitive financial information, again for the purpose of identity theft. Companies spend enormous sums of money to ensure their computer systems are protected from threats. In many companies, only a few people within the organization understand the systems that protect the company information. Any company that gathers personal information from consumers needs to protect this information.

A company that's careless with personal information may be held liable in a civil action: a consumer can take the company to court to assert a claim for damages related to violation of their privacy rights. The careless release of sensitive personal information could cause the consumer to suffer losses and damages, a logical basis for a claim for damages in a civil court.

As an example, the Privacy Commissioner's office rendered a decision recently that it is not sufficient that a company throw sensitive personal information into the wastepaper basket. Personal information should in fact be shredded before being thrown out. All real estate brokerage companies should maintain these same safe practices in protecting their clients' personal information.

Before you give personal information to your buyer or seller salesperson, find out what steps the brokerage company takes to keep your personal information secure.

Principle 8 – Openness Concerning Policies and Practices

Members shall make readily available to consumers specific information about their policies and practices relating to the management of personal information.

Every organization needs a privacy policy that clearly sets out what the company does with personal information. The policy should be available to anyone who asks about it. Every brokerage company you deal with should have its own privacy policy. Ask about it when you interview your buyer or seller salespeople. You should be satisfied that they take their privacy obligations very seriously.

Principle 9 – Consumer Access

Upon request, members shall inform a customer of the existence, use, and disclosure of his or her personal information and shall give the individual access to that information.

This is another common-sense principle of privacy law: consumers should be permitted access to whatever information of theirs a company has in their files. An example: all of us have the right to call a credit reporting agency and make an appointment to review our files. If we find any inaccuracies, we can apply to have a credit error corrected. This principle applies to any organization that holds your personal information. An organization must, upon request, make personal files available for review, usually within thirty days.

In most cases, real estate offices do not keep files containing any personal information that's already available in the client's lawyer's file. You probably won't ever have to review the personal information contained in your salesperson's file.

Principle 10 – Challenging Compliance
A consumer shall be able to address a challenge concerning compliance with the above principles to the designated accountable person or persons in the member office.

As a consumer, you have the right to challenge any privacy policy you do not agree with.

RELATED PRIVACY QUESTIONS

The ten principles of privacy create some issues that may arise during a real estate transaction.

Collection and protection of sensitive personal information
Mortgage brokers are in the business of collecting as much personal information as possible to qualify buyers for financing to buy a home. Because most of this information is sensitive, mortgage brokers should take all necessary measures to protect it, including shredding any unwanted personal information.

Passing information on to the buyer salesperson

When it's time to waive conditions regarding financing, the buyer salesperson can ask for written assurance that the buyer has in fact been approved for the financing. However, buyers who are pre-qualified for a mortgage may be reluctant to reveal the upper limit of the approval, so the buyer salesperson doesn't disclose the amount during negotiations with the seller salesperson. There is no reason for buyers to disclose this information to their buyer salesperson if they do not want to.

Weisleder's Wisdom on the Privacy Act

1. Every fact about your home is personal information.
2. Before a company can use any of your own personal information, it must tell you why it needs the information.
3. Every buyer and seller must consent to the use of personal information in any real estate transaction.
4. Ask to see a copy of your brokerage's privacy policy.
5. Be vigilant whenever you reveal personal information.
6. No privacy rule can change a seller's obligation to disclose what should be disclosed.

CANADA'S DO NOT CALL LIST

The Canada Do Not Call list lets you limit the number of annoying telemarketing calls by registering your home phone or fax number on the government Do Not Call Registry. Your work number is not protected.

Exceptions

Even if your number is registered on the Do Not Call list, you may still receive calls at home from:

registered charities;

political parties;

opinion polls or surveys that do not involve sales or services;

people to whom you've provided consent to call; and

businesses that have an existing relationship with you.

If your home number is on your business card, and you hand your card to a business, that business can call you at home, because the Do Not Call list does not include business telephone numbers.

MAINTAINING AN INTERNAL LIST

Besides the government Do Not Call Registry, every business that telemarkets to consumers must also maintain their own internal list. This is important for every consumer to know. If for example, your cable supplier calls you because they have an existing relationship with you, to sell you new services, you can immediately ask them to take your number off their own telemarketing list. The same is true for any charity or political party that solicits you over the phone. You can ask them to take your number off their own internal list and to stop calling you in the future. If someone from their organization does call you after you told them to stop, then you can complain about their activity, in the same way that you can complain about other private telemarketers that violate the Do Not Call Registry.

HOW DO YOU REGISTER YOUR NUMBER ON THE DO NOT CALL LIST?

You can register your phone, cellphone, and fax numbers by going to www.lnnte-dncl.gc.ca or just google the Canada Do Not Call list to find the link. The website says you can register a maximum of three numbers online, but I have registered more than three. There is no cost to register. When you register, you'll be advised that there is a thirty-one-day grace period during which you may be still called by telemarketers. If a telemarketer calls you after the grace period, you may register a complaint. Your contact numbers will stay on the Do Not Call list for five years, at which time you'll have to reregister your numbers to maintain your protection.

HOW DO TELEMARKETERS ACCESS THE DO NOT CALL REGISTRY?

Telemarketers pay to find out whether a phone or fax number is on the list. If a number is on the list, it's off limits to the telemarketer.

HOW DOES A CONSUMER COMPLAIN?

The easiest way to complain is to go to www.lnnte-dncl.gc.ca, where you'll provide your number as well as information about the company that called you without your consent. You must register your complaint within fourteen days of receiving an unwanted call. The National Do Not Call list operator will investigate to determine whether your complaint is valid.

If a complaint is valid, an individual telemarketer may have to pay up to $1,500; the maximum penalty for a telemarketer company is $15,000. Penalties are paid to the Do Not Call Registry, not to the complaining consumer.

NEW TELEPHONE CONTACT RULES

Telemarketers may solicit only between the hours of 9:00 a.m. and 9:30 p.m. on weekdays, and between 10:00 a.m. and 6:00 p.m. on weekends, based on the consumer's time zone. Telemarketers must display the number they are calling from. They can no longer use blocked phone numbers to make solicitation calls.

These limits apply also to those annoying recorded solicitations. You can complain about taped calls as well, if your number is on the Do Not Call list registry.

Weisleder's Wisdom on Canada's Do Not Call list

1. Register your number on the list as soon as possible, to reduce the number of telemarketing calls you receive.
2. When a company or charity calls, tell them you wish to be taken off their internal Do Not Call list.
3. Do not hesitate to complain if you are called by any telemarketer, including any recorded message, after your number has been on the Do Not Call list for at least thirty days.

CHAPTER 11

Legal Proceedings:
Are They Worth the Trouble?

I went bankrupt twice in my life. The first time when I lost a case.
The second time when I won.

— Voltaire

One of the main goals of this book is to help you avoid legal
actions against you when you are buying or selling a home. To
demonstrate why you don't want to be part of any legal proceeding, I will now take you through what occurs in a typical
legal action involving real estate buyers and sellers. Most
people understand that a civil proceeding — a lawsuit — will
end up costing a substantial sum. However, ask a litigation
lawyer what most commercial litigation is about, and the
lawyer will tell you that a vast majority of cases involve real
estate disputes. Real estate is expensive, therefore worth fight-
ing over. In the Toronto and Vancouver real estate markets, the
sale of million-dollar homes is a regular occurrence. When
things go wrong, the amounts of money involved justify legal
proceedings.

THE LEGAL PROCESS

Here is a description of a legal proceeding in progress, including time frames and fees.

You get a letter saying someone has decided to sue you. You experience surprise, shock, and indignation that anyone would institute proceedings against you. Even Martha Stewart felt this way: I saw her being interviewed after she was sentenced. Here was the queen of advice on almost everything related to domestic life, from cooking to decorating to raising children. Yet she was quite frank in admitting that there were no books or magazines offering advice that could adequately prepare her for the stress and the complexities of the legal process.

Once you've calmed down a bit, hire a lawyer to represent you. Most lawyers demand a substantial retainer before they take on any case, whether you're suing or being sued. Always remember, when you're contemplating any kind of legal action: the lawyers always get paid first.

The lawyer you hire will want to meet you to review the allegations made by you or against you, and will ask you to produce any documents, e-mails, or notes that relate to the issue. Most buyers and sellers will not have much in the way of written documentation other than the agreement of purchase and sale. The lawyers — both yours and the other person's — are going to ask for precise details of the transaction; the more documentation, the better.

Set aside five working days for the first interview with the lawyer, to look for and review any documentation that may be involved, and make any changes to the claim that you are making or that is being made against you in your dispute. If you're being sued, you prepare a statement of defence to answer the allegations made in the claim. If you're suing, there may be motions to strike out any offensive paragraphs in the statement of claim, such as a reference that you deliberately tried to commit fraud on the other party. Usually both sides have to file a supporting affidavit. Then you review all the material, and it gets filed.

Both lawyers ask questions about any affidavits that have been filed. Set aside some more time to prepare for this and to attend at the actual cross-examination. The cross-examination is recorded; it may be used in a motion and during the trial. A motion usually takes about three days of your time, including preparation and attendance.

Did I mention the lack of sleep on the night before any examination? You'll be thinking about the questions the lawyers are going to ask you. We're not even close to a court hearing, yet you've already lost two weeks of time that could have been used in other ways. Think of how upset you get when you prepare for court to fight a simple traffic ticket. Now multiply that stress by a hundred, and you'll begin to understand what a lawsuit is like.

Then you need to prepare an "affidavit of documents." Both sides must provide a list of all the written documents that will be produced during the trial to support their positions. You'll have to dig up everything you can find that relate to the matter: e-mails, phone records, personal diaries, and anything else that's relevant.

After the affidavit of documents comes discovery: both lawyers ask questions of both you and your adversary, to learn what facts and legal positions you'll be relying on at trial, and what documents will be used, so there will be no surprises at trial. The lawyer for the opposition will ask many detailed questions about your business background and education, looking for a way to discredit your testimony. Your lawyer will do the same with your opponent.

The discovery proceedings are recorded, and any information in that recording can be introduced at the trial as well.

Your lawyer may ask you to attend while he or she questions your opponent, so you and your lawyer can work with your opponent's responses. The discovery process usually takes a full week.

After the discovery and before the trial, both lawyers can make more motions; you may have to attend to answer questions and sign affidavits.

The trial usually takes one to two weeks, depending on the complexity of the facts and the number of witnesses. The preparation for trial usually takes at least a week, during which you review your examination for discovery. Often it takes three or four years to get to the trial part of the process, and you should attend the entire trial. The hours spent in court are often very exhausting. Don't expect to get any other work done while the trial is in progress; you'll be totally consumed by it.

Most people involved in a lawsuit are amazed by the amount of paper it generates. Even something as small as a "slope in the kitchen" (as we soon will see) could result in detailed structural engineering reports, being prepared by experts, who will have to give evidence at trial.

You may spend the working equivalent of two full months from the time you start a lawsuit until your trial, to say nothing of the stress hanging over your head for three or four years. Can anyone quantify how much is lost during the process? Imagine the money you could have earned if you weren't working on your case, and the stress. Medical researchers and doctors say that stress contributes to health problems, including heart disease and cancer.

The results of your lawsuit may become public knowledge; all legal proceedings are public information. You may read about your case in a newspaper article or the Internet; the publicity can be negative. People reading about you don't care who was right; they know you were involved in a legal action, so you carry a stigma.

In the next few paragraphs I'll describe a case summary of proceedings involving a buyer, a seller, and a listing and buyer salesperson, from the time the claim was issued until the matter was decided. The case is *Wood v. Lautenbach*, and the action commenced in 1998. The trial took place in the spring of 2004, six years later, and lasted four weeks.

The matter began simply enough. The property was listed by a seller who had lived in the house for several years. Some minor renovations had been done on the property. The buyers saw a for-sale sign while driving by and immediately contacted their buyer salesperson because they wanted to see the house.

The property had a slope in the kitchen, which some witnesses said was visible when they inspected the house; others said it was not. The buyers and their salesperson did not notice the slope in the floor. Another person put in an offer at the same time; that person did notice the slope. The slope was measured, and was eleven inches from one end of the house to the other.

The buyers admitted there was some discussion about having a home inspection but they decided not to have an inspection. The buyer salesperson did not make a strong argument for a home inspection.

The transaction closed. Sometime after closing, the property began to deteriorate. It turned out that the slope in the floor was a symptom; there was a problem with the foundation. Some years after the buyers moved in, the house had to be demolished. The buyers claimed damages from the sellers, the buyer salesperson, the seller salesperson, and the town.

There were two issues at trial. First, was the listing salesperson aware of the defect? (If yes, that agent had a duty to disclose it.) Second, should the buyer salesperson have inspected the property more carefully and made a strong recommendation that the buyers obtain a home inspection?

The case began when a statement of claim was served in 1998. The trial was completed in the spring of 2004. At the end of the trial, the buyer salesperson was held responsible for not recommending that the buyers conduct a home inspection, which could have uncovered the defect. The township was also held partially responsible for not ensuring that the house complied with Ontario building codes, and for failing to conduct proper inspections during construction. The trial required complicated expert engineering evidence, so it took sixteen days. It is safe to say the legal fees exceeded the total value of the property. The costs and the six years of stress could have been avoided if the seller had disclosed everything related to the property before the offer was signed by the buyers, and if the buyers had hired a qualified home inspector.

STEPS INVOLVED IN A LEGAL PROCESS

1. The complaining party (the buyer, in most cases) meets with a lawyer and provides all facts, so the lawyer can prepare a claim.
2. The salespeople and the seller meet with their lawyers to provide all documentation so the lawyer can prepare a statement of defence.
3. Everyone involved finds any documentation, notes, or e-mails for the affidavit of documents; everyone attends personally to execute the affidavits of documents.
4. Everyone attends examinations for discovery and gives evidence under oath while in answer to questions from both buyer's and seller's lawyers.

5. The next step is mediation; lawyers provide everyone with a copy of the mediation brief, for review and comment. Then all lawyers and their clients attempt to resolve the matter out of court. Mediation usually takes a day, or part of a day.

6. The rules of civil procedure in legal actions generally require that everyone attend a pre-trial settlement conference. (This is the same as mediation, only with a judge.) Pre-trials generally take one hour; everyone is required to attend and participate.

7. Preparation for trial comes next, and can take a lot of time as everyone gathers information for lawyers, then meets with the lawyers. Lawyers and clients review reports from experts and decide whether the experts will give evidence at trial. Everyone attends the trial and gives evidence, and there is cross-examination by lawyers in open court.

INSURANCE ISSUES

Real estate salespeople carry insurance, called errors and omissions insurance. Some buyers and sellers assume it will be easy to sue a real estate salesperson because the insurance will pay any damage. Not a good assumption!

Insurers who don't see liability will not agree to simply write a cheque to resolve a matter, and insurance companies have far more resources to pay their lawyers than buyers and sellers have. Insurers don't want people to think it's easy to bring a claim against a real estate salesperson and collect a quick settlement from the insurance company. When an insurance company thinks a claim has no merit, they'll defend the case.

SETTLE!

If you do become involved in a legal proceeding, try to reach a settlement, and the earlier the better. In my opinion, the very worst settlement is still preferable to the best legal position. Once a matter is settled, it is over, and since the terms of a settlement are usually confidential, there is no publicity, either. I have heard too many times the phrase, "It's not the money; it's the principle." Forget it. It's always about the money. And if you factor in what it really costs you, in terms of time and stress, you are almost always in a better financial position by settling.

USE SMALL CLAIMS COURT

In Ontario, the small claims court limit is $10,000, but on January 1, 2010, this amount will be increased to $25,000. If your dispute fits into this dollar category, use small claims court to resolve your issues. Although small claims court may take one or two years, the legal costs should be significantly lower.

For proceedings under the *Privacy Act* and the Do Not Call list, most of the expense is undertaken by the government investigating the complaint, and there are no legal fees to make any claim.

Weisleder's Wisdom on legal proceedings

1. No one wins any legal proceeding – except lawyers.
2. Most legal proceedings take three to six years to resolve.
3. If the opportunity arises to settle a claim, take it. Remember, "The worst settlement is still better than the best lawsuit."
4. Use small claims court, if you can.

Conclusion

FOREWARNED IS FOREARMED: THE FOURTEEN STEPS OF SUCCESS

The goal of any buyer or seller should be to have a stress-free experience. By following the principles set out in this book, you'll be able to achieve this, and you'll be able to avoid unwanted legal proceedings.

Some basic principles to increase your chances of success:

1. Hire the right real estate professional to assist you.
2. Conduct your own neighbourhood and Internet research of areas that interest you.
3. Be prepared, especially if you become involved in a multiple offer.
4. Carefully review every detail added to the agreement of purchase and sale form – including all chattels and fixtures you expect to receive on closing – before you sign the agreement.
5. As a seller, practice full disclosure of all legal, physical, and psychological defects that affect your property.

6. Understand your rights as a landlord or tenant; know how being a tenant or a landlord may affect your real estate transaction.

7. Before you sign it, understand every clause in the printed form in the agreement of purchase and sale.

8. Know why you need conditions, representations, and warranties.

9. Be wary of Internet brokers and no-money-down real estate offers.

10. In a resale condominium, it is all about the status certificate.

11. With new builders, it is all about good references and about your provincial new home warranty program.

12. When buying under a power of sale, take extra care to conduct a detailed home inspection.

13. Understand why you need an up-to-date survey, and know how helpful it can be if there is a property dispute.

14. If you are ever involved in a legal proceeding, try to settle the matter.

Special Clauses to Consider

THE AUTHOR ASSUMES NO LIABILITY FOR THE UTILIZATION OF ANY OF THE CLAUSES OR PROVISIONS HEREINAFTER SET OUT.

Buyers and sellers are encouraged to seek expert advice in the drafting of all agreements of purchase and sale.

1.1.a Chattels and Fixtures – Good Working Order, Broom Swept Condition

The seller represents and warrants that the chattels and fixtures as included in this Agreement of Purchase and Sale will be in good working order and free from all liens and encumbrances on completion and the property will be in a broom swept condition on completion. The Parties agree that this representation and warranty shall survive and not merge on completion of this transaction, but apply only to the state of the property at completion of this transaction.

1.1.b Chattels and Equipment – Good Working Order

The seller warrants that all the mechanical, electrical, heating, ventilation, air conditioning systems, air compressors, elevators, conveyor systems, sprinkler systems, boilers, and all other equipment on the real property shall be in good working order on completion. The Parties agree that this warranty shall survive and not merge on completion of this transaction, but apply only to those circumstances existing at the completion of this transaction.

CONDOMINIUM

1.2 Condition – Review of Condominium Documents, By Specific Date

This offer is conditional upon the buyer and the buyer's lawyer reviewing the Status Certificate and Attachments and finding the Status Certificate and Attachments satisfactory in the buyer and the buyer's Lawyer's sole and absolute discretion. The _____

(buyer/seller)

agrees to request at the _____ expense, the

(buyer's/seller's)

Status Certificate and Attachments within _____ days after acceptance of this Offer. Unless the buyer gives notice in writing to the seller not later than 5:00 p.m. on the _____ day of _____, 20 ____, that this condition is fulfilled, this Offer shall be null and void and the deposit shall be returned to the buyer in full without deduction. This condition is included for the benefit of the buyer and may be waived at the buyer's sole option by notice in writing to the seller within the time period stated herein.

INSPECTION OF PROPERTY

1.3.a Condition – Inspection of Property by a Home Inspector

This Offer is conditional upon the inspection of the subject property by a home inspector at the buyer's own expense, and the obtaining of a report satisfactory to the buyer in the buyer's sole and absolute discretion. Unless the buyer gives notice in writing delivered to the seller not later than _____ p.m. on the _____ day of _____, 20____, that this condition is fulfilled, this Offer shall be null and void and the deposit shall be returned to the buyer in full without deduction. The seller agrees to co-operate in providing access to the property for the purpose of this inspection. This condition is included for the benefit of the buyer and may be waived at the buyer's sole option by notice in writing to the seller within the time period stated herein.

1.3.b Condition – Inspection of Property by a Home Inspector – Condominium

This Offer is conditional upon the inspection of the unit and common elements by a home inspector at the buyer's own expense and the obtaining of a report satisfactory to the buyer in the buyer's sole and absolute discretion. Unless the buyer gives notice in writing delivered to the seller not later than ____ p.m. on the ____ day of _____, 20____, that this condition is fulfilled, this Offer shall be null and void and the deposit shall be returned to the buyer in full without deduction. The seller agrees to cooperate in providing access to the unit and common elements for the purpose of this inspection. This condition is included for the benefit of the buyer and may be waived at the buyer's sole option by notice in writing to the seller within the time period stated herein.

1.3.c Inspection – Pre-closing Visits

The buyer shall be entitled to visit the property on 2 occasions prior to closing, upon providing 24 hours advance notice to the seller.

INSURANCE
1.4.a Condition – Arranging Insurance

This offer is conditional on the buyer arranging insurance for the property satisfactory to the buyer in the buyer's sole and absolute discretion. Unless the buyer gives notice in writing delivered to the seller not later than _____ p.m. on the _____ day of _____, 20____, that this condition is fulfilled, this offer shall be null and void and the deposit shall be returned to the buyer in full without deduction. The seller agrees to co-operate in providing access to the property, if necessary, for any inspection of the property required for the fulfillment of this condition. This condition is included for the benefit of the buyer and may be waived at the buyer's sole option by notice in writing to the seller within the time period stated herein.

1.4.b Condition – Arranging Insurance, Cost Not to Exceed

This offer is conditional upon the buyer arranging insurance on the property for the following named perils:_____, at a yearly cost not to exceed _____, excluding applicable taxes. Unless the buyer gives notice in writing delivered to the seller not later than _____ p.m. on the _____ day of _____, 20____, that this condition is fulfilled, this Offer shall be null and void and the deposit shall be returned to the buyer in full without deduction. The seller agrees to co-operate in providing access to the property, if necessary, for any inspection of the property required for the fulfillment of this condition. This condition is included for the benefit of the buyer and may be waived at the buyer's sole option by notice in writing to the seller within the time period stated herein.

1.5.a Condition – Lawyer's Approval, Buyer

This Offer is conditional upon the approval of the terms hereof by the buyer's lawyer. Unless the buyer gives notice in writing delivered to the seller not later than _____ p.m. on the _____ day of _____, 20_____, that this condition is fulfilled, this Offer shall be null and void and the deposit shall be returned to the buyer in full without deduction. This condition is included for the benefit of buyer and may be waived at the buyer's sole option by notice in writing to the seller within the time period stated herein.

1.5.b Condition – Lawyer's Approval, Seller

This Offer is conditional upon the approval of the terms hereof by the seller's lawyer. Unless the seller gives notice in writing delivered to the buyer or to the buyer's address as hereinafter indicated not later than ___ p.m. on the _____day of _____, 20___, that this condition is fulfilled, this Offer shall be null and void and the deposit shall be returned to the buyer in full without deduction. This condition is included for the benefit of seller and may be waived at the seller's sole option by notice in writing to the buyer within the time period stated herein.

MORTGAGE
1.6. Condition – Arranging a New Mortgage
This Offer is conditional upon the buyer arranging, at the buyer's own expense, a new _____Charge/Mortgage for not less than _____ ($_____), bearing interest at a rate of not more than ____ % per annum, calculated semi-annually not in advance, repayable in blended monthly payments of about _____ ($_____), including principal and interest, and to run for a term of not less than _____ years from the date of completion of this transaction. Unless the buyer gives notice in writing delivered to the seller not later than _____ p.m. on the _____day of _____, 20_____, that this condition is fulfilled, this Offer shall be null and void and the deposit shall be returned to the buyer in full without deduction. This condition is included for the benefit of the buyer and may be waived at the buyer's sole option by notice in writing to the seller within the time period stated herein.

1.7. Power of Sale
The buyer understands and agrees that the Chargor/Mortgagor has the right to redeem the property up to the time of waiver or expiration of all rights of termination or fulfillment of all conditions and this Agreement is subject to that right. In the event of redemption by the Chargor/Mortgagor, this Agreement shall be null and void and any deposit monies paid will be refunded in full without deduction. Where a court of competent jurisdiction prevents the completion of the within sale by an interim, interlocutory or permanent injunction or otherwise, then the seller (Chargee/Mortgagee) is not obliged to complete the said transaction and the Agreement shall be terminated and the deposit shall be returned to the buyer in full without deduction. In no event shall the seller be responsible for any costs, expenses, loss or

damages incurred or suffered by the buyer and the seller shall not have any further liability to the buyer whatsoever. Notwithstanding other provisions of this Agreement, the seller shall not be required either on or before closing to discharge its own Charge/Mortgage or any existing Charges/Mortgages, liens or other encumbrances subsequent in priority to the seller's Charge/Mortgage, which may be registered against the Property.

The buyer also acknowledges that the seller makes no representation and/or warranties with respect to the state of repair of the premises, inclusions of chattels or fixtures, or ownership of fixtures or appliances, and the buyer agrees to accept the property "as is." Chattels and fixtures on the premises may or may not be included with the premises but the seller shall not be obliged to remove any chattels or fixtures. All the provisions of the Mortgages Act shall supersede any part of this Agreement which may be in variance thereof or in conflict therewith.

1.8.a Condition – Septic System

This Offer is conditional upon the buyer being satisfied, in their sole and absolute discretion, that:

(1) all sewage systems serving the property are wholly within the setback requirements of the said property and have received all required Certificates of Installation and Approval pursuant to the provincial Environmental Protection Act;

(2) all sewage systems serving the property have been constructed in accordance with the said Certificates of Installation and Approval;

(3) all sewage systems serving the property had received all required use permits under the said Act or any other legislation; and further, that on inspection, the septic bed is in good working order.

The buyer shall be allowed to retain at the buyer's own expense, a professional in the septic business to make an examination of the septic system. Seller agrees to allow access to the property for the purposes of a septic inspection and agrees to allow the buyer to request information as outlined above from the appropriate authorities having jurisdiction. Unless the buyer gives notice in writing delivered to the seller not later than _____ p.m. on the_____ day of _____, 20____, that these conditions have been fulfilled, this Offer shall become null and void and the deposit shall be returned to the buyer in full without deduction. These conditions are included for the benefit of the buyer and may be waived at the buyer's sole option by notice in writing to the seller within the time period stated herein.

1.8.b Condition – Water Supply, All Well Types

This Offer is conditional upon the buyer being satisfied, in their sole and absolute discretion, that:

(1) there is an adequate water supply to meet the buyer's household needs;

(2) the pump and all related equipment serving the property are in proper operating condition; and

(3) the buyer can obtain a Bacteriological Analysis of Drinking Water from the authority having jurisdiction indicating that there is no significant evidence of bacterial contamination. Unless the buyer gives notice in writing delivered to the seller not later than _____ p.m. on the_____ day of _____, 20____ that these conditions have been fulfilled, this Offer shall become null and void and the deposit shall be returned to the buyer in full without deduction. These conditions are included for the benefit of the buyer and may be waived at the buyer's sole option by notice in writing to the seller within the time period stated herein. The seller agrees to allow access to the buyer's inspector at any reasonable time or times.

SURVEY

1.9.a Seller to Provide Existing Survey with Declaration

The seller agrees to provide, at the seller's own expense, not later than
__ p.m. on the ____ day of _____, 20____, an existing survey of
said property showing the current location of all structures, buildings,
fences, improvements, easements, rights-of-way, and encroachments
affecting said property. The seller will further deliver, on completion, a
declaration confirming that there have been no additions to the structures, buildings, fences, and improvements on the property since the
date of this survey.

1.9.b Seller to Provide New Survey

The seller agrees to provide, at the seller's own expense, not later than
__ p.m. on the ____ day of _____, 20____, a new survey of
said property showing the current location of all structures, buildings,
fences, improvements, easements, rights-of-way, and encroachments
affecting said property.

1.9.c   Seller to provide Survey, Building Plans, Mechanical Drawings, Warranties

The seller agrees to provide, at the expense of the seller, a survey of
the property, completed by an Ontario Land Surveyor, showing the
current location of all buildings, structures, additions, fences, improvements, easements, rights-of-way and encroachments affecting the
property. The seller also agrees to supply all building plans, mechanical drawings, and any other plans, and all warranties and service
manuals, if available, applicable to any equipment or chattels included
in the purchase price.

SWIMMING POOL

1.10.a By-Law Compliance

The seller represents and warrants to the best of the seller's knowledge and belief that the swimming pool, its equipment, and the
fencing of the said pool, comply with all applicable by-laws, regula-

tions, and legislation. The Parties agree that this representation and warranty shall survive and not merge on completion of this transaction, but apply only to the state of the property existing at completion of this transaction.

1.10.b Good Working Order, Warranty

The seller represents and warrants that the swimming pool and equipment are now, and on the completion date shall be, in good working order. The Parties agree that this representation and warranty shall survive and not merge on completion of this transaction, but apply only to the state of the property existing at completion of this transaction.

1.10.c Winterization

The seller agrees to winterize the swimming pool and equipment prior to completion, and shall provide a written undertaking on completion that the seller shall be responsible for any costs or expenses incurred by the buyer if the swimming pool and equipment are not properly winterized, provided only that the buyer gives written notice of any claim to the seller not later than _____ p.m. on the _____ day of _____, 20__ , failing which the seller accepts no responsibility for costs.

UFFI
1.11.a Acknowledgement – UFFI Present in Building

The seller discloses and the buyer acknowledges that the building contains urea formaldehyde foam insulation. The buyer accepts the property in that state and further acknowledges that the seller does not warrant the quality or quantity of the insulation or the quality of its installation.

1.11.b UFFI Found But Corrective Action Taken

The seller represents and warrants that the building was insulated with urea formaldehyde foam insulation but has undergone the following corrective actions: _____. The Parties agree that this representation and warranty shall survive and not merge on completion of this transaction, but apply only to the state of the property at completion of this transaction.

1.11.c UFFI Removed from Building

The seller represents and warrants that, although urea formaldehyde foam insulation (UFFI) was installed in the building, such UFFI was removed in _____, _____, by _____, and the seller further warrants that, to the best of his knowledge, no UFFI has been installed in the building since such removal. The Parties agree that this representation and warranty shall survive and not merge on completion of this transaction, but apply only to the state of the property at completion of this transaction. As evidence of the removal, the seller attaches the following documents as Schedule "____" which shall form part of this Agreement of Purchase and Sale.

1.12 Representations/Warranties – Survive Closing – Specific Time Period

The parties agree that the representations and warranties stated herein shall survive and not merge on closing, but shall expire at ____ p.m. on the ____ day of _____, 20____, and be of no further force and effect unless the buyer, prior to such expiry, has given written notice of a claim under the warranty to the seller.

1.13 Vacant Possession Notice

The buyer hereby authorizes and directs the seller, and the seller agrees, when this Agreement becomes unconditional, to give to the tenant(s) the requisite notices under the Residential Tenancies Act, requiring vacant possession of the property for use by the Buyer or the buyer's immediate family, effective as of the _____day of _____, 20___, and the seller agrees to deliver copies of the requisite notices to the buyer immediately after service of the notices upon the tenant. The buyer and the seller agree in the event that the tenant fails to vacate the property prior to completion of this transaction for any reason, then the closing date shall be extended for a period not to exceed _____ days, to permit the seller to bring any court application that may be required to obtain vacant possession, all at the expense of the seller. If the seller cannot obtain vacant possession by the extended date, then the buyer shall have the sole option to either accept the tenant or terminate this transaction, in which event the deposit shall be returned to the buyer in full without deduction. If the seller is able to provide vacant possession to the buyer in accordance with this section, then the buyer agrees that the buyer or the buyer's immediate family will take possession and occupy the property after closing. The buyer agrees to provide the seller with a written indemnity on closing, indemnifying the seller from any action, claim or demand that may occur in the event the Buyer or the Buyer's immediate family does not take possession of and occupy the property as aforesaid.

Index

As Is Clause, 80, 87-89, 311, 312
Adverse Possession, 65, 67, 69

Boundary or Boundary Lines, xvii, 65, 66, 68, 85, 86, 101, 142, 192
Buyer Representation Agreement, xvii, 6, 15, 17, 18, 41-46, 48, 49, 50, 55, 58–62

Chattels and Fixtures, 110, 133-139, 191, 264–269, 343, 345
Caveat Emptor, 76, 156, 278
Closing Date, 111, 127–130, 259-262
Comparative Market Analysis, 3, 36, 58
Commission or Real Estate Commission, 11, 13, 22-27, 30, 41, 42, 45-50, 53–55, 58, 59, 61, 62, 121, 200, 201, 203, 252, 304
Commission Trust, 27, 30, 174, 175, 294
Conditions, 4, 79, 95, 97, 110, 125, 131, 132, 141, 143, 150, 157, 159, 169, 176–185, 187–189, 191, 193, 194, 235, 242, 245, 257, 279, 288, 298, 300, 344, 346–351
Condominiums, xviii, 45, 110, 222, 233–302, 304-309, 312, 313, 344, 346, 347
  Board of Directors, 239–241, 279
  Budget, 237, 239, 240, 243, 308, 313
  Bylaws, 237, 239, 242, 272, 275, 295, 297
  Common Elements, 233–235, 238–240, 249, 250, 272, 275, 277, 295, 298
  Common Expenses, 240–243, 245, 269, 270, 282, 308
  Condominium Corporation, 234–241, 245, 250, 270, 274, 275, 277, 279, 280, 282, 295, 299
  Cooling Off Period, 237, 307, 308
  Declaration, 234–237, 242, 245, 249, 251, 272, 275, 295, 296, 297
  Description, 234, 236, 237, 245, 249, 251, 272, 275, 295, 297
  Parking Space, 249–251, 269, 270
  Reserve Fund, 240, 282, 283, 298
  Reserve Fund Study, 240, 242, 244, 245, 298, 300
  Special Assessment, 241, 242, 244, 274
  Status Certificate, 242, 245, 250, 274, 278, 295, 298, 300, 344
  Statement of Disclosure, 237, 307, 313
  Units, 233–236, 238, 239, 241–245, 249–251, 269, 270, 274, 280, 295–298, 300
Consumer Reporting Act, 56, 168, 287, 316

Co-operative Agreements, xviii, 283, 296–298

Co-ownership Agreements, xviii, 299, 300

Credit Check or Score, 92, 95, 168, 287

Credit Report, 93, 168, 287

Deposit, 23, 111, 114, 120-125, 127, 143, 164, 173, 175, 178, 214, 217, 218, 237, 246–248, 251–257, 258, 284, 285, 308

Disclaimer Clause, 87–89, 99, 116

Disclosure and Full Disclosure, xvii, 17, 18, 30, 51, 72–85, 88, 89, 106, 117, 119, 137, 139, 148, 149, 151, 157, 269, 278, 279, 343

Do Not Call Legislation, xviii, 315, 318, 319, 330–333, 342

Dual Agency, 18, *See* Multiple Representation

Easement, 64, 67, 68, 73, 74, 100, 101, 114, 118, 119, 142, 144, 148–151, 154, 215, 216

Family Law, xviii, 34, 40, 229–234, 290

FINTRAC, 213, 214

For Sale by Owner (FSBO), 10–13, 62, 200, 201, 204

Foreclosure, 209, 210, 309, 310

Holdover Period 23, 25, 31, 47, 49, 55

Home Inspection, 4, 10, 55, 56, 79–81, 88, 92, 96-100, 107, 123, 134, 157, 176–178, 181, 183, 184, 193-195, 197, 235, 244, 245, 255, 266, 279, 298, 300, 309, 339, 346, 347

Home Inspectors, 4, 56, 75, 76, 78, 96–99, 134, 167, 176, 179–181, 266, 340, 346, 347

Identity Theft, xviii, 205–208, 219

Insurance or Home Insurance, 40, 60, 77, 92, 102-105, 107, 142, 143, 150, 157–159, 163, 283, 284, 341, 347, 348

Insurance Agent or Brokers 5, 85, 103–105, 149

Internet, viii, 2, 31, 71, 84, 90, 91, 107, 132, 194, 199–204, 207, 219, 338, 343, 344

Land Titles System, 63, 67–69, 117, 118, 141, 233, 234, 250, 273, 276

Landlord and Tenant Rights, xviii, 223–228, 350, 354

Lawyers, xvii, 4, 5, 14, 33, 62, 68, 72–74, 103, 105–107, 117, 119, 123, 128, 129, 131, 135, 141, 143, 147, 148, 151–153, 155, 161, 165, 166, 169, 171, 173, 174, 177, 178, 182, 191, 201, 202, 212, 213, 242, 252, 255, 257, 261, 273, 274, 276, 277, 280, 281, 284, 285, 289–291, 301, 303, 306, 312, 329, 335–342, 346, 348

Latent Defects, 56, 75–79, 83, 84, 97, 156, 157, 201, 278

Legal or Title Defects, 72, 73, 88, 104, 105, 119, 151, 273

Legal Process, xix, 335–342, 344

Listing Agreement, xvii, 6, 15, 17, 19–21, 25, 39, 40, 41, 51, 322

Matrimonial Home, 113, 114, 172, 228–230, 232, 248, 249, 292

Misrepresentation, 185, 186, 189

More or Less, 102, 114, 115

Mortgage Brokers, 4, 5, 27, 56, 94, 95, 105, 107, 201, 202, 329

Mortgage or Mortgage Loan, 10, 42, 64, 68, 92, 94, 95, 103, 107, 153, 155, 165, 195, 215, 241, 276, 309–311, 349, 350

Multiple Listing Service or MLS®, 19–21, 35–38, 45, 57, 84, 174, 175, 201–204, 294, 321, 322

Multiple Offers, xviii, 53, 81, 132, 183, 193–197, 264, 343

Multiple Representation, 15, 17, 27–30, 41, 50–54, 61

No Money Down Real Estate
  Seminars, 208–210, 219, 344

Open Houses, 6, 7, 18, 34, 54, 321

Patent Defects, 56, 76, 83, 97, 106, 278
Planning Act, 90, 159–161
Planners, 4, 5, 106, 107, 186
Power of Sale, 210, 241, 309–313, 349
Privacy Act, xviii, 315-330, 342
Property Condition Statements or PCS,
  10, 36, 74, 75, 78, 80, 81, 88, 97, 107,
  157, 186, 195
Property or Real Estate Taxes, 104,
  162–164, 243, 282, 283, 297
Psychological Defects or Stigmas, 72,
  82, 84, 85, 88, 106, 167, 197, 343

Real Estate and Business Brokers Act,
  20, 40, 43, 60, 121, 253
Real Estate Agent or Salesperson,
  xvii–xix, 1–62, 70, 71, 79, 82, 84, 90,
  91, 97, 99, 105, 111, 112, 119, 121, 122,
  130, 132, 134, 139, 147, 158, 169, 170,
  173–175, 183, 193–196, 199–204,
  211–214, 247, 255, 262–264, 280, 283,
  288, 293, 294, 303–306, 311, 312,
  321–323, 326, 328, 330, 339–341
Real Estate Fraud, 104, 211–214
REALTOR®, xvii, 1, 11, 15, 29, 61, 62, 107,
  112, 200–204, 214, 219, 247
Restrictive Covenants, 118, 144–147, 151,
  215
Registry System 63–65, 67–69, 117, 118,
  141, 233
Representations, 4, 14, 34, 37, 110, 125,
  137, 144, 167–169, 185, 186, 189, 191,
  257, 288, 344, 345, 352–354

Seller Property Information Statement,
  36, 79, 88, 106, 186
Staging or Home Staging, xvii, 7, 107
Survey, xvii, 65, 66, 68, 69, 73, 74, 86, 87,
  92, 100–102, 105, 107, 110, 115–119, 125,
  148, 153–155, 169, 190, 191, 213, 236,
  275, 276, 288, 311, 344, 352

Tarion Warranty Program, 301–303,
  305, 307, 309, 312
Timeshare Agreements, xviii, 295, 296
Title Insurance, 86, 92, 100, 104, 105,
  107, 118, 142, 153–155, 187, 213, 214, 219

Warranties, 4, 14, 34, 37, 75, 98, 99, 110,
  125, 136–139, 166, 167–169, 188–191,
  257, 267, 286, 288, 344, 345, 352–354
Work Order, 141–144, 149, 166, 271, 272,
  285

Zoning, 1, 77, 104, 106, 116, 142, 143, 145,
  146, 149–151, 153, 166, 213, 234, 285

Conclusion

FOREWARNED IS FOREARMED: THE FOURTEEN STEPS OF SUCCESS

The goal of any buyer or seller should be to have a stress-free experience. By following the principles set out in this book, you'll be able to achieve this, and you'll be able to avoid unwanted legal proceedings.

Some basic principles to increase your chances of success:

1. Hire the right real estate professional to assist you.
2. Conduct your own neighbourhood and Internet research of areas that interest you.
3. Be prepared, especially if you become involved in a multiple offer.
4. Carefully review every detail added to the agreement of purchase and sale form — including all chattels and fixtures you expect to receive on closing — before you sign the agreement.
5. As a seller, practice full disclosure of all legal, physical, and psychological defects that affect your property.

6. Understand your rights as a landlord or tenant; know how being a tenant or a landlord may affect your real estate transaction.
7. Before you sign it, understand every clause in the printed form in the agreement of purchase and sale.
8. Know why you need conditions, representations, and warranties.
9. Be wary of Internet brokers and no-money-down real estate offers.
10. In a resale condominium, it is all about the status certificate.
11. With new builders, it is all about good references and about your provincial new home warranty program.
12. When buying under a power of sale, take extra care to conduct a detailed home inspection.
13. Understand why you need an up-to-date survey, and know how helpful it can be if there is a property dispute.
14. If you are ever involved in a legal proceeding, try to settle the matter.

"In all my years in real estate, I have yet to see a more concise
and easy-to-read book about what you need to know before buying or selling
your home or condominium. This book should be read by every buyer,
seller, and real estate agent."

— Elli Davis, the #1 Royal LePage agent in Toronto for 22 consecutive years

"A very informative book that can help consumers through
the potential minefield of real estate transactions. This is a great resource
for anyone considering buying or selling a home."

— Pat Foran, CTV consumer reporter,
author of *The Smart Canadian's Guide to Saving Money*

Buyers will learn . . .
- How to find the right agent to represent you
- What research you need to do in advance
- How to deal with multiple offers
- What the agreement of purchase and sale means
- How to buy from a builder

Sellers will learn . . .
- How to properly prepare your home for sale
- What you need to disclose to potential buyers
- What the listing agreement means
- How to deal with special
- The impact of family law

Mark Weisleder has been a lawyer, author, instructor, and speaker in the
real estate industry since 1983. He has held senior positions in a major
law firm and at Bell Mobility. Mark is a regular contributor to "Real Estate
News" in the *Toronto Star*. www.markweisleder.com

ISBN: 978-1-55022-913-4   9 781550 229134